WRITING FOR
ACADEMIC JOURNALS

WRITING FOR ACADEMIC JOURNALS

Rowena Murray

OPEN UNIVERSITY PRESS

Open University Press
McGraw-Hill Education
McGraw-Hill House
Shoppenhangers Road
Maidenhead
Berkshire
England
SL6 2QL

email: enquiries@openup.co.uk
world wide web: www.openup.co.uk

and Two Penn Plaza, New York, NY 10121-2289, USA

First published 2005

Copyright © Rowena Murray 2005

A catalogue record of this book is available from the British Library.

ISBN 0 335 21392 8 (pb)   0 335 21393 6 (hb)

Library of Congress Cataloging-in-Publication Data
CIP data applied for

Typeset by RefineCatch Ltd, Bungay, Suffolk
Printed in the UK by Bell & Bain Ltd, Glasgow

For Phyllis

Contents

Preface

This book is based on the assumption that the writing skills you learned in school – which is when most people last learned about writing – do not equip you for your entire career. This is to say that we can all develop our writing skills throughout our careers, and that writing development – or whatever you want to call it – is not remedial; far from it.

When we come to the subject of writing for academic journals, there are other problematic misconceptions:

You cannot write for academic journals until you have immersed yourself in the literature and you cannot write for academic journals if you have not done any research.

These and other widely accepted conceptions about writing for academic journals have, of course, an element of truth in them; you do have to know the literature and you do have to contextualize your contribution in terms of the other work that has been done.

However, 'immersing yourself' in the literature is itself a long-term process. If you wait until you feel you have achieved that, you may never write. If you wait until you have found your place in the literature, you may lose the creative spark, the germ of your own idea and your commitment to write. In reality, it is the process of publishing a paper that helps you to establish your place in the literature.

If this is true, then you need strategies to write and develop your ideas while you are still learning about academic writing in your field. You also have to overcome the misconception that you cannot publish anything because you have not done any 'real' research. There are, in fact, many varieties of paper published in many fields.

Many see writing as a discipline-specific activity and will wonder how this book can possibly address new writers in every field. The answer lies in a generic approach, showing how, while each discipline is indeed in many ways quite different, there are similarities in writing published in journals across disciplines.

Yet each field does have its own rhetoric; in fact, each journal has, in a sense, its own genre, its own prevailing conventions and values. Detailed analysis of journal articles from different fields demonstrates the process of working out precisely what journal editors and reviewers are looking for.

On another level, if we look at practice – what people actually do when they write and how they manage to get it done – writing again presents challenges to new writers in all disciplines:

- Writers – particularly new writers – in all disciplines face the constant challenges of getting started and making time for writing.
- Academics in all disciplines have to raise the standard of their writing and publishing, as they move from postgraduate years to an academic career and as they progress through their careers.
- It is difficult to write regularly if you do not have productive practices, or if you do not even know what that might involve.

These are often seen as 'practical' problems, sometimes relegated to a lower order of thinking. In a sense, of course, these are practical problems, in that they concern practice. But, as we all know, it is difficult to separate out all the levels of activity that writing involves, to distinguish the purely practical from the cognitive, for example. They are closely connected.

This book therefore addresses the key challenges in writing academic papers in terms of actual writing practices:

- What are the activities that lead to a paper being submitted and, ultimately, accepted?
- How does it actually happen?
- What do you actually do?
- How do you really find time for writing?
- How do you improve the standard of your writing?

As for any research task, a range of strategies is available, and it is probably good to have more than one.

Throughout this book I include participants' diverse reactions – both positive and negative – to the strategies I suggest, because this helps to reveal not only the complexity of the writing process, but also what I see as learning stages.

What is new about this book is my argument that the way to regular, meaningful and enjoyable writing for journals is through an integrated approach: you can combine the conventional structuring strategies and the less conventional – though no less tried and tested – 'freewheeling' and generative strategies.

Acknowledgements

Once again, I want to thank Shona Mullen at Open University Press/McGraw-Hill – not only for her support but this time also for her patience.

Dr Morag Thow at Glasgow Caledonian University provided unstoppable support.

Many others, in many writing groups and programmes, have helped me understand what goes on when we write. Without all these rehearsals and airings, my ideas would not have developed beyond my reading, observations and my own writing. Most recently, writers in a 'mini-retreat' at Swinburne University (Melbourne, Australia) were astute, challenging and sympathetic sounding boards for my ideas, and they helped me to refine further the activities I propose in this book.

Introduction: Beyond reason and vanity

The title of this introduction, 'Beyond reason and vanity', echoes Skinner's *Beyond Freedom and Dignity*, the intention being not only to introduce, from the start, the important behavioural dimension of writing but also to reposition writing for academic journals: it cannot be reduced to a set of professional imperatives. Given the lack of immediate, or even long-term, reward for publishing, there must also be personal motives. The satisfaction that writing a paper brings only comes later, sometimes much later, long after the writing. Nor will publication necessarily bring any tangible reward.

Academics who publish regularly must therefore have somehow moved beyond 'reason', not in the sense that they have lost their minds, but in the sense that they do not, they say, find their deepest motivation to publish in organizational or political directives; ironically, the scoring systems used to value – and devalue – publications is, for some, the last thing they would think of if you asked them what motivates them to write.

Given that few academics who aim to be published in the top journals will ever achieve this, most must have other reasons to write. They must also have moved beyond 'vanity', in the sense that they aspire to more than making themselves look good by collecting a pile of publications. Nor is regular publication a guarantee – for everyone – of career progression; for most academics publication does not automatically bring status and promotion.

In fact, the dominant characteristic of academic writers is their persistence, as much as anything else, which keeps them going when others have given up:

> A writer needs obstinate perseverance to succeed. Writing is a fairly thankless undertaking. I think people get tired of it pretty quickly, so sticking with it is the greatest part of the battle.
>
> (Messud, quoted in Roberts et al. 2002: 50)

This makes developing effective motivational, behavioural strategies more complex.

Theoretically, what might be seen as the primary purpose of writing for publication – achieving 'hits' in some kind of audit – must, therefore, be broadened to encompass less rational motives: self-expression, creativity and enjoyment. In reality, however, the two types of motivation may work in opposition. There are those who would argue that academics are eternally plagued by a tension between 'idealism and practicality' (Rossen 1993: 5). Perhaps the competitiveness endemic in academic writing can be read as an externalization of this internal conflict.

This book is aimed at all academic writers, published or otherwise, since continuing to write and publish, and finding a purpose in doing so, is an on-going challenge. There is a persistent tension between 'scholarship as a means to an end or as an end in itself' (Rossen 1993: 3). In the present climate, the same could be said of writing for academic journals.

Do academics really need to learn about writing?

It has been argued that academics learn about writing in the course of their careers:

> Successful university lecturers are likely to have spent many years developing acceptable ways of constructing their own knowledge through their own writing practices in a variety of disciplinary contexts.
>
> (Lea and Street 1998: 163)

Yet many academics, even those with PhDs, report that this is not how it works; it simply does not prove possible to learn everything they need to know about research and writing as they go along: 'it was unspoken but it just seemed obvious: that's what one does. And then it turned out that I was terribly bad at it' (Ellmann, quoted in Hanks 2003). While it would be interesting – and worthwhile – to research why this might be, it is the purpose of this book to address the stated need for guidance and development in the demanding task of writing for academic journals, particularly for new writers: there is no need to pretend that you know all you need to know about writing.

Given the opportunity to experience writing development, many academics are surprised at how little they know about writing and some are relieved finally to be able to admit it:

> The writing process was something I hadn't given much thought to before starting the [writing] course. . . . One of the first topics explored was how is academic writing learned? The answer . . . seems to be by trial and error.

On reflection I cannot recall being given formal instruction on the specifics of academic writing during my undergraduate career. This trial and error process is not just confined to academic writing; it extends to all forms of writing.

(participant in Academic Writing module, Advanced Academic Studies course, University of Strathclyde)

What we learned about writing at school – without wanting to criticize that in any way – was not sufficient preparation for all the writing we have to do throughout our professional lives. How could it be? Yet there was an assumption that writing development or instruction was only for those who struggled with writing, perhaps non-native speakers, or those whose writing skills were poor. Although this assumption persists, there is growing acknowledgement that we ought to learn more about writing if we want to be published in academic journals. In some disciplines, some support is provided during the PhD, but in others there is nothing at all for new writers. What exactly we need to learn is, of course, still a matter of some debate.

Pressure on academics to publish increases year by year. In addition, as more institutions are granted university status and new disciplines join higher education, there is an urgent need for support in this area. Lecturers in these universities, some of whom are highly experienced, face even more intense pressure to participate in audit exercises that make publication targets very specific. Many of these lecturers will not have published in the past, but will be expected to do so immediately. They have to run to catch up with the other, more established disciplines with whom they will be compared. This pressure to publish is international, as, it appears, is the demand for development and support.

The stigma previously attached to what I call 'writing development' is thankfully being eroded, as academics and postgraduate students recognize that it is in their interest – and not just their universities' – to raise the standard of their writing by, simply, learning more about it.

Writing for publication requires a difficult transformation for those who have recently completed – or are still working on – a PhD thesis (UK) or dissertation (USA). It can be a complex transformation, involving several dimensions of change. Many new writers do not have rhetorical knowledge – knowledge of the techniques of persuasive writing that are the building blocks of scholarly writing. Consequently, they may make errors in their first papers, some of which, in my development work across the UK and elsewhere, I find recur across disciplines:

New writers' errors

- Writing too much about 'the problem'
- Overstating the problem and claiming too much for their solution
- Overstating the critique of others' work
- Not saying what they mean, losing focus through indirect writing
- Putting too many ideas in one paper

Defining the problem is clearly a crucial step in an argument. Yet many new writers spend too long on this, in their early drafts, and produce an over-long first draft that then has to be radically cut. Alternatively, perhaps they have a paper whose prime argument is that there is 'a problem', but new writers do not always perceive the gradations of argument that are available and end up overstating the critique, demolishing the opposition and drawing fire from reviewers. They are often able to say, immediately, when challenged, what it is they are trying to write: this is where it helps to have a colleague say 'write that down'. Balanced, usable sentences often appear in discussions about the paper.

Of course, any writer can make these errors at any time, but they do seem to feature regularly in new writers' texts. What these early errors have in common is the writers' lack of rhetorical development of their argument, too much stating of the point, without the necessary justifications. Once these flaws are pointed out to writers – as flaws – they can quickly modulate their tone, trim their critique and prune their paper.

Academics can, therefore, learn about writing; in fact, they do so very quickly, once the principles have been pointed out to them. This book will define and illustrate many of the key principles.

What difference will it make?

The popularity of the Writing for Publication programme that I designed demonstrates demand for writing development at universities and in other organizations, such as hospital Trusts. The programme helps those aiming to increase and/or improve written output. The structured approach to writing for publication helps academics, and others, develop this key professional skill over the longer term, rather than just 'playing the publication game'. It has changed some writers' conceptions of the writing process and of themselves as writers. Instead of sitting in the margin, occupying personal time, writing is more clearly positioned within the writer's working life. Evaluations, in questionnaires, focus groups and long-term follow-up interviews show evidence of impact in terms of participants' published output.

Writers develop both a knowledge base and the behaviours they need to become regular writers. While this book covers a wide range of approaches, the main theme is developing an integrated writing strategy. This involves working on all of the dimensions of the writing act. If you can create situations where you are able to work on all the dimensions of writing at the same time, it is possible to change your academic writing practices quite quickly. For example, in writers' group meetings, you can discuss the writing project itself, your progress with it and your goals for the next phase; more importantly, you would also discuss your feelings about the project, your sense of what constitutes progress and your levels of confidence in your writing. In this way, you include the rhetorical, psycho-social and cognitive aspects of writing. You will not just be talking about text.

The distinctiveness of this book is that it brings all these types of approaches together: rhetorical, behavioural (which academics learning about writing tend to call 'practical') and psycho-social. It is not just about one or the other. These are tried and tested approaches, refined in many different programmes and in discussions with writers about their papers.

What can research tell us about academic writing?

There is a body of knowledge on writing – about how it is learned and how it is done, about what constitutes good writing and how it is achieved. There is a substantial amount of scholarship on how undergraduate writing skills can be developed, but less on academic writers. Blaxter et al. (1998b) argued that research on academic writing is 'patchy'.

There is research on strategies used by one group of productive academic writers. Hartley and Branthwaite (1989) studied British psychologists and found that their results matched closely those of Boice (1987). Although the research is not recent, it does offer pointers that later researchers would endorse:

1 Make a rough plan (which you needn't necessarily stick to).
2 Complete sections one at a time. It may help to do them in order.
3 Use a word processor if possible.
4 Revise and redraft at least twice.
5 Plan to spend about 2 to 5 hours writing per week in term time.
6 Find quiet conditions in which to write and, if possible, always write in the same place (or places).
7 Set goals and targets for yourself.

8 Invite colleagues and friends to comment on early drafts.
9 Collaborate with longstanding colleagues and trusted friends.

(Hartley and Branthwaite 1989: 449)

What is interesting, and still useful, about this list is that it shows the way to a productive writing process. There is advice on how many hours you should try to spend on writing per week, which does not sound like much, but it is probably more manageable than the higher figure many new writers would set themselves. Point 6 recalls all that study skills advice that we give students. In this context it sounds a bit rigid, but this is what worked for the productive writers in this study. Perhaps, as psychologists, they were better at identifying productive behaviours. They would, for example, know all about the powers of goals and targets both in theory and in practice.

Boice (1987, 1990) developed writing strategies for academics, backed up by empirical evidence. His approach is still relevant, though contentious to academics who have developed a different mode: he advocates regular writing in short bursts, 'regular' meaning daily and 'short' meaning as little as 30 minutes, and for many academics this 'snack' approach contradicts their favoured 'binge' mode.

Elbow's freewriting – both public and private – is an invaluable technique for all writers, though some require more persuasion than others that this is so. The value of what he calls 'low stakes writing' cannot be overstated; although all writing is targeted at a specific audience, it is important to have a space to write that is removed from their potentially endless judgements.

The impact of writers' groups and development of an integrative strategy have been the focus of my own work for the past few years. Again and again, I have come back to the question, is it possible or sensible to talk about any one of the dimensions of writing separately from the others? Can we talk about rhetorical skills without, for example, talking about the need to – and skills of, having the confidence to – negotiate on a daily basis time to write? People tell me all the time that there is no time to write. The need constantly to be switching things around, stretching deadlines for other things in order to write – surely that too is a skill? Although, are we not already doing this kind of thing with other aspects of our professional roles? There are negotiating processes involved in writing and in time management and my work has opened up some of these individual and group negotiations. The main point about writers' groups is that we need to be able to link up, in discussion, the various dimensions of writing: rhetorical, psycho-social and behavioural. Can we make any progress if we only work to improve in one area?

One wonders why, if writing is so important in academic life, there has not been more research. There could, for example, be much more on what productive writers actually do; but perhaps they would be unwilling to share their 'secrets' in any case. The real reason may lie in the complexity of writing, involving potentially several different disciplines:

1 There is the psychology of writing, including motivation and meaning-making.
2 There is a social dimension to writing, usually a solitary act, but aimed at real people, and therefore benefiting from discussion and feedback.
3 There is the rhetorical dimension, including not only mechanics of writing, but also persuasive strategies.
4 There is a cognitive dimension, defining ways of thinking about writing.

Another block to research may, of course, be the residual stigma attached to writing development. Although it can be positively positioned as writing at a higher level, that old myth that 'those who can, do', along with the unspoken – and often spoken – belief that there must be something wrong with you if you need to be 'developed', has not quite gone. It only takes one influential and/or senior member of staff or senior officer to say that academics would be better spending their time writing than attending writers' groups, for example, to kill off the initiative of academics, staff developers and any others within earshot. They will function quite well without the explicit support of senior staff, but their active resistance or explicit criticism will make it very difficult to continue.

The argument about how academics' need for writing development occurs rages on. There are those who blame the schools; others blame new technologies for what they see as the degradation of students' grammar. In practice, staff are just as likely to be unsure of how to use the semi-colon as students. While we let that debate rage on, perhaps we can progress by admitting that what we learned at school about writing – whether that included grammar or not – was never likely to be sufficient for writing an academic paper.

There is also a misconception that writing can be separated from learning and research: I have heard it said, by a very senior keynote speaker, opening a conference that I had been invited to address on academic writing, that 'We all know that it is the quality of the research that matters, not the writing'. He singled out my session for this censure, not only putting me in my place, before I even had a chance to say a word about writing skills, but quite likely also discouraging anyone at his institution from seeking, or perhaps from providing, writing development.

This book

What distinguishes this book from others on the subject is that it deals not only with increasing or improving output, but also with the process of changing writing practices. Productive strategies are provided to help writers change their practices.

Change takes time. Stages in the process of becoming a regular, productive writer are outlined. By adopting and/or adapting these strategies writers will become more productive, will write more readily and will find more enjoyment in the process. There is also evidence that they will be successful. By working through this book writers can discover their own reasons for writing.

Each chapter includes writing activities that progress the writing project in stages, from start to finish, from finding topics to responding to reviewers. All the activities have been tried and tested in writers' groups at many universities, old and new, and in other organizations. Chapters are linked by questions or comments repeatedly raised by writers. Unless these issues are addressed the writing project falters.

In practice, some writers immediately take to some of the writing strategies described here; others find them counter-intuitive or not immediately productive. The trick is to adopt or adapt them, as appropriate, and, more importantly, to stick with them for long enough to see the benefit. Clearly, reading about a writing strategy, or even trying it once or twice, will have little or no impact on your practice or output.

This book argues that you may have to change your writing habits; in order to become a regular writer you may have to use *both* 'snack' and 'binge' strategies. Writing is not treated as a skill that you learn once and for all, but as a professional task that continues to present an on-going challenge to new and experienced writers alike.

Writing for academic journals is widely perceived as one of the most discipline-specific activities. Many academics assume that it is not possible to discuss writing in a generic way and that only someone in their area can provide useful feedback or instruction. Yet, this is to ignore the deep structures of published arguments across a wide range of subjects, illustrated in this book. This material is, therefore, relevant to all disciplines.

This book combines research- and practice-based approaches in order to help writers change their approach to writing and adjust their academic writing practices. There is some evidence that, once adopted, these new strategies can help writers with other, non-scholarly writing tasks.

The emphasis is on what writers do – or can do – rather than on what editors or reviewers do. Although the role of the reviewers is dealt with in this book, the focus is on how writers can respond to feedback in order to move their writing towards publication.

> That nature of the academy (and of academic work) is to foster rivalry through discrimination between various theories and ideas, which are largely – as critics of the academy delight in pointing out – subjective, which heightens the tension between scholars all the more.
>
> (Rossen 1993: 3)

Instead of fixating on this 'rivalry', like many of those who say they want to write but never do, or being distracted by your critics' covert 'subjectivity', you can focus on simply getting on with your writing.

1   Why write for academic journals?

What is academic writing? • Can it be learned? • Is it innate? • Reasons for writing • Reasons for publishing • Internal and external drivers • Career implications • Research profile • What is 'research'? • Reasons for not writing • 'I haven't done any research' • Intellectual capacity • Turgid writing • Narrow range • Pre-peer review • Guilt, fear and anxiety • Procrastination • The writing self • Team and collaborative writing • Barriers to writing • An integrative strategy • Checklist

This chapter explores the potential purposes of scholarly writing – why do we do it? What's in it for us? The aim is to prompt readers, particularly if you have not published much or at all in academic journals, to address your motivations. These can be quite mixed. New writers are often ambivalent about academic journals, even, sometimes particularly, journals in their field, and this can be a barrier to writing. It is crucial to address the issues that come up most frequently in discussions at this stage; if the issues are not addressed, it is unlikely that there will be any writing.

If you are not a regular writer, you may have counter-motivations; there may be factors, people or strategies holding you back from writing. Alternatively, there may be achievements that occur because you do not write, and you may be worried about losing these if you have to devote time and energy to writing.

You may not like the kinds of writing you see in journals in your field. Many new writers express a strong antipathy to what they see there:

'I don't want to write that turgid stuff.'

'I want to write something that I would want to read.'

'No one will read it if it's published in that journal.'

On the positive side, most new writers have something 'in the locker', something that they have been meaning to write about for some time. They may feel guilty, and may have to start by putting the sense of failure – at not having made more progress – behind them. In order to do this, some type of re-tuning of motivation might be necessary.

External drivers also impact on your motivation to write. Ironically, these sometimes interfere with internal, or intrinsic, motivations. Each writer has to work out his or her own answer to the question of why to write for scholarly publication. Important answers include developing your profile, progressing in your career and developing your understanding of your field. Once the ambivalence has been resolved, it is possible to reposition writing as valuable, feasible and enjoyable.

What is academic writing?

The craft or art of writing is the clumsy attempt to find symbols for the wordlessness. In utter loneliness a writer tries to explain the inexplicable.
(Steinbeck 1970: 14)

Academic writing is that set of conventions we see in a thesis or a published paper in our disciplines, a definition that becomes more precise once you scrutinize examples of published writing in your target journals.

Some argue that academic writing is a narrowly defined set of specialisms and knowledges, so narrow that it leaves 'huge gaps in our understanding':

It is the desire to think and write more, to fill some of these gaps that informs my desire to leave the academy – to think and write on subjects of my choice, in the manner that I wish to write, in whatever voice I choose.

There is so much emphasis on asserting a one-dimensional 'voice' in academic life. I enjoy writing about many subjects in different ways.

(hooks 1999: 141)

hooks argues that our subjectivity is 'colonised' in academic writing, and it is certainly true that across the disciplines subjectivity has traditionally had little or no value. This has begun to change recently, in some disciplines, but in others such changes are still seen as inappropriate to the enterprise of research.

Words associated with writing about research

- objective
- hierarchical
- focused
- conservative
- neutral

If hooks' argument applies, then there are gaps not simply in the literature, but created *by* the literature. The academic approach to research – and the academic style available for writing about it – is inherently limited. Those who find it limiting are not necessarily limited themselves; it is important to acknowledge that much of what we think, say and do in the course of our work can become invisible when we publish.

That accounts for academic writing, the product, but what about the process? A published paper creates an illusion of linear progression, when, as we all know, writing is a dynamic, cyclical process. While the merits of published papers are often discussed, there is relatively little discussion of how writing actually gets done: what are the stages and how do we fit them into our other tasks? How do productive writers manage to get so much done? – a question to be asked not so much in awe or envy as in anticipation of a practical answer.

Can it be learned?

Whenever I introduce the subject of paragraph structure – and its role in argument – to a group of academics I inevitably use such terms as 'topic sentence'. I ask them if they know what it means and, almost always, a silence falls. 'Is that the silence of "We know this already, move on . . . or the silence of we don't know, tell us now" ', I ask. Usually, a few immediately respond that they do not know. The point here is not that academics should learn jargon, but that they do have gaps in their knowledge about how sentences and paragraphs work. This can affect not only how they talk about writing with their students, but also how they manage their own writing.

Writing can, of course, be learned. The problem is there are very few formal, or informal, opportunities to learn. One editor, speaking at a recent world conference, said that it was the universities' job to provide training in academic writing, so that students coming through would be able to write well.

Feedback from journal editors and reviewers teaches us some lessons, but it is not advisable to set out to use them in that way. They will not appreciate it. Not all of them want to help writers learn; some would prefer all their submissions to be from 'learned' writers. Some of the more cutting reviews that we see may result from reviewers' frustration at having to provide what they see as basic guidance. Some report that, in any case, they find it difficult to give feedback on writing. They do not always have an explanation for why a piece of text does not work; they simply know that it doesn't.

If it can be learned, then can it be un-learned? People who do not write regularly, or who have stopped writing for a while, feel that they have lost the ability to write: 'I've forgotten how to write'. The cure is, as always, to start writing again – 'It's not till I write that I realize that I can' – but perhaps in new ways. It is possible to have a sense of your incompetence at the thought of writing, and this, if it goes on for long enough, can be aversive: it will stop you writing. This is something you have to find ways to avoid, if you are to write for academic journals.

Is it innate?

As for many other aspects of our professional roles for which we received no training or education, there is a tenacious myth that there are those who can write and those who cannot: 'Those who can, do. Those who can't, teach. And those who can't teach, teach gym/history/maths/law/education/writing/golf, other bias against a discipline.'

On the few occasions when writing ability is discussed in universities, there are popular assumptions about what makes some people productive writers, and it is not all about technical skill:

- These people are just good writers.
- Some are better at making time for writing.
- Those who publish are more selfish; they don't care about their students.

For new writers there is a potential double bind here: you should be able to write already on the basis on your education and experience, yet if you were really good enough you would already have written more than you have.

When academics talk about writing development, including training initiatives whose impact is evidenced in publications, senior colleagues, some initially and others serially, react with indifference at least and open scepticism at worst. This suggests that, across many different institutions, and in several countries, it is difficult to get past the remedial model: participation in writing development can be seen as a weakness.

The ability to write successfully for academic journals is not, of course, innate, although, interestingly, many people still think that it is. Yet, in the absence of formal training, perhaps it is true, ironically, that 'those who can, do', or can we rewrite that as, 'In the past, those who could, already did'.

This is not an excuse for avoiding writing development or, importantly, writing discussions. There are strategies for productive writing and ways of making time for writing in the average over-loaded academic life. Perhaps you do need to think about being more 'selfish', if that means putting your priority – writing – first. Perhaps you do need to overcome the sense that writers are a breed apart. Perhaps you need to learn new tricks.

Reasons for writing

Since it can have so many effects, there is potentially a wide range of personal and/or professional reasons for writing:

- working out what you think, clarifying your thinking or starting to think;
- having a 'rant', letting off steam, 'uncluttering' your brain;
- telling others what you think;
- persuading others to take it on board.

This list is no more than a starting point for thinking about where you are in what could be seen as a continuum between writing for yourself and writing for others: which is more important to you now?; which do you feel more ready to do?; which do you want to do in the short term? Starting today? If you have always had a feeling – as many have – that you would like to write, if only you knew how to go about it, then now is the time to start.

The general purpose of this book is to make a case for two kinds of writing: writing for yourself and writing for others. Writing for others, particularly for academic journals, can sometimes seem too constraining; writing for yourself, if you can silence your internal editor, is a crucial way to make sure that you develop your idea, your voice and your confidence.

Some writers argue that they like writing and do not lack confidence, but see no reason to get into print. They have other ways, they argue, of gaining professional recognition and other outlets for their communications than academic journals. Of course, this is always an option, as long as you are clear about and comfortable with any consequences there may be for your career. And what about consequences for your learning? Where will you find the kind of hard critique provided by journal reviewers?

Reasons for publishing

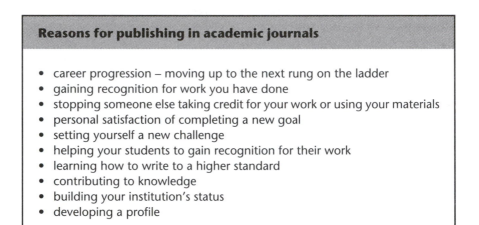

Your reasons for publishing may be much more closely linked to external drivers – and to other people's criteria – or, perhaps, to your awareness that you are expected to establish such a link.

Reasons for publishing in academic journals

- career progression – moving up to the next rung on the ladder
- gaining recognition for work you have done
- stopping someone else taking credit for your work or using your materials
- personal satisfaction of completing a new goal
- setting yourself a new challenge
- helping your students to gain recognition for their work
- learning how to write to a higher standard
- contributing to knowledge
- building your institution's status
- developing a profile

Some of these reasons are more altruistic than others. Co-authoring with students, for example, can help them in their search for a good job after graduation, in some professions. They will certainly have learned from publishing, provided you allow them to participate in the process, and you will have modelled a form of continuing professional development. In addition, if you have not published before, this is an excellent way of developing a small-scale piece of work for a journal.

Internal and external drivers

For writing, as for other professional tasks, there is a complex mixture of internal and external motivations. What is interesting is that when it comes to writing for academic journals, these motivations sit in opposition and can work against each other. Even in discussion among those who want to write for journals, there can be resistance to actually doing it.

Both external and internal drivers may combine if your aim is to get on in your career, yet this might be complicated by your ambivalence towards the writing you see published in the journal articles in your field. You may be ambivalent about joining what you see as a big 'game'. You may even develop feelings of antipathy towards those who regularly publish, particularly if they are in promoted positions. This may be compounded by your or others' scepticism at the whole promotion process, and this, too, can undermine your writing.

When I say, in an attempt at humour rather than cynicism, in writers' workshops that the quickest, surest way to get published is to change your first name to 'Professor', there is often rueful laughter, followed by an important discussion of the differences between papers published by those who already have a body of work and an established profile in the discipline and those published by 'unknowns'. Of course, reviewing should be blind, but sometimes it isn't, and even when it is, it is often easy to identify the authors from their references. The important lesson is that once you yourself have a body of work and experience, you too may write quite different types of papers; they may be very different from your first published paper.

Internal drivers include your intention genuinely to develop your writing skills, yet you may feel ambivalent about feedback you receive from peers and reviewers. You may invest time in researching a journal, yet feel that they have 'missed the point' of your paper, or been too harsh in their critique, or that they seem to be confusing it with another paper entirely. You may flat out disagree with the feedback. The criticisms may indeed be unfair and unhelpful, but your reaction may be as much about the emotional side of receiving criticism of your writing. You have, after all, invested so much of yourself in it. Until you have been through the process several times, you may find yourself taking criticism personally.

It will come as no comfort to know that as your knowledge of journal writing deepens, you may uncover new layers of ambivalence: you know what you are doing now and resent reviewers who still write as if they assume that you don't. This might be the best indication yet that it is an on-going struggle to bridge the gap between your internal and external drivers. You may continue to feel that what started out as your distinctive voice has morphed into journal-speak. It will be important, particularly when you are getting started, to have a way to refocus on what's in it for you to publish in academic journals.

There are those who will find all of this a bit pathetic; of course we all have to publish as part of our jobs – why all the ambiguity? Surely it is your responsibility to add to the store of knowledge and to keep yourself up to date for the sake of your students? If this is your view, you will, in theory, find it easier to make time and space for your writing, although when you start to, for the first time, there will be consequences for other people:

> You have to be very clear, if you want to write, what place it occupies in your life. I'm afraid that if you're ambitious, it often has to have first place – it sometimes has to take precedence over human relationships and anything else.
>
> (Mantel, quoted in Roberts et al. 2002: 75)

Even if you just want to 'get on' in your career, that is, you do not necessarily want to get to the very top – far from it, perhaps – there are those who will be ready to label you as 'ambitious'. Even if you simply want to be acknowledged for your work by promotion, there will be those who see you as selfish. No matter how much time and energy you plough into other roles, supporting students when no one else will, representing your department on more than your share of committees, and being course leader on more courses than two or more of your colleagues, there will be people in your peer group who refuse to see all your efforts. 'How did you find time to write', they wonder, 'if you really are so busy?' Come the day you actually do defer a task to finish a paper, there may be a cataclysmic reaction. You may be branded as someone who is prone to 'dropping the ball' for the rest of your career.

The point of this one-sided narrative is to characterize another type of external driver: the increasingly negative reactions – real or imagined, both can have real impact – that your writing may provoke in other people. These can drive against your writing, convincing you to make less time for it, not more. You do have to make writing more important than anything else at some point, in order to get it done at all. If you never make it the priority you will never do it. You have to ask yourself, what exactly are you waiting for?:

> Write as if you are dying. It works. Imagine if you've only got a year to live or something. I think that's the best motivator to get you to do it.
>
> (Gemmell, in Roberts et al. 2002: 57)

While this view will seem extreme to some, it does raise the question of how long you have, if you wait another year or two, to get started and to become a regular writer for academic journals.

Career implications

You may not enjoy the career appraisal or review process – that more or less statutory discussion with your head of department or director about your progress and goals, and you may not even find it useful, but it does give you an opportunity to make connections between what you want to do in your writing and what your department or unit values.

These connections are not always apparent to heads and managers, who, for various reasons, may never actually read what you write. The same goes for promotion time: do not expect senior officers to read your work, or even to have a grasp of its significance in your field, or in any sense. They are just as likely to read your publications as you are to read theirs – not at all likely. As long as they don't stop you doing what you want to do – in your writing – you can consider yourself to be in a fairly privileged position.

You may think that your work is so directly linked to your department's priorities that it hardly needs to be said. Think again. Take every opportunity to make that link explicit. As you develop your publication plans and intentions, think about how you can, if not 'align', then simply explain them in terms that are relevant to the department. In some disciplines, this will be superfluous; in fact, you may think the whole process of formal career review is superfluous. But in some areas, and perhaps at some times, it is much more important to make these links explicit. No one will do this for you; it may be that no one else could.

As you are contemplating the publishing dimension of a 'career', therefore, you may have to update your answers to three questions:

1 What are the precise or general targets for publishing in your area/ department?
2 Have you discussed with your head of department – as part of your appraisal or review – how you will meet those targets, including resources you will need?
3 Did you get general or specific, formal or informal, agreement to your publishing plans from your head of department?

Find out, if you can, how others would answer these questions, noting the interesting array of answers and areas of convergence. Note any dislocations, however minor, between the stated agenda and what is going on in practice, without, if you can avoid it, becoming too involved in what others are doing or not doing. You have no control over that, and is it really any of your business? If there is a problem with someone else's written work being published, surely it is your boss's problem?

If you feel that your work would be more valued in another area of the university, there may be possibilities for your publications to be entered into the local research 'accounting' system in another unit. In some disciplines, this would be ridiculous and possibly damaging to your career, but you might be surprised at the flexibility of the discipline bases when there are financial consequences. There are many ways in which being published in academic journals brings you external 'credit'; the question is how can you ensure that any credit also counts internally, whenever possible?

This is not to say that your output should be fixed for your entire career. You may want to do different types of writing for publication at different stages in your career, from 'initial career', when you might be developing publications from your thesis; to 'middle career', perhaps a time to write a single-authored book; to 'later career', when you might be asked to write a guest contribution to an edited volume (Blaxter et al. 1998a: 140). Again, it depends on your discipline and, above all, on your understanding of how people construct a programme of publications at different stages in their careers. Take a look at a few web sites: what and where are junior and senior researchers publishing in your discipline or sub-discipline?

Research profile

Are you thinking ahead? Do you want to be published in certain journals, not in others, and think you have no chance of getting into the 'big ones'? It may seem premature to be thinking of developing a research profile, but your first publication may present you to the research community in a particular way. It is important that you can live with that. Even better if you are making a conscious choice, even if it is a compromise determined as much by where you think you can get published as by where you would really like to be published.

If you want to develop a profile, will you have to focus your publications in a certain area, not publishing too widely? Or will you be able to use diversity, in your writing, to make a broader impact?

What is 'research'?

I discovered long ago in collecting and classifying marine animals that what I found was closely intermeshed with how I felt at the moment.

(Steinbeck 1962: 181)

This suggests that what constitutes 'research' will be closely related to your own interests. All sorts of studies count as research, in some disciplines, and the growing rigour and credibility of a range of qualitative methods has opened the door for those who do not want to learn statistics, for example.

Research is as much about the work you are currently doing, including teaching, as anything else. If you have expertise, experience and a profile in an area, then it makes sense to find your research in that area, unless you hate it with a passion. If you can find the right journal, and can construct a sufficient contribution, then you have a potential publication.

For example, a brief survey of the sub-field of social work dealing with residential childcare produced the following in published papers:

1 This is both a review of . . . as well as an attempt to place the issue in a practical and reasonable context (Anglin 1999)
2 A theoretical model is offered . . . (Pazaratz 2001)
3 The author draws upon 30 years of experience in . . . (Gavin and Lister 2001)
4 This article looks at how . . . There is a discussion of practical skills and training directions (Ziegler 2001).

The first example shows how what the author considers an 'issue' can be the subject of review and academic examination, while still being relevant to practice, a feature important to many new writers. The second example demonstrates that a new model, developed by the author, can make an important contribution. The third explicitly draws on extensive experience, making the case that this is itself an important body of knowledge. In the fourth, relatively non-academic terms such as 'looks at' and 'discussion' have clearly been judged sufficient for publication. Such options will not be available in all fields, but they are available in more fields than many new writers are aware.

In other fields, personal experience, the personal voice and the first-person, 'I', are off-limits, both stylistically and philosophically. In some disciplines, they simply cannot constitute the ingredients of new knowledge. This will be obvious to writers in those disciplines, but it is important that writers in other disciplines are not put off by these criteria. You will know what does and does not count as new knowledge from your reading. This is no time to be distracted by writing – and what other people say about writing – in other disciplines than your own.

Brew (2001) has argued that academic research – not just the writing that is published about it – is itself narrow, requiring closer links to living with uncertainty, ambiguity and the actual processes of researching. Calling for more 'reflexivity' and 'critical questioning', Brew opens up new possibilities, in some disciplines, for a rigorous critique of research itself and the development of new ways of thinking: 'we cannot escape seeing an outdated epistemology infusing practice' (p. 177). There is also a prompt here for analysis of practice. In other words, while experienced colleagues may attribute your views on the narrowness of academic writing in your discipline to your inexperience and naïvity, you have grounds for critiquing existing work and established principles. There is bound to be some such critique in your own discipline; you will not be the first to have these feelings or ideas about academic writing in your discipline.

Even failure – with, of course, a careful definition of what constitutes 'failure' – can be a fruitful topic for academic writing:

Research must acknowledge its disasters as well as its achievements; its rigidities as well as its creativity; its power and its powerlessness; its openness and its dogmatic blinkers.

(Brew 2001: 186)

Research can be quite narrowly defined, but acknowledging that narrowness, carefully identifying its nature and form, can strengthen your arguments. (Identifying the 'causes' of such narrowness would be a much more complex argument – cause-and-effect arguments are much more complex than the simple argument about the 'way things are'.) A key problem for researchers in many different fields is about how such critiques can be made credible and robust.

Brew (2004) has analysed the conceptions of research held by established senior researchers and has identified four categories of research experience:

> The domino (series of tasks), trading (a social phenomenon emphasizing products), layer (excavating reality) and journey (research transforms the researcher).
>
> (Brew 2004: 214)

Whether or not you feel you already have, or aspire to, one of these, it is as well to consider your own orientation as something real, part of your identity and, therefore, worth naming. Otherwise your concept of 'research' might remain amorphous and even internally contested. Work out where you are coming from, what definition of 'research' is meaningful to you and then you can start to give the tasks, trades, layers or stops on your journey some definition in real time and space and among real people. Brew's perspective, it should be noted, is underpinned by her research – phenomenography – uncovering the actual lived experience of researchers.

Of the orientations Brew describes, the 'trading' variation is interesting for its social nature:

> Whether the research outcomes are conceived in terms of publications, research grants, the achievement of objectives or social benefits, more often than not in this variation, research is described in terms of relationships, activities or ideas of other people (e.g. research assistants, collaborators or other researchers in the field).
>
> (Brew 2004: 221)

This implies that networks, collaborations and beneficiaries, in a variety of senses, are positioned in the research process at a more than conceptual level.

A related aspect of this variation, one that might link directly to writing – interesting that Brew uses the word 'variation', perhaps to emphasize plurality – is the idea that research is for an audience. Clearly, this suggests that it is important to develop not just an internal sense of audience, but also real external audiences, for our research and writing.

The strongest link to writing is, in fact, with this trading orientation, as Brew illustrates with a quotation from one of the participants in her study:

> I'm with the school that believes you should always be writing while you are researching and I always tell my . . . students too, that it's fatal just to

go away and read for a year. You should always be writing, . . . even if what you have written is discarded you should always be writing . . . Half the time is reading, half the time is writing.

(Brew 2004: 222)

This suggests that if you want to publish research regularly you should get yourself into the habit of writing during the research process, but that you should not try to do all this on your own; your social situation, including the social context of your life in academe, can enable or inhibit your writing. This last point may come as no surprise; many academics who want to write identify lack of support as a barrier. But you need to take steps to change this: take time to build peer relationships that will provide a forum, both critical and supportive, for your research. Develop some of this 'trading' mentality and find others who have it too. Brew (2004) argues that the trading variation is more likely to lead to publication.

You will, of course, come across others with whom you want to work, but whose orientation towards research clashes with yours. This may mean that they can, for a while, perhaps not forever, serve as research colleagues for you and you for them. Getting your different definitions of 'research' out into the open at an early stage will help you bridge the gap. This discussion may also sharpen your understanding of research.

To complicate matters further, you may change your orientation to research as you do more of it, or as you write more about it or as you learn more from feedback from reviewers. This too could be the topic of discussion, as long as the driver is the focus on external products (the trading variation).

Much of this, including what some will see as the potential narrowness of Brew's or others' conceptions of research, can itself be a topic for your writing. In fact, in some disciplines, the question of what does and does not constitute research is a recurring subject of debate, and not just in the academics-versus-practitioners direction. Looking across a range of disciplines, you can see that making the case for your research as sufficient to be given the name is often among the first steps in academic argument. This is another reason to write about it.

Alternatively, you can use this as an 'excuse' to get started: writing about potential orientations towards research, writing your response to Brew's 'variations', writing about your work in relation to what others have called research and constructing links between the two could be an important part of your re-orientation as a researcher.

You can take this a step further and consider writing in different forms – as a conscious development process, but with the possibility of publication in mind – such as narrative: outline your history as a researcher; describe your journey towards research; describe your attitudes, feelings and approaches at different stages in the process. What might start out as exploratory writing might become redefining, recovering and developing an identity as a researcher: how are you positioned as a researcher or writer in your scholarly community?; is there integration or alienation?

This is not just a matter of writing a 'how I see myself now' snapshot diary entry or essay, but more a matter of writing yourself back into research. Many people who are new to research, and to academic writing, have at some stage in their career written themselves out of research and, as their careers take shape, have found it difficult to write themselves back in.

Although academic writing in your discipline may not allow such subjectivity, there are potential benefits in developing a subjective response to research; it may be important for your long-term motivation. If academic writing – and a great deal of research – has its origins in a set of positivistic assumptions, then it may be productive to explore the limits of those assumptions. In some disciplines, their dominance is being eroded in any case. In others they are ripe for challenge: 'Historically, subjectivity has been the privilege of those with the power to control institutional discourses' (Bensimon 1995: 599).

Academic discourses have been constructed over time, they have been tried and tested and are now widely trusted; but this does not mean that the 'rules' will never change. It is not only cynics, the excluded and the disenchanted who take issue with what constitutes research. Some creative thinkers never tire of challenging the status quo.

In some disciplines, this will seem like wasting time; there is no need to develop an orientation, since researching – and writing about it – is obviously what researchers do. Yet Brew's research did include a wide range of disciplines, and so we can learn from that work what established senior researchers see as research, and there are even hints about how they do it. Surely this is a better way of learning about research than 'simply getting on with it'?

Reasons for not writing

Reasons given for actively taking up a position of not writing give insights into the nature of professional workplaces and the terms and conditions of those who are expected to write for publication at this time:

- I don't have any time for writing.
- I can't write in my office.
- I'm not ambitious.
- My teaching comes first.
- I review papers regularly, but I don't write myself.
- I don't want to play the publications game.
- I'm too tired when I get home to do any writing.
- I resent giving up so much of my personal time.
- I do a lot of writing, just not for publication.

- No one will read it anyway.
- I'm probably just afraid of rejection.
- I don't write well.

Many reasons for not writing have their origin in lack of confidence. This in turn is sustained by lack of education about the characteristics of high-quality academic writing – the product and the process – and lack of clear goal setting. Those who decide that the problem lies not with academic writing but with their deficiencies can congratulate themselves on being right: they are right in the sense that there is a gap in their knowledge about how academic writing is produced. Even those who do have some knowledge may have a 'knowing-doing' gap, whereby they have accumulated the knowledge without developing the practice.

In some cultures, identifying your 'deficiencies' or 'needs' helps to determine the content of courses or other activities you need to take in order to develop; in other cultures the very idea of 'deficiencies' amounts to an admission of failure and the line stops there. Yet, we can all theoretically, comfortably admit that no one can know everything about academic writing; everyone learns something about it from doing it. The paradox is that people still fault themselves for not having learned more when no teaching was available in the first place. The problem is that there is little or no discussion about how advanced writing – that is, beyond the level of high school – is learned, about who needs to learn or about which modes of learning might work best for them.

You may feel that you already know that your work 'makes a difference' and feel no need to 'publish for publishing's sake'; you may feel that there is really no point. Secure in your knowledge of your work's significance, you decide not to write.

There are, therefore, reasons behind the reasons: like many, many others, you may find that you lack the education, support and environment for writing. The sooner you admit that you can learn about writing, the better. Then you can set about looking for a course, group, mentor, programme or web site. The activities in this book will help you to start, progress and complete a paper, if, that is, you actually do them.

'I haven't done any research'

This barrier to writing is popular among academics in new universities or disciplines in which writing for publication is new. Many think they simply have nothing to write about.

Consequently, it seems to be an important part of the process of becoming an academic writer to take the time thoroughly to thrash out what does and does not constitute research in your discipline and, possibly, to broaden your definition of research for your area, a point covered in an earlier section.

The point to make here is that until you have reconfigured your work and your ideas – in writing – they will continue to seem far too modest for a paper in an academic journal. Yet, most papers do make modest contributions. Define what yours is, as this is an essential element of most papers anyway. Until you do, the voice telling you that you did not do that work as 'research', and therefore should not be representing it as such, will keep droning on and may stop you writing.

Intellectual capacity

Some years ago, in the midst of my discussion of ways to become an effective and efficient writer, one academic responded, 'Well, yes, that's all very well. But you're assuming that everyone has the intellectual capacity to write for publication. Not everyone does, you know.' Well, yes, I had been assuming that everyone in the group of academics in front of me was capable of finding something to publish somewhere. It was not my remit to judge writers' capacity; nor was I qualified to do so across the range of disciplines represented in the group.

It is a legitimate question, but what was he really asking? The intellectual capacity to do what? To analyse the literature, to work out what still needs to be done and to plan a piece of writing about that? And how would that intellectual capacity have been measured? Do we all need to have first-class undergraduate degrees? PhDs with distinction? Royal Society Fellowships? What would be sufficient demonstration of 'intellectual capacity'?

And how would that intellectual capacity have been developed in the first place; could it be that writing for academic journals is one way of developing it, teaching us how to raise the standard of our work and our writing? You have to handle the question of your intellectual ability very carefully; it can be transformed into a reason not to write. Much of what experienced writers know about writing for publication was learned through writing for publication.

Many people will challenge your ability to write for academic journals. This challenge may also be legitimate, though its relentless repetition can be wearing. Academics deemed 'non-research-active' may have to justify time devoted to writing. Most academics and professionals will have no dedicated writing time anyway.

Whatever your starting point, it is possible to develop your knowledge, understanding and skills – without wanting to get into the debate about whether or not that means developing your intellectual capacity – through writing for publication. Writing provides one of the few opportunities to develop. The purpose of your academic writing is to persuade readers to think about your ideas, at least, but it is also to develop those ideas. This requires you to accept that no matter how many hours you put into making your paper 'perfect' you will still make mistakes, produce weak arguments and overstate your claims. You will also find ways to strengthen your research.

In the end, I do still assume that everyone has something to write about. The question is, can you find the right place to publish it?

Turgid writing

> They make it so tedious – footnotes and bibliographies! They're just ridiculous. Who cares what you read? Just get on with it.
>
> (Ellmann, quoted in Hanks 2003)

New writers are often dismayed at what they find in academic journals. They reject the inherent value of papers published in a style they do not like. They resist the implicit injunction to 'write that way'. They reject the opportunity to transform their ideas into a new genre. They use the dominant styles and structures to construct an argument for not writing for academic journals.

This argument then provides a rationale for not writing at all; after all, the argument goes, who would want to join such degraded, self-serving, navel-gazing debates? They come to see the whole business of writing for academic journals as just 'playing the publications game'. In many discussions I have heard this literally transformed into a reason not to write for academic journals at all. Again, that is, of course, an option, but not one explored in this book.

Critiquing the dominant norms and forms of academic journals is an important activity. Negotiating the extent to which we choose to reproduce what we find there is an essential part of the writing process. Seeing publication as some kind of 'game' can stimulate new writers to find out what the 'rules' are and how the 'referees' apply them, so that they can then go off to 'train' and 'play'. Discussing the pros and cons of targeting journals that we do not enjoy reading – though they might 'count' heavily in external scoring systems – is an important stage in developing motivation to write at all.

The key point is that colleagues will not read our writing, no matter how fresh we think our style is, if we do not make some allowance for their perspective. Writing for academic journals is not about performance; it is about persuasion. This means that we always have to adjust our writing style to suit our audience. You have to at least consider adopting some features of the so-called 'turgid' style. This might require a change of your perspective: for example, if you think some points in the articles are too laboured, sentences too long and ideas too obvious, this might indicate areas that have to be very carefully argued in that journal, ideas that are more contested than you thought they were and/or the extent to which you have to embed your ideas in existing work *for that specific journal.*

The decision not to write for a journal because you do not like its style – or any other aspect of its content or presentation – is superficial. It may even indicate a lack of understanding of why the journal is written in a certain way. Accepting that you may have something to learn from analysing – and producing – a different style is more likely to develop your writing skills and your understanding of what it is that gets published in your field.

This is a contentious point; feelings run high in discussions of what constitutes 'acceptable' writing. Personal preferences are very powerful; people have very strong views on and feelings about what constitutes good writing. Once we have our preferences in perspective, we can begin to see that a range – not infinite – of options is open to us, one of them being to redefine what you think is 'turgid'.

Narrow range

For some, the range of writing options available in academic journals is just too narrow; others see this as a plus as it helps them decide what to write and how.

Finding options in the narrow range

Only certain topics are accepted   <>   I can relate my work to those topics
They do not publish my method   <>   I can focus on other aspects of my work

We're never allowed to write 'I'   <>   I can discuss subjectivity in the methods

---

Those who have not published are often uncomfortable with this approach, seeing it as exactly the kind of game-playing they despise. But it is about being rhetorical. It involves looking for a way to join a conversation that has been going on, in the literature, for some time.

Pre-peer review

Most people who have spent any time in a university will know how import-ant peer review is for many aspects of academic work. Fewer will be aware of how important it is to get feedback – 'pre-peer review' – on your writing before you submit it to a journal. You may think your writing is not ready to show to anyone else. It is probably a good idea not to expect that feeling to go away.

What makes people keep their writing from others? Lack of confidence? Unsure of how it might help them? Unsure of what sort of feedback they are looking for? A bad experience: they gave writing to someone once and were severely critiqued? Not leaving enough time; just wanting to submit it?

If you have had bad feedback on your academic writing before, why was that?: did you ask for the type of feedback you needed?; did you say you wanted constructive feedback?; or did you take it for granted that that was what you would get?; did you just react too emotionally or too analytically to the feedback?; did you ask the wrong person? All of these must happen sometimes, but the trick is to keep going.

In a 'pre-peer review' you might be looking for feedback on the continuity of your argument. Does it seem convincing? Does it make a contribution? Does it seem appropriate for the journal you are targeting? That might be plenty. Write these questions on a separate page, staple it to your paper, highlight them in colour, put it all in a plastic envelop so that the front sheet cannot become detached, give them or discuss with them a deadline by which your reader will return it to you.

I once asked a senior colleague for feedback on a paper that had been returned with major revisions required. Eight months later he put it in my mail tray with one comment written at the top of the first page: 'I presume this has already been submitted'. Why did that happen? In hindsight, I can see that he was not the right person, but I could only have found that out by asking him in the first place.

Another way of getting feedback in the early stages of the development of a paper is to email the editor to check that both your proposed subject and what you intend to say about it are of sufficient interest – as they see it – to readers of their journal at all. Without this early checking, it would be possible to write a paper that they are generally interested in, but that takes a direction that they consider moves away from their area of interest.

Pre-peer review	
Reviewer	**Type of feedback**
Mentor	Advice about journals and editors
Senior colleague	Guidance on writing about your subject
Someone who has published in your target journal recently	Specific information about editorial preferences
Colleague in any discipline	Feedback on your proposed 'contribution'
Colleague in department/discipline	Constructive critique of your idea
Constant ally	Encouragement to write at all

This is not to say that every writer has to have every type of feedback; it can be difficult enough to find one person who is prepared to supply feedback of any kind. The purpose of this list of pre-peer reviewers and their possible roles is to prompt new writers particularly to think laterally about finding feedback.

Don't forget to tell your reader what type of feedback you are looking for; it can save everyone time and effort. This is easier said than done: people are very busy; they do not have time to read each other's work.

Guilt, fear and anxiety

Many people report that they can be quite creative in finding ways to avoid writing: several cups of coffee, checking references or emails, putting on the washing. There have even, apparently, been one or two very clean bathrooms. There is potential distraction in an almost endless list of domestic and professional tasks. These avoidance tactics are probably related to uncertainties about the writing project, but they may also be related to writing itself. How many of us were ever taught a range of writing strategies for getting started quickly?

Some consider their displacement activity as an essential step in the writing process, even if they are not entirely happy with it. This is often cited as a reason for not trying the generative strategies that are proposed later in this book: 'What can I possibly write in half an hour? It takes me half an hour to get started.' They believe that they cannot simply 'start writing'.

Whatever the purpose or value attributed to such beliefs and behaviours, if they work to stimulate your writing, then all is well. If they do not, guilt follows. Guilt at not having done 'enough' is a recurring theme in writers' discussions.

Fear and anxiety recur so often that it seems important to spend some time building confidence (Moore 2003). If you want to become a successful academic writer, it might not be enough simply to learn more about the technical skills; it might be equally important to invest time in developing your confidence through new types of writing activity, dealt with later in this book.

The institution in which you work is not likely to change, in order to give you more time to write and more recognition for your writing, but you can develop an identity as a writer within that context. Over time, as you publish more, guilt, fear and anxiety diminish.

Before you start to see yourself as a neurotic or timid loser, you should consider the very real risks that you run by submitting your work to an academic journal. While 'risks' is perhaps the wrong word – some might say 'challenges' – it nevertheless feels risky:

- Your work is subjected to the hardest critique you have known.
- Experts scrutinize your research and your writing.
- You make mistakes.
- You 'put your head above the parapet'.
- You attract criticism.
- You unintentionally criticize an authority, causing conflict.
- You develop your argument beyond what you can logically claim and beyond the evidence.

These are not imaginary risks; writing for academic journals means writing at the edge of your – and perhaps others', though they may not admit it – certainty. Until your paper has been peer reviewed, you may not be sure that you have made a contribution. If you are submitting your first paper, there are more potential risks:

- What you have decided not to say is seen as a serious omission.
- Your critique of others' work is seen as too strong.
- Your statement of the problem is seen as too general, under-referenced.
- Linking your work with that of established figures is seen as presumptuous.

Once you are a successful, published author, there are new risks:

- Unsuccessful colleagues passively or actively loathe you.
- Your growing confidence is seen as arrogance.
- The area you publish in becomes devalued in your institution.

The trick is to get to grips with these potential risks, work out which ones are holding you back and discuss them with trusted colleagues who want you to succeed.

We have all had these thoughts. We all have our particular trigger, the one that makes us lose confidence from time to time. The bad news is that it may stay with you – simply publishing papers will not make all these rational and irrational fears and anxieties go away. The good news is that it will make you strengthen your arguments.

In practice, over time, these thoughts can become quite destructive prompts for writing, that is, prompts that tell you not to write (see Chapter 3 for more on writing to prompts). They can also make you lose focus in your writing, as you try too hard to strengthen your arguments. This may be why so many new writers put so much into their first drafts of their first papers. They often have two or three papers' worth of material, but feel that they need to bolster their paper, when, in fact, making the case for the work you did or making the proposal that it needs to be done may be publishable papers in their own right, in some disciplines.

This section has gone into fears and anxieties in some depth because new writers do seem able to find many reasons not to get started, or, once started, to give up when they are asked to revise papers. This is partly due to a lack of understanding of the process and partly to a lack of confidence in your ability to meet this new challenge, often without any training or support, and also partly to fears that may go back to your early education:

> Throughout my twenty years of teaching at a number of universities I have witnessed the terror and anguish many students feel about writing. Many acknowledge that their hatred and fear of writing surfaced in grade school and gathered momentum through high school, reaching a paralyzing peak in the college years.
>
> (hooks 1999: 169)

Submitting a paper to an academic journal can leave you feeling precarious, but that is not just because you are weak and inexperienced; it is the very nature of the writing act, some would argue, and it is embedded in your experience of writing at various stages in your life up to this point.

Procrastination

Putting off writing until you have 'more time'? Until you feel 'ready to write'? Convinced that if you had more time you would write more?

Tasks that have deadlines get done before those that do not. You already know that a deadline forces you to prioritize. Anything with a deadline is automatically more important than something that has not.

For some academics, teaching is always a priority. Marking examinations unavoidably consumes large periods of time at certain points in the academic year. For other professionals, caring for patients will be a priority. Writing is last in a long list of tasks and, as long as it has no fixed deadline, the first to be dropped. Even when you do give writing a time slot in your diary, it is very difficult to protect it. For some, it proves impossible.

There are, therefore, very good reasons for putting writing off, as other priorities arise. It may even feel quite subversive to be thinking about ways to lever writing into your timetable. Do you need to ask anyone's permission to do so? Who else will you tell? Who will support you as you do this? Who will undermine you? Is it simply easier to procrastinate, rather than risking the hostility of colleagues?

Some people will respect your efforts to stop procrastinating. How can you recruit their support and make sure you can access it to keep you going?

Those who write for a living can point to antidotes to guilt, fear and anxiety. They know what to do to keep writing. However, it is only by using such strategies that we can find ease, enjoyment and creativity in writing. You have to find your own antidotes and persevere when even those fail you:

> You need perseverance, courage, bloody-mindedness, a capacity for hard work, endurance . . .
>
> (Weldon, quoted in Roberts et al. 2002: 7)

The writing self

Academic writing is not neutral. It is gendered, raced, classed and, therefore, potentially discriminatory in many ways. These factors affect the role and status of the writer in academia and will impact on the new writer's learning needs in relation to academic writing. The community of academic writers is diverse, though the community of editors and reviewers may be less so. Some will see these issues as irrelevant to the development of the writing self; others will see the writing self as positioned by the organization of other writers and the position of publishing in their disciplines. For them, the whole enterprise may seem so fixed as to give the illusion of transparency, particularly to those who are already publishing in journals. Where does the new writer fit into all this?

Do you really need to let yourself be pinned down? There are ways of finding room for yourself in academic journals. For example, an interesting strategy is noted by Blaxter et al. (1998a: 146): 'You can, of course, use a number of different styles and voices. You might also use different names, as some academics do, for different kinds of writing.' While some will find this a bit extreme – and limiting to their developing profile – others will see that perhaps they have more options than the exclusivity of certain journals suggests.

However you choose to deal with the selectivity that operates in journals across the fields, it might help to think of yourself as a writer and to think through what that might mean in terms of your sense of yourself:

1 Have a reason to write that is not just about meeting other people's standards.
2 Make writing meaningful for yourself.
3 Reward yourself for making sacrifices for writing.
4 Take care of yourself, as a writer: physically, mentally, spiritually.
5 Find someone with whom you can have an 'open narrative' discussion about your writing, not just analysing barriers, but ranging over possibilities and experiences.

Many writers' experiences and perceptions of academic writing are of fierce competition. The sheer numbers of us trying to get published means that there is, in fact, literal competition to get into journals. But this need not be your motivation to write. Some people are simply not motivated by competition; they find it demotivating. If you expected collegiality in higher education, you may be disappointed. But there is no need to endure competition until you retire. This is not to say that opting out of the 'struggle' to publish is your best option – though it is certainly one option – but that you have to find some way of either ignoring other people's sense of the on-going competition or find other reasons to write, some of which you might just keep to yourself, if you feel they would put you at risk in your context.

Team and collaborative writing

This is a good way of not 'going it alone', or, as one new writer put it, 'We can begin to run in packs', and you may also be bringing some collaboration into this world of competition, with all the advantages – if you manage it well – of pooling strengths, skills and contacts. It might help, if you are just starting to write, to have someone who can help you make writing decisions, help you with writing dilemmas or who will simply listen.

You may be able to work and write with, and learn from, more experienced colleagues. You may be able to step outside your territory or tribe. There may be issues of voice, ownership, career implications, politics and time that you should discuss at the earliest opportunity.

However, there may also be disadvantages for new writers, and over the longer term this should not be your sole strategy: 'Those without sole publications are not rewarded for their team-playing skills' (Blaxter et al. 1998a: 144).

Barriers to writing

The greatest problem I can see for academics in post is not finding the motivation to write but the time amidst all the pressure and heavy workloads of teaching and administration.

(Anonymous reviewer)

This reviewer is right: time is definitely, absolutely and across all the disciplines *the* inhibiting factor for academic writers. This is evidenced in evaluations, focus groups, questionnaires and informal discussions where academic writers cited lack of time as the barrier they had not been able to overcome.

As the reviewer points out, even those who say that they have the 'motivation' to write cannot do so if the time does not exist in which to do it, or if they are so exhausted from other work that they have no energy left for writing. This suggests that even if you succeed in motivating yourself and are ready to write, you still have this problem to solve: finding time for writing and, even when you do find time, protecting it from other demands on your diary.

But are 'motivation' and our use of 'time' as separate as the reviewer makes out? Is your use of time not driven by your motivation? Do you not allocate your time to tasks that you decide to perform, knowing how much is needed for each task? Or is this too simplistic? Are you really free to decide how to spend your time, when there are so many external demands that simply must be met?

In theory, you know that you are the one who decides how much – or how little – time to spend on each of your professional tasks. In practice, however, there are so many interruptions that academics report that they rarely even get through their 'to do' lists. Moreover, there are priorities that cannot be deferred: when there is marking to be done, or when the department is visited by the auditors, inspectors, examiners or some other important body, we simply have to drop everything else and catch up with it in the evening or over the weekend or both.

This is the reality of many academics' lives. Can any amount of talk about your 'motivation' really make a difference in this context? In order to answer that question you have to go back to your motivation: obvious as it is, it has to be said that if you are genuinely – positively – motivated to write, then you will find a way to do so. If you are not, then you won't.

A key barrier, therefore, may be holding on to the idea that you have tried, really tried, to make time for writing and it simply does not work. I am not trying to make light of this predicament; there are many, many people who are at this point, but there are also those who have managed somehow to get beyond it. I do not in any way want to make light of what is a difficult journey – from not writing to regular publication. In fact, I would argue that there are some situations where the barriers are, in fact, insurmountable: anyone with a family and/or others to care for, anyone going through a break-up or a bereavement, or anyone who is ill should, in my view, let themselves off the hook for a while. Having said that, some people would find such a new challenge gave them just what they needed to take them out of themselves, to look beyond their situations and to move forward in their lives. It is a very personal matter. They may also judge – rightly or wrongly for their own wellbeing – that it is too risky for their careers to take time out.

Whatever your situation, the purpose of this chapter is not to analyse reasons for not writing – though that can be very instructive – but to progress the discussion of ways of solving the problem of finding time to write, even when it seems almost impossible.

If you are in the position of not being able to find time to write, it is time to face up to the need for change. You may need to cast off some of the writing strategies you currently use – they aren't working. There are other ways to write that take up less time, use up less energy and reduce the need for endless, demotivating revisions.

An integrative strategy

Writing can be integrative in the sense that it is related to other academic roles, and you can find many types of outlet for the types of writing that you could develop from your different roles: 'biographical, confessional or developmental' (Blaxter et al. 1998a: 139).

Writing can be integrative in another sense: it is one of the themes of this book that new writers can – and should – work on more than one dimension of writing. Rather than using just one of the strategies proposed in this book, or sticking with the one that you have, this book encourages you to move towards an integrative strategy, combining several different strategies.

For example, you can get words down on paper and then work on them later, filling in the blanks, making improvements. Or you can structure your paper in detail before you start writing. Either way, you can start a project – without procrastinating – and make progress.

The strategy you use may depend on the time you have available, the type of writing you have to do or your familiarity with the subject. You can choose the strategy that suits the stage of writing you are at, at any one time. You can adapt as you go along. In other words, having a range of strategies – rather than just one – can help you to write through the various challenges that writing presents.

Having said all that, it would not do to give the impression that writing is forever integrated and 'flows' once you have mastered these strategies; there is no way round the 'interruptedness' of writing, nor is this a state unique to writing, of course. Continuous flow of writing may not be an achievable goal; what you can do is adapt and adopt strategies that will help you connect the various stages of writing among the diverse activities of your life.

Checklist

- Consider writing about your current work; don't wait until you have new 'research'.
- Find personal reasons to write, reasons that matter to you.
- Don't let your views on published papers stop you writing.
- Combine different writing strategies.
- Consider changing your current writing habits.

2   **Targeting a journal**

'That's interesting!' • Getting to know the journals
• Peer reviewed or professional? • Instructions for
authors • Journals that 'count' • Analysing a journal
• Working out what is acceptable • Becoming a scholar
of the journal • Analysing abstracts • Defining genre
• Joining the conversation • Cloning or creativity?
• Mediating • Personal negotiations • Contacting the
editor • Wait time • Editors' responses • Checklist

The key point in this chapter is that, as with any other form of communication, you have to address the needs of your audience. Of course, you will have some – or considerable – knowledge of the journals in your field from reading them over the years. But now that your intention is to write for them, you have to pay closer attention to both your target journal's instructions for authors and its published papers in order to work out what type of paper editors and reviewers are looking for.

What is acceptable can be defined in terms of what editors and reviewers have already accepted, that is, what they publish in the journal. When you write for a journal you have to find a way to bridge the gap between what you want to say and what editors and reviewers, at any point in time, want to hear.

You have to research the journals, becoming a scholar of the journals, identifying the dominant issues and conventions operating in the journal you choose to target first. It also means, as with any other aspect of research, keeping your knowledge of journals up to date.

There is, of course, information that this book cannot supply: it would be impossible to provide advice for targeting every journal in every field. What this chapter does provide is advice on how to go about becoming an expert in your target journal and, equally important, how to start writing your paper at the same time.

This is what 'instructions for authors' do not tell you: when you start to scrutinize journals for the first time, you might well find them off-putting, for many different reasons. All the more reason to develop your writing, in writing, as you go along. It is a mistake to wait until you feel sure that you can produce what the journals want before you write anything. In fact, if you have been avoiding writing for some time, that thought may be what has been stopping you.

'That's interesting!'

'That's interesting!' may be the last thing you want to say about papers you read in academic journals. Once you have started to study them closely, you may be more tempted to say 'That's obvious', or 'That's boring', or even 'Who cares?' Yet someone found something 'interesting' – perhaps not new theory, but something sufficiently new – in every paper published in your target journal.

Some time ago, a paper with exactly this title, 'That's interesting', described research into what makes a paper 'interesting' to readers (Davis 1971). The author concluded that it is not just papers that follow a journal's lead that get published; papers that go against the grain may be even more interesting:

QUESTION: How do theories which are generally considered interesting differ from theories which are generally considered non-interesting? ANSWER: Interesting theories are those which deny certain assumptions of their audience, while non-interesting theories are those which affirm certain assumptions of their audience.

(Davis 1971: 309)

This does not, however, mean that the published papers studied broke all the conventions, but that they offered a clear contribution that explicitly stood out from the rest of the work in an area. Of course, you can do this while still following the conventions of your target journal; you do not have to break all the conventions in order to inject your papers with a 'that's interesting' factor.

Davis provided a useful question to help us work out what would constitute the 'interesting' factor at a certain point in a journal's history: if an interesting paper attracts the attention of readers, you have to work out 'Where was the [readers'] attention before it was engaged by the interesting?' (p. 310). It might, in fact, be valuable, if you have not already developed this knowledge, to learn about the types of 'interest' represented in a recent selection of issues of your target journal over the past year or so. This analysis would give you a very real understanding of what is – and is not – likely to be published in that journal.

A further implication of Davis's argument is that you should have developed not only your knowledge of your subject, but also 'an intense familiarity' (p. 337) with your audience's assumptions about your subject:

- What does your audience assume about your subject?
- Which aspect of your subject do they assume is still open to question?
- Which aspect of your subject do they assume is not open to question?
- Will you challenge either of these assumptions in your paper?

On the other hand, you have to be wary when certain areas are branded as important for research and writing, careful that these areas do not lock you out of other areas that are equally worthy of research, areas that you might have an interest in researching.

Nor is there only one way of being 'interesting', of challenging existing thinking in a rational and well-argued way. Nor can you avoid the task of making the case that your work is as interesting as you imply it is or in precisely the way you say it is.

Your job, as a writer for academic journals, is to work out what constitutes the 'That's interesting' factor specific to your target journal, noting exactly how that quality is put into words. If you do not find any of the papers interesting, you may have to revise your definition of what constitutes 'interest' for this context. You may have to admit – at least to yourself – that you have a different set of criteria. You may even have to review your understanding of what constitutes publishable work.

Getting to know the journals

In order to choose a journal, there is probably no way of avoiding having a look at them all. Browse the journals in your field. Identify the types of journal. For example, Blaxter et al. (1998a) define six types: popular, professional, applied, academic, multi-disciplinary and electronic (p. 150). Is there the same range in your field? Do you have all these options?

You can develop a profile of the journals in your field. Rank them in order of status. Some would say that you should aim for the top-ranked academic journal with your first papers, but that clearly depends on the quality of your work, the extent to which it is considered relevant by your research community and, perhaps, other factors specific to your discipline.

Are there articles published in some of the journals to which you could refer in your paper? This would make a direct connection between your work and that of the journal. Starting with this question is not 'cheating'; it makes you begin to read a few papers with the eye of a writer, rather than as a reader.

You would have to make explicit the connections between your work and the work of other published authors, showing how you are taking the work forward, complementing it or taking the field in a different direction. Thinking this way may already begin to shape your paper. Or you could be drawing up a list of possible topics.

More specifically, browse the titles of the papers published. Think about how you might package your work in one of these types of titles. Examine a few types of title in detail. For example, you may find that some titles are definitive, while others are more tentative or propositional. Some signal what type of paper it is – such as a review paper or research paper. Others foreground methodology. Then there is the title-plus-subtitle option, allowing two types of heading to be combined in one; perhaps there is a topical title before the colon and something more 'dull' or descriptive after the colon. Is this used in your target journal? Other possibilities – though you may have other ways of describing them, appropriate to your discipline – include the descriptive, allusive, elusive, humorous, ironic, topical, generic, specific, alliterative, ambiguous, puns and titles using quotations. Some of these, you will know already, would not fit at all in any of your journals. Some of them will seem to you useless. Write yourself a short list of options you are prepared to consider.

Writing activity

A key writing task at this stage is to write several different working titles for your paper.

This is not just about making it up, pretending to write a paper, but about beginning, with an appropriately modest goal, the process of writing a paper. Of course, your title will change, possibly many times, as you write, but, on the other hand if you choose a title that will fit easily into your target journal's agenda, then you may find that you have a useful focus for the rest of your writing process. Moreover, by writing a working title, you are, it has been argued, creating a link between your developing identity – as a writer – and the titles of your works: 'the titles of published papers also help to frame an academic's public identity' (Blaxter et al. 1998a: 147). Your titles may be an initial expression of your developing identity. Once you see them in writing, you may realize what that means in a way that is not possible if you simply keep possible topics running around in your head.

Over the longer term, it is worth thinking about creating a pattern of titles in your papers, if this works with the range of journals you target: 'it is worth giving some attention to the ways [the title] may contribute to creating a sense of cohesion across . . . several research projects' (Blaxter et al. 1998a: 147). This helps you to develop a body of work, a profile and a focus in your chosen area. You may find it helpful to read whichever of the many books on writing for journals in specific disciplines relates to your field, such as Sternberg's (2000) *Guide to Publishing in Psychology Journals*.

As you begin more and more to look at the journals as a prospective writer, you can also be thinking about your options. Take time to think – and, above all, write about – your developing ideas, however half-formed or half-baked they seem to you.

Read a selection of papers from your potential targets and try to define and distinguish the 'spin' or argument of each. Think about how it positions the writer and reader. Are there any ways in which you can adjust the 'spin' of your paper? It might be a mistake to use the word 'spin' here, since it has particular associations, but it is used here to mean adjusting your argument and to characterize the scale of that adjustment. It need not always be a huge adjustment.

For example, if you want to write a critique of current developments, methods or concepts, as many new writers do, you could well end up by putting your head above the parapet, drawing too much fire, being too critical, or over-relying on your own perspective and motivation. An alternative could be to make the case – and write your article around the argument – that lessons could be learned or should be learned about the subject. This is a more positive line of argument. It can mean that you can write about the very same topic, but from a different, more positive perspective. Another alternative might be to argue that future developments should take into account, or be founded on, even partly, lessons learned from the past. Or you could argue that while lessons have been learned, there are underlying issues that have not yet been resolved. You might want to question whether lessons have been learned from the past or suggest that those lessons have been influenced by certain factors, results or approaches. Can you connect your perspective to a different set of factors, results or approaches? In other words, you do not need to turn your field on its head in order to critique it. This type of adjustment of the overall pitch of your argument can sometimes more quickly be achieved in discussion with colleagues, perhaps in a writers' group (see Chapter 8).

This type of topic is a popular one among new writers, who see – and feel – the need for change and have that as a focus and motivation for their writing. There is no need to abandon this focus; rather, there should be a moment in which you consider how to covert it into a reasoned argument. Above all, write about it, in any form, before it slips away. This subject may be one of your prime motivators to write. If you lose that, you may decide not to write. You may, of course, decide, after looking at the available journals, that this is not for you, that you would rather devote your time to other types of writing or to other professional tasks. But this decision would, at this stage, be based on a partial analysis of the field. There is more analysis to be done before you really know what is expected of you as a writer for a particular journal.

Peer reviewed or professional?

New writers often spend a fair amount of time debating the pros and cons of publishing in 'academic' or 'professional' journals. The academic journals, they argue, will reach a minute readership, while professional journals will convey their ideas to the people who can implement them. At this point I usually ask the question, 'How many papers have you published in this or that journal?', and the answer is 'none'. In other words, there is a quantity of informal knowledge about these two types of journal that is not based on experience or even on hearsay.

This is not to say that new writers are lacking in ability, but that they have often formed fixed beliefs about journals and readers that can inhibit their motivation to write. Although this discussion is a crucial moment in a writer's development – without it they may never overcome their resistance to writing for academic journals – it can lead to a block.

It is important to see the value in both types of journal and to consider, over the longer term, whether you could or should publish in both. 'Academic or practitioner' is, therefore, less a dilemma than a set of rhetorical choices. In practice, there are journals in some fields that bring the two together:

Academic	*Professional*	*Both*
• Research	Practice	Study of practice generates new knowledge
• Small audience	Large audience	Mixed
• Values theory	Values experience	Researches experience

You can probably identify the journals in your field that combine 'theory' and 'practice'. This may involve you in updating some of your assumptions about what constitutes an academic subject.

In practice, however, this discussion of choice has to be much more specific to your subject area, and this would be a good topic for you to write about now, even using the informality of style and writing in the first person singular in order to explore what you really think:

Writing activity

- What experience can I draw on?
- What do I want to analyse?
- What is the underlying theory?
- What theory can I relate my work to?
- What new perspective do I want to bring?
- How can I relate that to others' perspectives?

Practitioner journals may have less status, particularly if they do not use peer review. It is worth checking, however, whether this traditional distinction still applies to the journals you are considering.

You may see the low/high status decision as a kind of 'stepping stone' model: aim for journals with less status first and work your way up to the higher ones later. Being strategic about where you publish is not just about matching what you want to say with what they currently print; it may be much more about having outputs that count. Frequently, new writers have enough material for both types of journal, but they do not realize it. Hence the need for some deep discussion with more experienced writers about your potential publications. You do not have to limit yourself to one type of journal, and you may argue that this is not a healthy, motivating strategy in any case: 'it is dangerous for us to allow academic institutions to remain the primary site where our ideas are developed and exchanged' (hooks 1999: 140).

Remember that there is plenty of information about journals, about their impact factors, half-lives and the role of citations indices in establishing a journal's status. If you are not sure what these terms mean, or doubt whether they are even used in your field, enlist the help of a librarian. Librarians know all the latest information sources and can probably teach you a thing or two about writing for publication in your field. At the very least, they can probably update your literature searching.

Instructions for authors

Many editors report that, incredible though it seems, writers often ignore their journals' written requirements. This section is here to spell out the point, however obvious, that you must follow the instructions for authors to the letter.

What not to do

- Invent your own referencing style, use the wrong one or provide incomplete references.
- Go well over the word limit.
- Omit abstract/summary, author biography or other requested elements.
- Submit your paper single-spaced or double-sided.

Instead, use the recommended style manual or the journal's house style. Of course, you probably know all this already, and cannot believe that an astonishing number of writers do not follow the journal's guidelines. If you need any further motivation, some editors claim that they will not even consider papers that do not follow their guidelines.

Another part of your 'instructions' as a writer is the journal's aims and scope. Unlike the guidelines for presentation, these are open to interpretation. If possible, talk to someone who has been published in the journal recently and try to develop an understanding of how these aims are being delivered in practice.

There may be other important requirements for submissions, such as ethical approval, statement of potential conflicts of interest and any financial support you have had for the work you are writing about.

Journals that 'count'

Who decides on the status of the journals? In some countries, such as South Africa, there is a list of journals that academics have to publish in, if their publications are to count. However, that list may change from time to time. Writers have to know how to keep up with such processes.

Some journals will count in research audits, some do not. Some count for more than others. This might depend on the scale being used in your system or institution. You can always check the citations index for your discipline to determine a journal's status:

Citations have three merits: they reflect the view of the international community rather than that of a small expert panel; they are objective and transparent; and they are immune to grade inflation. Drawbacks include bias towards established researchers and against excellent work in obscure fields. Poor work may sometimes be cited in order to correct it.

(Smith and Eysenck 2002: 15)

You may not agree that citation counts are so important in measuring the status of publications, but you will have to acknowledge that others see them as a kind of 'gold standard'.

Of course, it should not just be your publications that count; it would be nice if you could get some credit for making what is, for some, the not insignificant effort of starting to write, for, as one institution sees it, 'getting off zero'. At the University of Swinburne Business School, for example, there is a system of rewarding those who take early steps, such as joining a writers' group. While many systems reward the successful writer, others reward those who are getting started.

In some disciplines, and at some times, it is difficult to get a definite answer to the question of a journal's status. Be ready for a confrontation with different value systems as you research this question. One academic's top journal is another's *Journal of Insignificant Studies*.

- Ask the editor – editors know about citations indices.
- Review citations indices yourself – ask the librarians.
- Check web sites of top-rated departments: where do they publish?
- Look up web sites of those you read and admire: where do they publish?

This list suggests that, rather than waiting to be told what to do, you should take an active role in researching the journal. In the absence, in some fields, of definite answers about the relative status of journals, you will have to use several different types of information to make the choice about the one you want to target first.

Analysing a journal

In the same vein, there are other features of the journal itself that you would do well to analyse in some detail. Again, this is not to say that you are a complete novice, if you already read the journals; instead, the point is to develop your knowledge of the journal further through systematic analysis.

How to analyse a journal

1 Read the full instructions for authors.
   Some journals only publish an extract in certain issues.
   Check the web site. Read/print titles and abstracts.
2 Skim and scan last few issues for topics and treatments:
   which topics appear most often and how are they treated?
   How can you adapt your material to suit the journal's agenda?

3 List the headings and sub-headings used in two or three papers.
How are the papers divided up: number of words per section, proportion of whole paper?
4 Which methodologies or theoretical frameworks are used?
How long, and how defined, is that section of each paper?
5 Discuss your analysis with experienced, published writers in your field, preferably those who have been published in your target journal recently.
Ask them: 'Are the editors/reviewers likely to go for a paper about . . .?'

Look at how structure is signalled in each paper. Even in short articles, there are versions of the generic structure of academic writing – rationale, aims, methods, results, meanings, though not always in these exact terms – but in what form for your target journal?

How the structure of the article is signalled

At Oxford Radcliffe Hospitals NHS Trust we have been rolling out a programme in which . . .
The key components of the US programme were: . . .
. . . of 441 patients who contributed to the survey
This illustrated that . . .
The findings suggested that . . .
The infection control team . . . to disseminate . . .
. . . it was decided to roll out . . .
Learning points [heading]
The success of the programme . . .
This programme is not a panacea . . .
What we have done . . . is not in itself new . . .
. . . is not the whole answer, but . . . is a big part of the solution.
J. Storr (2000) Hand in hand, *Nursing Times*, 96(25): 28–9

Note the clever qualification, at the end, of the significance of the findings: 'not a panacea . . . not in itself new . . . not the whole answer, but . . . part of the solution' – is this the kind of thing you find in your target journal? Will you have to write this kind of qualification on or weighted judgement of your work in this, or in some other, way?

Develop a profile for each journal, reviewing it from time to time. You will have internalized a lot of this information, but it can help to make your observations explicit. You can then check them against others' observations.

Taking this type of analytical approach can also help you to move beyond scepticism about the journals' agenda; for example, as you take a closer look at what is going on in the papers, you might see that they are not all as narrowly circumscribed as you think they are. More importantly, once you have defined more specifically the range of types of paper, you will probably find that you are already generating ideas for how you will shape your paper.

You – perhaps along with colleagues or in a writer's group – can analyse a journal in some detail by looking at how the arguments are articulated across all the abstracts in one issue:

Analysing every paper in one issue of your target journal: example

British Journal of Educational Technology, 32(1), 2001

1 Ford & Chen

Starts with 'This paper + verb': 'This paper presents results'.
Followed by specifics of the study.
Results take up the bulk of the abstract.
Key word at start of sentence: '*Significant* differences in'
Implications in second-last sentence in propositional style: 'The findings provide support for the notion that'.
Last sentence refers to future research, but is not specific.

2 Pedler

Starts with background/context statement in general terms.
'This paper + verb' comes second: 'This paper examines'.
This structure in also used in sentences 3 and 4: 'It first describes . . . It then presents . . . and finds that'.
Sentence on findings included.
Implications stated as a proposal statement, minus the phrase, 'The findings suggest': 'Spellcheckers need to use'.

3 Morris

Starts with 'This paper describes'.
Method is described in general terms: 'A summative evaluation study'.
'However': good link word to signal balance of interpretation.
'The implication of this research outcome is considered', but not specified.

4 Holsbrink-Engels

General opening statement.
Almost half the abstract is background.

General statements in the continuous present tense.
Then 'The results are described': good sentence variation, but too cryptic?
Explicitly signals 'The main conclusion'.
Wordy (in my view): 'is considered as having the potential to assist'.

5 Sandberg, Christoph & Emans

Change of style: 'In this article *we*'.
Uses narrative structure, with time words: 'First we established . . . Then the
requirements were . . . description . . . evaluations . . . Conclusions'.
Pros and cons of findings referred to, not specified.

6 Salmon

Starts with 'This paper describes and discusses critically'.
Claims study is 'unique' in first line.
'Useful lessons' learned from the study are semi-specified.

The next step is, of course, to analyse a whole paper in your target journal.
Once you have decided what type of paper you want to write, choose one of
that type and take it apart. Work out exactly how it is constructed and how
that construction is signalled in words. What stylistic choices and rhetorical
devices are used here?

The following two examples are from the Manufacturing Strategy:
Operations Strategy in a Global Context Conference (London Business School
1996).

Analysing an abstract: example 1

Neely et al. 'Developing and Testing a Process for Performance Measurement System Design

Abstract

- First word is '**Traditionally**'.
- Second sentence defines problem with 'tradition': '**Dissatisfaction** with these traditional . . . systems'.
- Scope of this dissatisfaction?: 'widespread'.
- The solution?: 'balanced scorecard . . . in an attempt to overcome **this problem**'.
- Link with next sentence, and next step in this mini-argument: 'For **such** frameworks to be of practical use'.
- The research question: 'the process . . . **has to be understood**'.

- Aim of this paper is to research the process: '**This paper documents** . . . which has sought to understand this process'.
- **Focusing** on 'methodological issues' [that is, *not* the whole study].

Introduction

Each element is developed in the introduction, for example, 'Dissatisfaction' is developed in 'short-termism . . . lack . . . fail . . . encourage [a negative] . . . minimise . . . fail'.

Note how the sequence of ideas is signalled in topic sentences:

1 '**Traditionally** businesses have used financially oriented measures of performance, derived from criteria such as DuPont's return on investment (ROI).'
2 'The main performance measurement tool of **today** is undoubtedly the balanced scorecard.'
3 '**The paper begins by explaining** how the authors developed a process for performance measurement system design through a programme of collaborative action research.'

Notice the use of the three-part sentence structure:

'The paper **provides** justification for these research questions, **demonstrates** how the researchers collected and analysed the necessary data, **and documents** the learning that ensued.'

The authors forecast the elements of paper; they define the function of each section in advance. Note links between this forecast and the headings and topic sentences that follow:

'The paper begins by explaining how the authors **developed a process** . . .'

'DEVELOPING THE PROCESS'

Background literature

Use of listing: '. . . three main steps. The first involves . . . The second encompasses . . . The third focuses . . .'.
    Use of author's name + date + verb in summary of literature, for example 'Wisner and Fawcett (1991) also assume . . .'.

Developing the process

Two graphics placed together for comparison, but no detailed comparison done.

Testing the process

As throughout this paper, listing:
'Maskell (1998) offers the following seven principles of . . .' (p. 472).
   'It was decided that to answer this question comprehensively, five research questions had to be addressed' (p. 475, para 1).
   Note use of sentence variation:
'The learning from the two clubs was quite different' (p. 476, line 1).

Conclusion

Strong statement of what has been achieved:
'This paper has demonstrated how a process . . . was developed.'

Analysing an abstract: example 2

Voss et al. 'Learning, Benchmarking, and Manufacturing Performance'

- Statement of result in abstract: 'The results **show**'.
- **Definitions** at the start.
- Statement of research **gap**: 'This paper addresses that gap by . . .' (p. 689).
- **'In this paper, we focus** on **two** mechanisms. . . . First, . . . Second, . . .'.
- Substantial theoretical review, pp. 689–90.
- Passive voice in methodology section:
  'A structured interview was used to gather the data . . . Data were gathered . . . respondents were asked . . . questions were taken' (p. 691).
- Forecasting: 'Each is further defined below' (p. 691).
- Short (compacted?) statement: 'Thus, Optimism Index is expected to be negatively related to Performance' (p. 691).
- Language of work-in-progress: 'We expect . . . therefore we expect . . . This leads to our first research proposition . . . are likely to be . . . we predict . . .' (p. 692).
- Highlights outcome: '**This study clearly points to** a link between . . . The results of the regression analysis show . . .' (p. 693).
- Conclusion highlights implications for theory and practice.

If you find this analysis too detailed, you will have to find some other way of establishing the type of paper that you have to write. The value of the analysis is that it defines your task. Without it, you may have no more than a generalized idea of what form your paper should take. This will mean that you have to develop the form as you go along, with none of the certainty that this type of analysis provides. As you write, you will not know whether your paper will meet the journal's expectations. This additional uncertainty may undermine your confidence as you write and may even stop you completing and submitting your paper.

Working out what is acceptable

What is acceptable might be quite narrow in some journals and quite wide in others. Some journals have only two or three types of article; others have several types: 'conventional academic articles . . . research notes, viewpoints, work in progress, responses to previously published articles, review articles, autobiographical pieces and poems' (Blaxter et al. 1998a: 146).

Although it is contentious, the case can be made that you can define what is acceptable for publishing in your target journal in terms of what has been accepted, although there are, of course, exceptions in some fields: 'Many of the more recently established journals . . . allow for and even encourage less conventional kinds of writing' (Blaxter et al. 1998a: 146).

You may find that you resist or reject this approach to targeting. You may even be uncomfortable with the idea of targeting. Yet this is what constitutes effective writing – writing that persuades its audience – and it also, it has to be emphasized, defines the work you have to do.

Becoming a scholar of the journal

You can take the analytical and targeting processes one step further, making your study of the journal as thorough as your study of your field. It might even help to put aside your current 'reading knowledge' of your journal, and look at the journal as if it were in another area.

You already know the journals. The purpose of this section is to argue that you could and should know them better. You certainly will have absorbed subconsciously certain features of their style, structure and layout, in the course of reading articles for content, but what you need now is an analysis of the writing.

My use of the word 'scholar' is quite deliberate; it is not enough, I would argue, to 'familiarize yourself' with the conventions; that is an important process, but you can bring your considerable analytical ability to all the features of academic writing, not just its conventions. After all, once you have studied the conventions, how will that produce appropriate writing?

This argument is not targeted solely at those writing outside their own fields:

> Because disciplines vary, you should familiarize yourself with the conventions of the field in which you are publishing. If this is the field in which you have done most of your research, you probably have absorbed such conventions subliminally. You will have to make a special effort, though, if you are writing in an area outside your usual territory.
>
> (Luey 2002: 10)

In any case, if you are writing your first journal paper you are, in a sense, doing exactly that. This argument is aimed at writers staying within their own 'territory' who may therefore assume that they know enough already, when more detailed knowledge would improve their chances of communicating with their readers.

If you take a research approach to understanding your target journal, you might even go as far as to conducting a mini-survey of its readers:

> . . . start by conducting a small, informal survey among members of your intended audience to see who really would like to know what you're planning to tell, and what the general level of ignorance is. Then you can avoid alienating readers either by dishing up background they already have or beginning your discussion on too advanced a plane.
>
> (Appelbaum 1998: 71)

Even if you think this is going too far, or wasting valuable time that could be spent writing, you can see the sense in trying out the idea for your paper with real people. An added benefit is that it works as a rehearsal of your paper, making you articulate the main message and perhaps thereby clarifying one or two points. The trick would be to capture the sentences that seem to make most sense to the potential reader by writing them down. If you don't, you will be potentially starting all over again when you finally do sit down to write, and, more importantly, you may have lost the essential focus on audience.

Even if you think that having material that is 'too advanced' is unlikely, there may be other adjustments that you need to make. You may, for example, be thinking about your subject on too esoteric a plane. Discussion will show you where you have to make adjustments. Whether you actually make them all or not is, of course, a complicated decision in itself. This is where writing – rather than just thinking – can help you to clarify your purpose. The kind of writing that works well at this stage need not necessarily be 'academic'; paradoxically, it is sometimes best to work in quite un-academic ways (see Chapter 3).

Analysing abstracts

This section is about learning to look for the shapes of argument that a journal has accepted recently. It is also about seeing the patterns that occur across disciplines: problematizing sentences, methods for approaching the problem, contingent answers to your chosen question and so on. Abstracts begin with what is known, then move to what is not known and needs to be researched, then to the justification of the work done, followed by the argument that it needed to be done and so on.

Three abstracts from one field – probably, deliberately, not your own – are analysed in some detail in this section. If you think the field of academic writing – as an area of research in itself – is likely to be narrow, wait until you see the range of current research and the different journals in which it is published. This means that in this area – as in many others – different types of writing are available to writers, but for any paper they are writing, they have to carefully match their research and writing with the journal they are targeting at any particular time.

These examples also illustrate an important point for new writers, touched on in an earlier section: if you can adjust the pitch of your argument you can write about your topic in different ways for different journals. In doing this, you do not just re-hash your material, but develop it in new ways, sometimes even taking your thinking or research in a new direction. These abstracts deal with different kinds of research; yet you could write about the topic in different ways without always doing new and different research. In fact, it may be essential to do so in order to truly test and develop your ideas.

Although higher education is not your field, there is a purpose to this exercise for other disciplines: this section shows the kind of analysis that you need to do on abstracts in your area. Doing this analysis outside your area, in the first instance, is a good way to avoid being distracted by the articles' content. Since you might not care too much about the content of the papers in my selection, you can focus more on the analytical approach I am demonstrating and arguing that you should adopt yourself.

Perhaps more importantly, although this activity is meant to be analytical, it often draws out academics' personal preferences. Some people just do not like certain styles of writing. Of course, there is nothing wrong with that in itself, as long as you put your stylistic preferences on hold in order to produce the type of writing that is acceptable to your target journal.

The first abstract begins with a good example of that clever rhetorical device, the 'uncontentious opener', marked in bold. The opening sentence problematizes an issue without drawing too much fire. While it makes a sweeping statement, the terms are general enough to stay on the right side of overstatement and familiar enough not to require references at the end of the sentence. The case is made for the work conducted without critiquing the work of other researchers.

Abstract 1: the review paper

During the last two decades the higher education system in the UK has moved from an élite to a mass orientation, while academic careers have become less secure and more demanding, and a greater accountability has been imposed upon the system. In the light of these changes, it is appropriate to ask what is known about the nature of academic work. For the purposes of this article, academic work has been conceptualised as involving one or more of five overlapping roles: the commonplace triumvirate of teaching, research and managing, plus writing and networking. **The existing literature** on each of these roles, and on academic careers in general, **is reviewed**. At the time of writing, there was **no single comprehensive text available** on academic work in the UK. While much has been written in recent years on the teaching role (and, to a lesser extent, managing) **relatively little** of a cross-disciplinary nature **appears** to have been written on academic researching, writing or networking. **The future development of** these, and other, areas of writing on academic careers, **is considered**.

177 words

Blaxter et al. (1998b) Writing on academic careers, *Studies in Higher Education*, 23(3): 281–95

The second sentence creates a brilliant, economical shift of gear from context to the work reported in the paper: 'In the light of these changes, it is appropriate to ask'. The authors do not say, 'We have to consider' – which would be much more debatable – nor do they propose that this is a neglected area of study. This is also relatively uncontentious: in many fields, it is indeed always 'appropriate to ask what is known about' many subjects. This is an excellent way of introducing a review paper. The authors build a solid foundation for the sentence, 'The existing literature ... is reviewed', so that their review develops logically from the context.

One statement in this abstract often strikes academics as overstated – 'no single comprehensive text available' – yet, on closer examination, we see that while it might be foolish to claim that 'no text was available', what the authors have said is that there is no 'single comprehensive' text, a claim that is not as extreme as it first seems. Likewise, 'relatively little' qualifies the statement 'little has been written on', as the authors suggest merely that there could be more work in this area. The word 'appears' prevents the authors from sounding too categorical in their assertion – a standard device in academic writing, by means of which authors acknowledge that much of what they are saying is open to debate.

Finally, what the authors provide that is new is described only in the most general of terms – 'the future development of . . . is considered'. We are not told the outcome of their review, analysis and 'consideration'. For some readers, this is unsatisfying; they want to know whether or not it is worth their while reading this paper, and they make that judgement based on the abstract. However, the fact remains that this paper was published and therefore was judged adequate in its present form. This is not to say that no papers published in this journal ever specify the outcome of the research in the abstract, but it does mean that this is an option, whether or not every writer would choose to write that way.

The purpose of this analysis is to make two points, particularly for new writers:

1 There are established rhetorical devices that can be used in many disciplines to set up and develop academic arguments.
2 If you analyse abstracts you will learn what these are in your discipline.

This abstract is particularly relevant to new writers, including postgraduate students who are extremely well placed to write review papers: they are at the cutting edge of research in their areas and are up to date with the literature. Since they normally have to review the literature, in some form, in any case, writing a review paper will not take them too far from the writing of a thesis.

In the second example – same subject of research on academic writing, same field of higher education – the writer does more work to establish that there is a gap in the literature.

Abstract 2: defining the research gap

A review of literature on released-time programs shows a trend away from uncritical acceptance. Emerging skepticism about released time from teaching or service **stems from a lack of evidence supporting** its usefulness and from the mixed messages it gives about the value of teaching. **Four demonstrational experiments** confirm that skepticism by **showing that (1)** verified assessments of normal work loads contradict faculty claims of being too busy for additional scholarship; **(2)** faculty given released time usually persist in old habits; **(3)** new faculty showed no obvious benefits of a typical released-time program; and **(4)** faculty in released-time programs verbalized real doubts about how to use extra time for meaningful scholarship. **A fifth experiment suggests an**

alternative to traditional released-time programs: faculty who claimed too little time for regular scholarship learned to produce significant amounts by finding time for brief, daily writing sessions.

142 words

Boice, R. (1987) Is released time an effective component of faculty development programs?, *Research in Higher Education*, 26(3): 311–26

The opening sentence, 'A review of literature on . . . shows a trend away from [or towards]', is one we could all write regularly. This is not to say, of course, that we should all plagiarize this paper, or any published writing. The point is that there is a limited range of rhetorical techniques that work in each discipline, and a limited number of ways of saying that your work needed to be done. What is interesting about this variation is that the author did not write, '**There is** a trend away from', but rooted his assertion in literature, or at least the review of it, which 'shows' such a trend.

'Emerging skepticism' develops the point that such programmes are no longer viewed uncritically, while the term 'released time' is given more definition. This sentence also identifies that ubiquitous trigger for research: 'lack of evidence'. It is logical to assume that if we had more evidence of effect, we might be more willing to consider a programme. It is a useful, reasonable and recognizable argument for research.

The essential link between the literature, and the question it leaves unanswered, on the one hand, and the author's research, on the other, is implied, rather than made explicit: 'Four demonstrational experiments'. The link between the statement of the need for the work and the beginning of the description of it is made by repeating the word 'skepticism'. Like the first example, this abstract tells us nothing about the author's methodology. We do not know how the 'experiments' were conducted, or how the data were analysed. Yet, clearly, this was judged appropriate for publication in the journal at the time of publication.

Some academic readers like the listing and numbering – 1, 2, 3, 4 – of research outcomes. It makes for a very long sentence (66 words), but each element of the list follows the same pattern, making reading easier. Yet many feel relief when the last sentence breaks the pattern with 'A fifth experiment'. Others find the style very difficult. Whether or not you like this style, the point is that there are certain recognizable, generic rhetorical manoeuvres that Boice used that you will see, in different guises, in your field. Again, the main point is that the paper was judged acceptable by the reviewers and editors.

Finally, a third example – same discipline, same research area, different journal – shows a different approach. There is no contextualizing opening sentence, uncontentious or otherwise; instead, we go straight into a description of the study.

Abstract 3: straight to the study

Three different two-day thesis writing courses were designed and evaluated. Forty-one graduate research students completed a product-centred course which taught grammatical and stylistic rules for good research writing. **Thirty** students completed a cognitive strategies course which introduced heuristics for generating and organising thesis content. **Thirty-three** students completed a generative writing and shared revision course which entailed the production of an unplanned draft followed by extensive revision on the basis of reviewing by peers. **All three courses** were well received by the students, **but** those who attended the product-centred and generative writing courses **showed significantly greater improvements** in productivity than did the students who attended the cognitive strategies course. **These findings suggest that** short writing courses **can be of benefit** in teaching research writing to graduate students **but** that such courses should focus directly on the production of text rather than on strategies for generating and organising information and ideas prior to composing.

152 words

Torrance et al. (1993) Training in thesis writing: an evaluation of three conceptual orientations, *British Journal of Educational Psychology*, 63: 170–84.

Knowing from the first word of the first sentence that we are about to find out about three studies, we then follow a pattern of reports on each, as each of the subsequent sentences starts with a number, again setting up a pattern. Unlike abstract 2 (Boice), with all its results presented in one long sentence, here each result has a sentence. A synthesizing sentence, beginning 'All three courses', neatly pulls them together and makes a positive statement about them, quickly qualified in 'but'.

'These findings suggest that' is another generic phrase which we will probably all write at some time. Certainly, there is no avoiding the word 'suggest' in academic writing, particularly at the conclusion of academic argument, implying as it does the process of interpretation – rather than proof – so important in research.

We would all probably be happy to say that our work led to 'significantly greater improvements' in our field (whether or not that means statistically 'significant' will, of course, have to be clarified, but not, obviously, for abstracts in this particular journal). Some form of branding of your paper's 'contribution' will be required for some journals: does your work contribute something 'new', 'fresh' or something that 'can be of benefit'? How are contributions described in your field – exactly which words are used in the closing sentences of abstracts and conclusions in journals in your field? Significantly, in this third example, the claim to a contribution is qualified, again in the word 'but', so that the authors not only clarify their claim but also do not appear to claim too much. Is this current practice in your target journal?

These three examples show the range of rhetorical choices made by writers in one discipline. Although the three are, in some ways, quite different, there is not an infinite variety across any one field; if you study your journals in this way, you will have a better understanding of how successful, accepted papers are put together. Without that understanding, how will you make your rhetorical choices? If you become a scholar of abstracts in your own discipline, conducting this level of analysis, then you are more likely genuinely to have learned about how writing is produced in your discipline's journals. If you are not a scholar of your journals, how will you make all your writing decisions? – confusingly, some will be straightforward, but others may be shots in the dark.

What we can learn from studying abstracts

- How to write uncontentious openers
- How to make the case for your work
- How to link what is known/not known and your work
- How much to write about your methodology
- How much detail to give of your results
- How to define your contribution

You can use recurring phrases – or what almost seem like 'catchphrases' at times – as prompts for your writing. They need not be a constraining factor in the expression of your own ideas in your own voice. However, if you decide you do not need to write regularly – see Chapter 7 – then you may find this analysis inhibiting or even insulting. Others will immediately see the point of understanding the rhetorical norms of writing in their journals, even seeing it as learning the 'formula' for a specific journal. Wherever you stand in this debate, you can surely at least see the sense in working out what your audience – editors and reviewers – have judged acceptable in the recent past.

Defining genre

There are distinctive ways of thinking, stating ideas, and constructing and pacing arguments in each academic discipline. There are what could be called sub-genres within disciplines, represented by or within different journals.

There are also features of the genres of academic writing that appear across disciplinary boundaries. These can be considered generic features of academic writing.

I thought this was a relatively uncontentious position until I was vigorously challenged by a scientist who strongly disagreed: 'How can you say that there are such generic features? How do you know? What is your evidence?' The fact that we were, at the time, analysing examples from his and other disciplines which included similar features did not make him see it that way. This is not to say that he was being obtuse, but the strength of his reaction was interesting. Some academics are so invested in the distinctiveness of their discipline that they feel they can learn nothing from the others, that there are no common-alities and that we are wasting their time talking about the genre of academic writing because each discipline is different. Can it really be true that his discip-line was so distinctive from all the others that no comparisons could be drawn?

This is what I have come to call the 'tribal' response. Meaning no disrespect to anyone or to any discipline, I want to make the point that while it is crucial to study the genre of your discipline, it is equally important to learn about the generic forms available to all disciplines. Later in this book examples from different disciplines are used to illustrate effective strategies in academic arguments. Will you only read those from your own discipline?

It is probably important to warn new writers that, even as you learn about genre, there may be others in your discipline who think like our colleague mentioned above. They may think that you are just being naïve, that you still do not really know what is going on in journals in your field, that you are just too new to the game. Some may even think that you are proving too slow at picking it up, particularly if you seem to want to debate their views, rather than just acting on their suggestions. Clearly, you will have to gauge for your-self which, or perhaps whose, advice to use and how to express your responses to it, but as you learn more about writing you may find that you have opened a new debate in your department.

Perhaps we can agree that academic writing is not infinitely various; there are recurring patterns and dominant norms and forms within and across dis-ciplines. Consequently, the range of structures and styles at your disposal is not infinite. Your writing choices are limited by the conventions currently operating in your target journal. Each journal has its own genre, certain types of arguments that are privileged over others. There are those who have made a study of genres:

Gould's synoptic history of evolution **unfolds as a kind of narrative**. **Life begins** (prokaryotic cells), **develops** (eukaryotic cells), **diversifies** (Ediacara and Tommotian creatures), **explodes** into the modern fauna of the Burgess Shale and **then subsequently subsides** through large-scale attrition **until we arrive at** the ever diminishing number of extant species co-habiting the planet **today**. To make his point Gould rewrites Darwin's model of evolution as a puzzling story, whose climax (the Burgess Shale) is clear, but whose interpretation is a matter of considerable debate.

(Halliday and Martin 1993: 36)

Narrative is a genre linked by time words, with implied or stated continuity between stages, which themselves may be open to question – does everyone agree that these are the key stages? – and perhaps avoids the more complicated cause-and-effect mode. Simply saying that one thing followed another is still open to question, but it may require a different type of evidence than causal analysis. Some might question the link made by the words 'we arrive at', since it implies a connection that either has already been well argued or is about to be.

The point is to identify the genres that are used not just in your discipline, but in your target journal. If not narrative, then what?

Joining the conversation

This does not mean that your writing should be 'conversational'; although there is a place for informal writing as part of your writing process, it may not appear in your paper. It depends, as always, on the journal.

Lack of rhetorical education – lack of awareness of the skills of written debate – leads some new writers to write in ways that are closer to conversation than is appropriate, but, again, it depends on your field and your aims as a writer. New writers' personal engagement with their topics and their concern about finding their own voices can lead them to make their writing too personal.

What you are doing, in writing an article for a journal, is joining an on-going conversation. It may have been going on for many years. You can analyse this conversation:

- Who is already participating in this scholarly conversation?
- Who decides who can join in?
- Do you know anyone who is already taking part?
- Who has been excluded?
- What are they all talking about?
- What is already being discussed?
- What have they not talked about for a while?
- What do you want to tell them?
- What do you need to do and know in order to join the group?

Your answers to these questions could, in some fields, be topics not only for exploratory freewriting but also for your academic writing.

You have to establish your place in the conversation: on what terms can you join the on-going debates in your field at this time? Even when you have thoroughly analysed the conversation, make a clear case for your contribution, as persuasion counts more than performance in this type of conversation.

You can use writing at this stage to develop your ideas. If you do no writing at this stage, as you study the writings of others, there is a chance that you could get distracted from your own ideas. In fact, writing regularly can help you to develop your ideas, perhaps exploring several potential lines of argument.

Besides, it should be clear to you now that even those whose papers you find dull or unoriginal have put a fair amount of blood, sweat and tears into getting published. They may be well aware of the flaws and deficiencies in their writings. Yet, experienced people at the journal judged them to be adequate.

To say that we can have compassion for other writers will seem, to some, to be taking it too far, but something in that direction helps you to see published papers not as part of some great game or fraud, but as the efforts of real people to make a real contribution to knowledge. Perhaps others will see your writing in the same light. Imagining readers giving your writing this more receptive response can help to maintain motivation; in which sub-group of your target audience is such a compassionate or collegial response likely to occur? Can you usefully focus on that sub-group as your audience for at least some of the time? Of course, it is also important to consider the voices of those who will be critical of what you say and write: who are they, what will they say, how will you respond?

Taking this one step further: can you see yourself as part of a community of writers, all facing the same challenges? If so, you can position yourself, as a writer, not on the outside looking in, but on the inside looking around at how other people are getting on with their writing.

Cloning or creativity?

It is precisely because common structures of evaluation and advancement in various academic jobs require homogeneous thought and action ... that academia is often less a site for open-minded creative study and engagement with ideas and more a space of repression that dissenting voices are so easily censored and/or silenced.

(hooks 1999: 140)

Some academics feel that targeting a journal by becoming a scholar of it is like 'cloning', losing your identity as a writer, losing your own voice. Some new writers say this feels like compromising, blending in, losing your originality.

One even put it as strongly as 'prostituting' the work, although he immediately withdrew the remark, stating that he had taken it too far.

Yet, it can be exactly the opposite: targeting is about working out where, within the on-going discussion in your discipline, what you want to say can be rendered relevant and, at the same time, original. This is not about losing creativity; it is about applying your creativity to finding ways to have your say.

This is not a way to lose your voice; it is a way to choose how to give voice to your message, rather than just expressing it in the way that suits you. This is a process of giving external voice to your thoughts and ideas. Finally, if you do not test your writing, by submitting it to peer review, then you will have no voice, only thoughts and ideas.

In any case, as has already been acknowledged in this chapter, you may be very far from 'cloning' if your paper is going to fill a gap in the journal's publications:

Matching your subject to a company's [or journal's] strength may be the single best placement strategy, but matching it to a company's [or journal's] obvious weakness can make sense too.

(Appelbaum 1998: 81)

You can see an area in which your target journal has not published as a 'gap' in a different sense.

. . . pick a topic from within a journal's remit on which it has published little.

(Blaxter et al. 1998a: 152)

There is pressure towards 'homogeneous thought and action', but this need not silence you altogether; perhaps the challenge of writing in your field is finding ways of saying things that go against the grain but still find an acceptability within your field.

The best strategy is to know what is dominant in that sub-field of your discipline represented by those who are published in your target journal, and to let that influence your writing, while, if it is feasible, still being able to move away from that when you choose, and still get published. It may be that to write with too much of an eye on the business of what 'counts' may change 'the nature and spirit of the words that come together on the page' (hooks 1999: 163). This may be inevitable, but it does not always mean that the 'change' will be negative and limiting. Nor is it predictable, and this is one of the things that makes writing both frustrating and exciting.

Mediating

Rather than take yourself out of the running, there are ways in which you can build the apparent interrogation of your ideas into your writing. Anticipate the refutation of your work and build it into your paper. Show the debate in your writing. Establish a mediated position for your paper.

You can redefine some of the terms that you think might be thrown at your writing: 'practice' orientation, for example, can be defined in many different ways, not all of them pejorative. If you check the literature, you will probably find many of these definitions, allowing you to recover the term for the purposes of your argument. If you cannot find a sufficient range of definitions in your own field, of this particular term, check out other fields.

Your work could be based on a body of practice, draw on practice-based research, use research conducted at one institution to prompt research at another or establish connections between practice and research orientations, arguing that this is, in some cases, a false distinction.

Any potential tensions between what you want to write and what they want to hear can be built into your writing: you can make it the subject of part of your paper. In some fields, this might be the subject of an entire paper.

Personal negotiations

Do I contradict myself?
Very well then. . . . I contradict myself;
I am large. . . . I contain multitudes.

Walt Whitman, 'Song of Myself'

It is not certain that you will hold to the same position, in the scholarly debates you enter, for your entire writing life; you may change your mind. As your ideas develop, you may take a different slant, or you may disagree entirely with something you wrote earlier. You may have new findings that contradict the old. Or you may find that you finally do accept to modify your argument in light of recurring responses. Whatever the reason, there is nothing wrong in making this shift, as long as you signal it, define and justify it, and make it as explicit as is appropriate for your discipline.

Contacting the editor

This may be one of the most important steps in your paper-writing process. It can provide you with information that is not available anywhere else.

Many new writers are surprised by the suggestion that they email the editor of the target journal directly and immediately, as a first step in the process. Yet only by doing this can you genuinely check that the journal you have decided to target is interested in (a) your subject and (b) what you want to say about that subject. Because this is only an initial enquiry, you can legitimately email several editors at once, to see if one is more likely than the others to be interested in your paper.

This strategy has worked for many new authors, helping them to adjust the slant or emphasis of their papers so as to achieve a better 'fit' with the journal and thereby to increase their chances of being published. For example, I wanted to write a paper about writing development for academic staff and emailed the editor of the journal I wanted to target to that effect. He replied that his journal was a 'research' journal and thus not receptive to papers on staff development. I adjusted the pitch of my paper to focus more on the evidence of impact in my work: focus groups, questionnaires and actual published output showed that my programme worked. I could still write about the same subject but could demonstrate research outcomes: there was evidence of an effect. I emailed this back to the editor. He was much more receptive to this approach. I wrote my paper that way, and it has since been published. The point of this narrative is that I would have wasted several months of my time had I not sounded out the editor initially. The editor's one-sentence response was enough to guide me in shaping my paper to fit in with his agenda, while still – important point – writing about the subject I had chosen. This is not to say that we should all ask editors how we should write our papers, but should be sounding them out at the earliest stage to see if they are interested at all in what we are writing.

As always, there may be disciplinary differences: according to one senior scientist, emailing the editor with an initial enquiry about your paper is absolutely the wrong thing to do. What you do, this scientist stated, is write the paper and send it in; everyone knows what they have to do, he argued, and discussing it with the editor is wasting everyone's time. This point was put so strongly that either you have to believe it is true all across the board in that discipline or it is, in some ways, challenging to this senior scientist's practice. However you interpret his response, it would be worth getting a response from more than one published author in your field, particularly if you are new to the game, but it might also be fruitful if you are not new to the process but trying to raise your game. It has to be said that there is no great risk in trying this strategy – if editors think it is wrong to approach them in this way, they will surely tell you so.

Besides, can all journal editors in any one discipline really be using exactly the same practice? How likely is that? And how would you know? Will there be none at all who see the benefit of initial enquiries from authors? In order to find your own position in this debate, you ought to note that some journals – including scientific journals – explicitly ask you, in their 'instructions for authors', to contact the editor before submitting a paper or abstract. Some want to see a summary first. Some make no such request, but this may not mean that they are not amenable to the practice.

First check whether your target journal explicitly invites or forbids such early dialogue. If it is not explicitly discouraged, and if you make it clear in your email, if you feel the need, that you are trying to save the editor time, rather than wasting it or, worse, looking for writing tips, then it is no more or less than good professional practice.

A further reason for and benefit of this practice is that it can produce a confidence boost when the editor responds to say that he or she is interested in your topic. Such a positive response, from such a senior figure in the field, is the first many new authors have had. Even new authors understand that this brings no guarantees of publication; but they appreciate being given the 'green light' to write the paper. There is, at last, a real audience for the paper-in-progress.

A further argument for such early discussion with editors is that it saves you and them time: you do not waste time writing a paper on a subject that you know they are interested in, but that they would prefer to be treated in a different way, and they do not waste time wondering whether or not to bother reading and reviewing your paper.

We all know that in some disciplines what is and is not required for a paper is very prescribed in some journals and much less so in others. Presumably the senior colleague who objected to this strategy was used to the former. He certainly stated his case so strongly that there was no debate on the matter. New writers might find such definitive advice quite refreshing; yet, again, unless the journal explicitly forbids early contact, we have to bear in mind those advantages.

Send an email with the subject 'Initial enquiry' to the editor. Say three things:

Emailing the editor

1 State the subject of your paper.
2 Say what you are saying about that subject.
3 Say why you think this paper would be of interest to readers of the journal at this time – unless it is obvious, make the connection explicit.

With this version you are not giving the editor any work either in trying to work out what you want to know or in making the connection between the journal and your proposed paper. Alternatively, you could end your message with a question, since this prompts a response: 'Do you think this would be of interest to readers of the journal at this time?'.

Example

| Subject | *Journal of X Studies*: Initial enquiry |

I am writing a paper on XXX which argues that YYY. . . . This could be of interest to readers of the Journal because it contributes ZZZ . . .

It may be important not to say that your paper is already written, meaning that you can still act on the editor's feedback. Keep your message short and you are more likely to get a quick – sometimes immediate – response. Three sentences is plenty. Keep the sentences short enough that your reader does not have to scroll down at all.

Editors' responses

Some respond within two minutes. Some take longer, perhaps 20 minutes. If an editor has not responded to your initial enquiry within 24 hours, email him or her to check that your message was received. If you still hear nothing back, try emailing another editor, if the journal has more than one. If you still hear nothing, you will just have to go ahead and submit your paper.

Wait time

After you have submitted your paper put a date in your diary, six or eight weeks on, or whenever the editor has said feedback will be sent to you. When that day comes, if you have not heard from the editor, send an email to ask about the progress of your paper through the reviewing process. If you are going to be out of the office for any length of time, this is the moment – or find another excuse – to contact the editor.

Checklist

- Analyse your target journal: focus on structure, style and rhetorical features.
- Develop an idea for your paper that either fits or challenges the dominant norms and forms of your target journal.
- Email the editor at the start of your writing process.

3   Finding a topic and developing an argument

Finding a topic • Conference presentations • Thesis
• Freewriting • Generative writing • Writing to prompts
• The writing 'sandwich' • Finding readers: critic,
mentor, buddy and others • Finding a voice • Finding
an argument • Formulating a hypothesis •
Constructing an argument • The quality question
• Calibrating your topic • Writing a working title
• Checklist

The first part of the title of this chapter may sound odd – surely everyone knows what their topics are. They are obviously to be found in your work and research, so you already know what you are going to write about. Yet in some disciplines academic work does not automatically translate into topics for papers. There is still work to be done in developing a topic for a paper.

The purpose of this chapter is to suggest ways in which you can (a) shape your ideas into topics for papers – this is particularly aimed at those who have not already done so – (b) develop your idea beyond just thinking about it, and (c) start writing.

This may mean starting to write your paper before you feel 'ready', 'sure' or 'certain' of your topic or argument, but, as you are probably well aware, if you wait until you feel ready to write you might not start at all. Getting to the point where you can say to yourself, 'Yes, I am ready to write today; I have the time and I now know exactly what I want to say' is perhaps not an achievable goal at this stage.

This chapter introduces the notion of writing as a social act that benefits, at times, from interaction with and feedback from others. Productive writing strategies are introduced and illustrated. Their pros and cons are illustrated in a range of different writers' reactions – positive, negative, contemplative and inquisitive. The emphasis is on the value of these strategies for both starting a paper and generating ideas for your future publications.

The value of these strategies is that they produce what Elbow has called 'low stakes writing'. They help writers to defer editing to a later stage in the writing process. The 'high stakes' question of whether or not the writing you do is 'good enough' is, without doubt, ultimately highly important, but may be destructive, or at least dysfunctional, at this early stage.

The purpose of writing in these ways at this stage is to develop topics along academic lines without applying too heavily the standards of academic writing. If this sounds counter-intuitive – and it does to some academics – this may be because you did not learn about these strategies during your student years or in your training for higher education teaching, for example. The methods are well established in pockets in higher education, but are nowhere near to being universally adopted. This chapter, therefore, offers what will be, for some, a set of challenging new strategies, not difficult in themselves to apply, nor requiring extensive reading to understand, but potentially demanding reform of some of your most cherished – even if unproductive – writing habits.

It is also, perhaps, time to face up to the important fact that these strategies do, almost always, generate text. Some academics will see this as a simplistic goal; yet we all know how crucial it is – how excruciatingly difficult it is – to find ways to force ourselves to write when we are tired, stressed and generally in need of a break. We need new strategies to do this, strategies that will not consume even more of our personal time – since that may simply be impossible – but allow us to fit academic writing into our professional lives.

Finally, it may be that these strategies help writers to find a space for writing that is unmediated and unconstrained. This is not just about finding a space that is free from evaluation, but about recovering creativity, pleasure and authority in writing. This is the theme of this chapter; the rest of the book makes the case that a productive academic writing process is likely to include both mediated and unmediated writing. The case for a combined strategy is developed further.

For those who have published in the past, but are looking for a way back to writing, or for those who are mentoring new writers, these are important talking points.

Finding a topic

It helps to have strategies that are specifically designed to let you write when you feel neither sufficiently ready nor informed about your topic, even if you have been thinking about it and teaching it for years. If you have not written for publication before – or if you have been unsuccessful in your submissions – you probably feel that you have much more reading to do before you can even think about writing a paper for an academic journal. However, you can start to write with what you have already:

Finding a topic

- What I am interested in is . . .
- I did a couple of small studies that looked at . . .
- I could do better than . . .
- That paper on . . . by . . . is exactly the type of thing I'd like to do.
- I'd like to write about . . . but that's already been done by . . . who . . .

In many disciplines these are topics for writing, not just for continuing to mull over. For new writers, some of their new topics, like the last in this list, are accompanied by their old barriers and fears. All the more reason to start writing, to get the ball rolling.

A key point – particularly if you are not convinced by the above paragraphs – is that writing for publication does require you to think about your ideas in a new way; you are about to take your ideas to an on-going conversation. You have something to say that you think needs to be heard, something that will improve things in some way. You not only have to argue your case for your idea, you also have to make the case that your idea was needed in the first place. You may have to make the case that what you see as a 'problem' or 'issue' to be addressed is, in fact, a problem: why is it a problem?; how did it become a problem?; who else thinks it is a problem?; and, last but not least, who does not? In order to say what you want to say about the subject of your paper you have to negotiate with what has already been said by others.

This does not mean demolishing the work of those who are already in print – as many new academic writers do, at first – but making the case that aspects of your topic 'remain in dispute . . . [and] still invite contention' and that you have identified an area that 'has not been sufficiently explored' (Selzer 1981: 70–1). In some disciplines, and perhaps for some – not all – journals in your discipline, you have to develop the delicate art of identifying an area of contention without being too contentious yourself; in other disciplines, of course, it is more cut and dried, but you still have to make a case for your work in writing – as you had to do for your grant proposal, perhaps – without being unfair, inaccurate or inflammatory in your assessments of others' work and writing. You may, of course, have to find out what the literature contains and where the gaps are, but sometimes this is a retrospective writing task, once you have started to develop your topic; it need not be your first step in writing your paper.

There may also be a need for an important reorientation: rethinking your work in terms of potential papers. Some people see this as just a bit too mechanistic, but the intention is to prompt you to think differently about your work, and that is certainly not mechanistic:

1 What are your topics?
2 How many can be made into papers?
3 Can any of these be subdivided to make more than one paper?
4 Which one could be developed most easily/quickly?

The approach here is not to look for topics in the literature, but to start with what you know, developing topics from familiar subjects. In a sense the topic is already there, before you start. Based on the body of knowledge that you currently have, the body of experience that you already have and the reading that you have already done, you can write a paper for an academic journal, if you find the right journal for your topic. This will probably mean adjusting your topic to achieve a good 'fit' with one target journal. This will help you to extend your knowledge, gradually, not all at once, and to see for yourself that it is not necessary to do so before you write. Rethinking your topic for a particular, high-level, academic audience is hard work, but if you can focus at this early stage, you will progress your paper, rather than just read more.

You may then, of course, extend your reading, doing a highly focused search and some highly selective reading, so as to maintain your focus. This is easier said than done, as it can be distracting and diverting to start seeking out more new – to you – reading. But, some will say, 'Surely you have to immerse yourself in the literature before you write?'. Some will tell you that you should not be writing at all until you thoroughly know the literature; this is, potentially, a recipe for deferring writing. Every academic knows the importance of referring to the literature. It is not just a game of who cites whom and mentioning all the big names. It is difficult conceptual work linking your writing to others', particularly the first time you do it for publication. But the importance of literature in your field should not develop into dependency on it. The literature provides a scaffolding, or structure, on which to build your work.

I understand that this discussion is appropriate for some academic disciplines and heresy in others. I have found that some writers – old and new – are adamant in holding their 'immerse yourself in the literature first' position. This suggests that they may not be starting their paper for between six and eighteen months, or whenever they decide that they have done sufficient reading. This is an acceptable route, and it may indeed be the only route in some fields, or where there are multiple authors. But this route can also involve writing, writing as you read, developing your understanding as you read. Just because you, or some influential person in your field, has said that you have to 'immerse' first and write second does not mean that you should not write as you read. If you do not write at all during this phase, the risk is that you will find the idea you started out with has diminished to the point where you can no longer see any reason to write about it. You will also have missed out on all the other potential benefits of writing: from clarifying your understanding to getting into the writing habit.

Of course, you have to contextualize your work, for the purposes of your paper, in the literature, but this means your writing task is to produce a highly selective piece of whatever length your target journal likes literature reviews to be. You can probably write the overview piece of your literature review now, since you know the 'big names' already, and you can top that up with their more recent work in due course, but only if their more recent work is directly relevant to your paper. It may not be.

Conference presentations

You may think that even your most recent presentation is well out of date. You may think the presentation you gave to your faculty or department is just too small-scale. You may not even have thought about these as potential topics for papers. You may be right, but the fact remains that for any presentation you have put in a fair amount of work, have developed the idea and given it structure and have brought closure to a piece of writing about it. More importantly, you have had feedback on, or at least a reaction to, it. This means that you have what you could see as a draft of a paper already.

If you have a presentation coming up, see if you can miss the session after yours, and take that hour or so to write notes on participants' responses and feedback.

Writing session at a conference

1 Write down all the questions and responses from the audience.
2 Write down your responses.
3 Copy and paste your overheads or Powerpoint presentation into a new file.
4 Keep a copy of the paper for conference proceedings, if requested.
5 Reformat the text to 12-point font.

> 6 Fill in your oral comments, as you gave them in your presentation.
> 7 Do a word count. Check your target journal's requirements.

Take a few recent issues of your target journal to the conference and adapt your format, layout, style, headings, title and so on to suit the journal. If you find it difficult to make a connection with the journal's agenda, you might be able to make this struggle part of the paper. You may want to adapt the focus and key words of your paper – probably explicitly linked to the conference theme – to the journal's style and current agenda. You may feel that you have to develop a whole new outline for your paper, but that may not, in fact, be necessary.

Check the word count again. How far short are you of the journal's requirements? Is that including references or not? Do you have any figures, diagrams or tables to include? Plan the additional writing you have to do section by section: for example, how many more words do you have for your introduction, methodology/approach and so on? Or are you over the word limit? What can you cut?

It is a mistake to spend all your time – in this post-presentation writing session – outlining or reading articles in the target journal. Perhaps this implies that you should do a bit of reading of the journal on the way to the conference, a bit of browsing at a coffee break or a bit of scribbling during a boring presentation. Of course, some of your attention and time should go on outlining, but you also need to write. Your outline is, after all, a list of the topics you need to write about, and there are others:

Write for five or ten minutes (in sentences) on

- Questions asked during/after your presentation
- Discussions you had with people who are interested in your work
- The key message of your journal paper
- The key themes you will develop in the sections
- Other references mentioned by participants – do you need them?
- A paper published recently in your target journal – can you use it?

So there is no excuse for not writing. If, at the end of your hour's 'time out' from the conference, you have a detailed outline, but no writing, take another ten minutes just to write in sentences. If you have done two or three short blasts of writing, you will probably have both a decent outline and between 500 and 1000 words of text, in addition to the headings from your presentation and your notes on what you said about them.

Counting the number of words is – or is not – important, depending on where you stand on the issue of what constitutes a useful writing goal and, equally important, how you measure whether or not you have 'achieved' anything in your session of writing. Setting yourself a goal to write for a fixed amount of time and/or to produce a certain number of words strikes some writers as too simplistic. Yet, it can be an effective antidote to the impression – so quick to set in – that you have not achieved much. If you complete all the tasks suggested in this section during that hour after your presentation, you can be justifiably pleased with yourself. Time for a rewarding coffee/drink/ workout/swim/phone call/visit to the bookstore.

If you have not already done so, contact the journal editor while you are at the conference. (See Chapter 2 for guidelines on what you can say in your email.) A response will help you further focus and develop your paper.

Take this time, while you are away from other commitments, as writing time. If you leave all this until you get back to your workplace or home base, you know what will happen: you will quickly be swept up in a wave of catch-up tasks. The priority you give to writing may be highest when you are preparing for a presentation. The energy and enthusiasm you have for your ideas may be at their highest levels during and just after your presentation. The trick is to capture both the energy and focus of that moment and translate it into writing.

Just as important, of course, is to plan your next writing session: when will you be able to spend another hour on this paper? The secret to connecting up your writing sessions is to write an instruction for yourself, so obvious that you will know exactly what to do when you come back to this paper next week or next month, such as 'My next writing task is to summarize the research of Brown, Jones and Hoolihan in 300 words. I'll do that in 20 to 30 minutes. My prompt for starting is "Brown argues . . . Jones confirms . . . Hoolihan combines . . ." '. If your writing instruction is specific, in terms of content, scope, word length, time and prompts, then you will know exactly how to start where you left off, rather than going back through what you have already written – also important, but perhaps stalling your progress. This is one of the ways to become a regular writer, even if you do not have regular writing time at the moment and do not envisage having it when you return to your workplace.

Thesis

The same applies to your thesis as for conference papers, only more so, since you probably think your Masters or PhD thesis is now so old – which it is to you, since you have lived with it so long – and out of date, which it may be, but this does not mean that all your findings are useless. Nor does it mean that you have to spend six months catching up with the literature.

Even the review chapter could be an important paper, since you are up to date with the literature, your work is at the cutting edge of your area and you are well positioned to give an educated guess about possible future directions of research in your field. Clearly, you will have work to do to 'translate' a chapter of your thesis into a paper for a journal, but you can follow the steps outlined in this chapter.

Freewriting

If your response to the idea of doing any writing – let alone freewriting – is that you have nothing to write about yet, then these could be the very words to start a session of freewriting: 'I don't have anything to write about yet. I don't feel ready. I don't see how this leads to writing a paper anyway. This is not how we write papers in my area', and so on. The aim is to start writing.

By starting in this way, new writers are often freer to generate ideas and possibilities, without evaluating them. You start to write, even if you are, in fact, not sure about where the writing is going. Even your reactions to writing are legitimate subjects for writing. Writing about writing can help new writers get into the writing habit while they identify writing barriers and motivations.

There is an old cliché that you should 'write about what you know'. For the purposes of academic writing, 'what you know' may be an accumulation of your experience, education, experiments, reading, worries, feelings, conversations and teaching. This may be constituted as a solid body of work or as something that seems to you to be more transient and intangible. The point is that you can write about it in any form; it is not necessary to wait until you see it taking some kind of 'academic' shape. As a writer, you must actively set about giving it that shape, perhaps even reshaping your work as 'academic'.

This cannot be done in one easy step and this is where freewriting comes in, since it lets you write from where you are now:

> Freewriting was good. I normally write in a more structured format, but this gave me a chance to just get what I needed down on paper.
>
> (Writing course participant)

For those who are further down the line towards academic writing, or who work in disciplines where the connections between their work and academic writing are obvious, freewriting also has uses. You can use it in two ways: (1) as a bridge between experimental work and writing, and (2) to make the step from outlining to writing.

How to do freewriting
• Write for five minutes • Without stopping • In sentences • For no reader • Without structure

Writing without stopping helps you to silence your internal editor. You might think this is a mistake, since you will cease to apply the criteria for academic writing, but writing without stopping can help you to write by stopping you from compromising on content for the sake of grammar or punctuation. This does not mean that you have to completely ignore grammar and punctuation, which might be impossible in any case, but that you can ignore that level of writing choices for a few minutes.

Writing in sentences can help you to make connections and, paradoxically, to persist with writing when you do not see any connections. Freewriting sometimes produces new connections. You may prefer to work with a list of bullet points. Many do. Yet this will not produce the same benefits. This is not to say that you should never use bullet points; the point is that you should do some 'writing in sentences' for your writing project every day.

You may feel that you write best when you have a plan first, rather than just 'diving in' to writing. Again, the point is not that you should abandon all planning activities; instead, you can combine planning with freewriting (Chapter 4).

An even greater challenge in freewriting may be the 'snacking' approach; many academic writers insist that they can only write in large chunks of time. Freewriting takes only small chunks of time and this, too, seems counterintuitive to those who think that they need plenty of thinking time before they can write.

The unstructured, possibly even disjointed, nature of freewriting is also a challenge for academics. Yet much of our thinking and research is not laid out in the linear structure required for papers in our journals. Freewriting can help us to capture some of the different types of analysis and reflection that do not immediately seem to fit the paper, yet which we can transform into academic writing at a later stage. Does this seem like making extra work for yourself, creating more stages in the writing process than are strictly necessary? All I can say to that is that you might want to let go of what I would argue is an illusion: that you can match the way you think to the way papers are written. Undoubtedly, some people do, but it has probably taken them time and practice. You can always ask them.

Some people are prepared to articulate what it is about freewriting that they do not like. This can be an interesting discussion, and it can make writers more aware of what writing means to them. In the course of talking about freewriting they reveal their assumptions about best practice. Since some of these are based on anecdote and a kind of academic hearsay, they merit periodic scrutiny. For example, many academics reveal a belief that all of their writing should be of an acceptable 'quality', in many cases meaning a level that is not achievable in the early stages of writing. In reality, writing is a series of sketches and drafts that could all be called 'rough' or even – why not? – 'free'.

In fact, the quality end product you are striving for, or even your topic, will not always emerge immediately. Ideas you have been thinking about for some time do not necessarily constitute a topic for a paper. They are perhaps only the starting point. What do 'topics' look like? Presumably they can take all sorts of forms, at different stages in the writing process: what do they look like, and what types of words are used, at the working title, rough title and final title stages? In the context of your discipline, you will know what they look like in the final stage, but that tells you nothing about what the topics looked like at the earlier stages.

Freewriting may serve different purposes at early and later stages in your writing project. It may also serve different purposes early and later in an academic writing career. There is further unpredictability of outcome: will you use your freewriting text or not and does it matter? You may develop your thinking through freewriting, but not produce text you can use.

Once you have started, freewriting is habit-forming: it is easy to make time to do it, but not as easy as you think. It requires a tiny amount of your time – five minutes – but a large change in your behaviour. Try regular freewriting: for example, writing for five minutes two or three times a week. Then assess its effects.

As you do so, it is probably as well to decide on a purpose that is meaningful to you, even if you are writing without a topic in mind. Over the years, in workshops with academics, we have generated a wide range of potential uses for freewriting:

Uses of freewriting for academic writers

- As a warm-up for academic writing
- To overcome procrastination
- To start writing
- To develop confidence – that you can write
- To develop fluency – ease of writing
- To write your first draft
- To clarify your thinking or your argument
- To stop yourself editing and getting bogged down
- To generate topics for your papers and sections

- To start developing the habit of writing in increments
- To develop 'snack' writing

Can you live with freewriting's initial unpredictability, not knowing in advance whether or not you will produce useful, useable writing? Because freewriting is done quickly, without planning and without attention to structure, spelling and grammar, you will probably think it has little value, but you could be wrong. Those who persist with freewriting, twice a week for ten minutes, find that it is useful. They identify a wide range of benefits on, interestingly, their thinking, writing and, in some cases, general wellbeing. Many writers report that freewriting lets them produce text that they can then work on for their paper.

While responses to freewriting may be discipline-specific, academics are able to analyse what is going on here and to extrapolate some potential uses and even to observe some immediate effects on their writing and thinking. They can also see potential uses and effects that are arguments for continuing to use freewriting over the longer term.

What academics say they use freewriting for

- For self-discussion, thinking about both sides of the issue
- To think through alternatives to your own view
- For linking different ideas
- Developing the writing habit
- Thinking through ideas
- Breaking through rigid or established ideas that do not fit the outline
- Doing the first draft
- Getting initial thoughts
- Generating ideas – it's OK to abandon one and go back to other work
- Preparing the analysis
- Emotional expression
- 'Ventilating' feelings and ideas
- Thinking beyond your patterns
- Breaking free of existing structure in your thinking and your discussion
- For notes, revision or confirming your understanding
- Summarizing knowledge

What is striking about this list is the number of references to what I would consider intellectual development. This is surprising, given the wide disciplinary mix – academics in the sciences and arts. This list suggests that freewriting has potential to bring many different types of benefit to many different types of writer.

Some of these – for example, 'thinking beyond your patterns' – are quite creative, not in the sense of 'creative writing' but in the sense of finding new ways to think about your material. Some academics find that freewriting fulfils several different functions at once – for example, 'notes, revision or confirming your understanding'.

Oddly, you may think, some find it useful to have a writing activity that is completely separate from their academic writing; although it assists academic writing, it sits apart from it in some way. Scientists may be thinking at this point that it is patently obvious why freewriting sits apart from academic writing. Yet the above list shows how it can also be connected to both academic thinking and writing.

For me, and for the purpose of this chapter which deals with how papers get started, the main benefit of freewriting is that you can start to write, using writing to develop potential topics:

What are you going to write about?

1 What is your area of special interest/concern/study?
2 Can you combine two or three of your areas?
3 What are all the possible angles for writing about it?
4 Write about two or three of these in a little more detail.

This approach is like brainstorming in sentences – a contradiction in terms designed to make the point that you can use freewriting in the exploratory phase of writing an academic paper, as you generate topics, make connections, establish distinctions and change your mind.

Over the long term, the key benefit of freewriting is that it lets you have your say, say what you think and, perhaps, achieve both more quickly. In the process of accommodating your writing in the on-going debate, the mountain of knowledge and the phalanx of experts in your area, it is easy to lose sight of exactly what you want to say or why you ever thought it was sufficient to make some kind of 'contribution' to your field. You can say exactly what you think in freewriting. You know full well this will have to be modulated for your paper, but it helps you to focus on the key point.

This effect may be related to the impact of freewriting on writers' motivation: it gives you a space to voice your commitment to making a contribution, however small, about your topic. As soon as you lose this commitment, writing becomes much harder. As research or publication audits of one kind or another begin to bite, paradoxically, for some people they undermine their motivation to write. In any case, even if they put research-monitors on people, it will not necessarily change how they write or how they think about writing. Some people love being able to meet targets, but there are others who simply do not believe in them. Wherever you are in this debate, it is important that you have a way of getting back on track with your own special interest.

You can also use freewriting in your teaching role, since that is what it was developed for in the first instance, and this is one way of finding time to do it: as your students do their freewriting in the classroom, you can do yours; in the midst of a supervision session, you and your postgraduates can do some freewriting, thus building writing into supervision and, possibly, supervision into writing. This may make for a talking point in itself and students are often intrigued to find out that academics face similar challenges in writing.

If this whole argument has passed you by: you tried freewriting and hated it; you know that could mean something, but you frankly cannot see the point of working out what it is; if freewriting is just too 'unacademic' for you to even want to begin to make sense of it, even though you know you need something new in your writing, then you are not alone among academics and researchers:

Why [some] academics reject freewriting

- It bears no relation to the 'real thing' – academic writing.
- It is a waste of time.
- They are afraid of it (some say).
- It produces 'bad writing'.

It is, of course, important to question any new approach. Ideally, you would go back to the original source, Peter Elbow, and read his very interesting books, check his web site for current publications and read his papers for evidence of impact. Yet, most of us do not have time to do all that. If that thorough follow-up seems a bit of a luxury to you, then perhaps freewriting critiques – be they elegant or emotional – are also a bit of a luxury. Surely, it would be a good idea to try the thing out for yourself before you reject it on the basis of a semi-informed reaction?

At the very least, you can use freewriting as a warm-up for other kinds of writing. All that time you spend getting ready to write – some people say they cannot do any writing in five minutes because it takes them half an hour, some even an hour and a half to get started – what is that all about? This makes getting started so time-consuming that you really do need a fair amount of time, or it will not be worth it, and this too can become another reason not to write. Freewriting can help you to get started without delay or delaying tactics.

Even if freewriting is ephemeral – like the newspaper, you discard it when you are finished – it is still writing. If writing is a skill – without wanting to get into a great debate about skill acquisition and maintenance – then you need to practise it. If you do not practise, the skill becomes that much harder to perform. The standard of your performance may also fall. This is not simply a metaphor for writing; there are, for some, very real benefits from regular short bursts of writing.

Writing warm-ups

- I really do not feel like writing now because . . .
- I really want to watch the football/soaps/film/clouds in the sky . . .
- I really want to spend time with my partner/kids/volleyball team/TV . . .
- I know what I want to say, but can't be bothered . . .
- I have no energy right now for writing about . . .
- This is all such a big game anyway . . .
- I am bored with this paper because . . .
- My methods section needs more work than I have time to do . . .
- The feedback is just too much to . . .
- I am not looking forward to the reviewers' comments on . . .
- There is little chance that this will be published because . . .

The list of potential negatives is probably endless. The point of this list is to illustrate that even strongly negative feelings about writing and actual weaknesses in your paper can themselves be the subject of a five-minute warm-up for writing. For some academics, the person they have to work hardest to convince that they have something to say that constitutes a contribution to the literature is themselves. If this is true for you, then you have to attend to that internal critical voice in some way: define the weaknesses – we all have them – assess their seriousness and address them in your paper, as appropriate. Alternatively, cut them out. The internal critic can, if handled properly, be helpful in strengthening your paper.

Whatever your current thinking about your paper, you can write for five minutes on that. Many people surprise themselves by coming up with a solution to a problem in the paper. If that sounds just too good to be true, then I can only repeat my suggestion that you try it before you dismiss it. I can accept that if you have never used writing this way, it would seem unlikely to you, and I have been in hundreds of conversations where I have tried to point out the potential value of freewriting for academics. At the end of the day, all my cognitive persuasion will have no effect; you have to do freewriting to see the benefits.

You can use freewriting to vent the feeling or thought that might be stopping or inhibiting your writing. In 'ventilating' you sometimes see a way to reframe your writing. You might actually calm down. Some people find that they can relax into their writing in this way. This is probably a very different process from simply discussing your writing, or talking to someone about one or more of the items on the above list. You could engage in lengthy speculation about why that might be so – what is the mechanism? – or you could simply use it for the benefits you know that many other academics, in many disciplines, have observed quite soon after they started to use freewriting.

Finally, freewriting is a way to force writing – and to stop procrastinating. You can write even when it is the last thing you want to do, even when you are tired. This is not to say that it is right or fair that you should have to write when you are tired, but it is useful to have a way to get a certain amount done in a limited time and on a restricted amount of energy and motivation. In fact, if you do not expect too much to come out of your freewriting, so much the better, since you have lowered the stakes, and this makes writing, and thinking about writing, less daunting and draining.

Freewriting, or some variation of it, is the perfect solution to the new writer's lack of confidence in writing, lack of time for writing and potentially crushing uncertainty about the value of their writing – even before they have done any – to any reader. Fears of writing build up over many years; they are not going to be easily dismissed. Freewriting is one way to start to unravel many fears and bad habits and to become immediately more productive.

Writers who use freewriting report that writing is a completely different experience when they know that no one is going to read it. Then, when they look at their writing again later, they are surprised at how good it is, or at least useable. They find great relief in knowing that they can get on with their writing, get something down on paper and work on it later. Freewriting, therefore, seems to work well in staging writing, breaking a complex process into a series of manageable steps.

Generative writing

As with freewriting, ideally you should go and read Robert Boice's *Professors as Writers* (1990) to understand this approach. Alternatively, for reasons I have argued above, you might be as well to try it first and see what you think.

Generative writing is the same type of routine as freewriting – more 'snack' writing – but with a couple of differences that generally appeal to academic writers, apart, that is, from the last feature in the following list:

How to do generative writing

- Write for five minutes
- Without stopping
- In sentences
- Without structure
- Write about one part of your freewriting or the subject of your paper
- Let one other person read it

This type of generative writing activity combines well with freewriting. Some academics prefer it. Some decide that their freewriting was actually more like generative writing anyway, because they are used to writing with a topic in mind. If you find this, it could be a moment to pause and think about whether you have to stick with your current writing practice: rather than adapting this writing activity so that it resembles what you 'normally' do when you write, could you not, instead, practise writing differently to see if it makes you more productive?

In many writing workshops, academics find that knowing one other person will read their writing immediately changes it in ways that you might be able to predict: some writers are more hesitant, some feel they have to provide more explanation and definition, some write more, others much less. Asking them to show such early pre-rough-draft writing to a colleague seems to some to be unfair and unhelpful. Yet if the writing is at an early stage, your colleague will lower his or her standards accordingly. In addition, they know that they can ask you about anything that seems unclear and you can fill in the gaps.

The purpose of including this feature is, of course, to help you overcome your fear of peer review at an early stage and, if possible, to get you into the habit of showing your writing to your colleagues. You can also begin to develop the skills of giving and receiving feedback on writing.

A productive writing process will probably involve both freewriting and generative writing, and you can probably see that the combination of the two could establish a progression in your writing, as you gradually, step by step, move towards more structured and 'academic' writing.

Writing to prompts

The downside of freewriting is that you can feel that you are drifting, not focused, and even wasting your time. There may be no sense of moving towards achieving your goal of structured academic writing. As an alternative, writing to prompts can work as a good compromise, the best of both worlds: you can engage with a topic, perhaps in academic terms – or a writing problem – without the constraints of building an argument at the same time. This approach involves writing questions or fragments – incomplete sentences – that actually prompt you to write more.

One of the most effective prompts, in many different settings, is perhaps one of the simplest:

Starter prompt

What writing for publication have you done and what do you want to do?
    If you have not done any writing for publication yet, what is the closest thing to it that you have done? – write about that.

This prompt gives everyone something to write about. It always generates text. It actually gets people started with their papers. There is no more beating about the bush, no more delaying. It is probably important to use the word 'want' rather than 'must' in this prompt, as that is more likely to focus you on what motivates you.

As a next step, you can follow this up with freewriting and/or generative writing. Or you may prefer to do freewriting and generative writing first and follow them up with writing to prompts. The key point is to try all three strategies, perhaps in different combinations, perhaps for different purposes in your paper-writing process.

If, in practice, you find that your prompt does not actually, literally, prompt you to write, then it is failing. There may be something in it that stops you from starting. Rather than seeing yourself as failing at this task, change the prompt. Perhaps you chose too big or too wide a topic to cover in one block of writing – perhaps, instead, you should plan two or more blocks. Perhaps, as in the above starter prompt, you had two prompts in one – separate them out and write about one at a time. Perhaps your prompt is written in an academic style, and that is inhibiting the flow of your thinking and writing. Change the style: use personal pronouns, simple language and short questions or fragments.

Try using different forms of prompt:

Fragment   **Question**
What I want to write about next is . . .   What do I want to write about next?

You may find that prompts in the form of a question lead to open exploratory writing, as you generate several possible answers, while the fragment form keeps you more focused and produces one sentence. Alternatively, you may find the opposite is true for you in practice. The point is to try them both. Otherwise, how would you know if they work and how?

This particular prompt is, of course, one that you can use again and again. It can help you to take stock, noting your writing achievements or outputs so far, and then look forward to your next writing goal or task. Because of this it works as an effective warm-up activity, enabling writers to focus on the task in hand.

These are not the only prompts that you will have: it is interesting to study the internal prompts that you already have, some of which may not be very positive or productive:

Internal prompts that can inhibit writing

- I had better do more reading first.
- The reviewers are not going to like this bit.
- I should have had more done by this point.
- I said I would submit this by the end of last month.

You will have to learn from practice – from what works and what fails – how to write good prompts for yourself. For example, you will find out whether the question or incomplete sentence form works best for you. Does the academic or informal style prompt writing best? Or is there another style that you can develop?

It may also be important to keep the informal style for some of your writing, or, more importantly, to frame your prompts differently:

Poor prompt	Effective prompt
What literature is there on this subject?	Where do my ideas come from anyway?
Who has researched/written about this?	Who has influenced my ideas?

The so-called poor prompts can lead writers to be overwhelmed by the literature – a common complaint among new writers – whereas the effective prompt leads to an immediate, relevant and manageable selection of the literature, and perhaps of particular works by a few authors. In this way, you can write prompts that help you to do some of the thinking that you need to do for your paper. You can also, of course, write prompts that are much more specific to your target journal, as long as they actually produce writing.

The point is that you are your own prompt writer. It is up to you to tackle poor prompts and to create productive ones. It may help to write these down, so that you can consider them, analyse them and, if need be, revise them so that you have ones that work.

As time goes by, and as you are more successful, more published, you may find that you no longer need to write your prompts down; you have internalized them. As more time goes by, and perhaps you become head of department and have to put your writing to one side for a year or two or more, you may find it useful to revert to the tactic of writing down your prompts, finding which ones work for you to actually generate writing and so on. But, above all, you will always have a strategy for producing text.

The writing 'sandwich'

The idea is quite simple: you combine writing and talking in a kind of 'sandwich', with alternating layers of writing-talking-writing.

Step 1   **Writing** in a short burst, for example ten minutes' private writing.
Step 2   **Talking** for ten minutes with a peer, 'writing buddy' or writers' group participant about what you have both written, five minutes each.
Step 3   **More writing** for five or ten minutes, building on what you discussed.

The challenge of this activity is to make time for discussion – that is to stop writing, even if you feel that you could go on writing for another five minutes or even for longer, since that is, usually, what academic writers do. The point is to use the five minutes to set out, in writing, the main point of your paper – and, it has to be said, sometimes just to see what comes out in your writing – and to use the very short deadline to force you to focus. The argument for this is that if you had more time you might range more widely in your writing. Not that this is essentially a bad thing, but the focus that the five-minute deadline brings can sharpen your thinking.

The most important feature of this activity is to do more writing after your discussion. At first, you may find that you end up talking for much more than ten minutes; in time, you will have to make sure that you are able to cut that short, at least some of the time.

In order to find someone with whom you can do this – if you are not already in a writers' group, and perhaps even if you are – you will, of course, have to discuss and agree with your colleague(s) what you are trying to do, that this has purpose and how exactly you are going to manage your time. You will have to agree to just try it and to learn about how to manage this kind of session as you go along. It is not a complex process to manage. You just need someone to keep an eye on the clock so that you do move from writing to talking and back to writing.

There is a temptation, in many of these group and peer activities to spend much or all of your time just talking about writing, promising each other and yourselves that you will actually do the writing at some later date. This is to miss an opportunity to get some writing done and, more importantly, to get some of the essential thinking done.

The value of this mode of working is that it captures the positive response of your peer discussion and lets you use the impact of that to motivate you to write more. Such discussions often throw up other subjects for your writing, and you can capitalize on your writing time by doing it right away, rather than trying to remember what you wanted to write about later. In addition, you are rehearsing your arguments, and verbal feedback can help you to sharpen them. For example, subjects for further writing that can be prompted by such discussions include:

- I have to define this more carefully . . .
- I need to add a bit on . . .
- I can move on to write the bit on . . .
- I have to elaborate on what I wrote about . . .
- I have made a bit of a jump here, the connection is . . .

These new writing topics are not just responses to your peer's comments; they arise from the thinking about your writing that carries on while you are talking or listening. This does not mean that you should direct your writing towards your peer – you might have to watch out for that – unless he or she actually reads your target journal and is, therefore, part of the audience for your writing and is prepared to respond appropriately; instead, you are using him or her as a sounding board – and not just for your ideas, but for your writing practices. By doing this you are opening up the many stages in academic writing, often left unspoken in academic environments, revealing your on-going choices, decisions and uncertainties. The more you work with each other, the better your understanding will be of what you are both trying to achieve in your papers.

Peer discussion is also important for motivation to write. Giving each other mutual encouragement can be even more motivational, as you are helping someone else, in a small way, to get on with their writing. In these short discussions, there can be valuable consolidation of work that you have already done, thereby preventing you from getting bogged down in your sense of what you still have to do to finish the paper.

These discussions also provide feedback on your writing. You can use them as an early form of peer review. You can discuss the types of feedback you are looking for – structure, content, style, 'contribution', focus and so on – and can make it as 'hard' or 'soft' as you want at any given time.

In fact, the writing 'sandwich' structures feedback into your writing practice. Rather than waiting until you have brought your paper to a stage of completion, and you are ready to submit it, you get feedback at several much earlier stages, and from someone who knows what you are trying to achieve in your paper, and who is, therefore, potentially well placed to tell you whether or not you are achieving it.

An added benefit of this, as an academic writing practice, is that it normalizes incompleteness. Clearly, any paper is incomplete for a certain amount of time, but this rather obvious statement can become problematized, particularly for new writers, or for anyone who does not have a clear sense of writing as a process, to the extent that they lose sight of the writing goal, only seeing a messy, incomplete paper where there could be a gradual progression towards completeness. In other words, these regular discussions of your on-going writing project can help you to be realistic and positive about your developing paper, not just in an emotional sense but also in an intellectual sense: the writer who does not see the paper as gradually developing may be tempted to add further points, with the aim of strengthening the paper, that actually detract from the main argument by blurring its focus. More is not necessarily better.

The 'writing sandwich' is another strategy for getting into the writing habit. In such 'sandwich-structured' meeting you are building writing into work time, and not just giving up your personal time. Perhaps more significantly, you are bringing writing into peer interactions. Workplace discussions that might previously have been limited to the topics of teaching, marking and meetings can now also include your writing. Initially, you might want to share this with no more than the select few with whom you work in this way, but later you might alert others to the fact that you are actively writing.

For example, it might be politic to remind your head of department of what you are doing – and how much you are producing – in these 'sandwich' meetings, even if you do not use precisely that term in such discussions. You might even want to go a step further and externalize your goal: tell your head of department exactly what you are writing about, which journal you are targeting, and roughly or exactly when you expect to submit. If your paper has developed out of a conference presentation, funded by the department, be sure to say that too. Mention your progress towards your goal of submitting your paper the next time you see him or her. Later, of course, you can happily report submission as and when that great day dawns. Do not worry if the response is complete indifference; the purpose of the conversation is to give information not to seek reinforcement. On the other hand, you may actually pick up a tip or two about the journal that will help you to target it more effectively, although if the information provided is liable to take you down a completely different tack in your paper, you might want to get a second opinion.

Above all, in the sandwich meetings you are protecting time by putting writing, cloaked or disguised as a 'meeting', in your diary. If these meetings are not in your diary, they are not in real time, and it is highly likely that they will be displaced by one of your other responsibilities or tasks.

It has to be emphasized here, as for other writing activities in this book, that someone in another discipline can give you useful feedback, even if you are not initially convinced of the possibility; sometimes this is better than feedback from someone in your discipline, 'better' in the sense of holding the focus on what you want to say, rather than adding all sorts of related issues and potential topics. People in your discipline are likely to react to the content of your writing; discussion is likely to range over debates and definitions. This may not help you to keep going with the argument you are formulating; it may stimulate you, instead, to add new points and may, thereby, disrupt the focus of what you want to say and unravel your argument. Of course, at some stage, feedback from colleagues in your discipline will be crucial; I am not arguing against it. The point is to be aware of the pros and cons of feedback from both types of reader, particularly since many academic writers – because our discipline base is so central to our writing and thinking – are not aware of the benefits of trans-disciplinary discussions of this type.

How often you do this 'writing sandwich' will, of course, depend on a number of factors, but if you feel that it has to come last in a long list of other tasks, then either you might be on the way to deciding not to do it at all before you have really given it a proper chance to work, or you might make the sensible decision to meet once a month at first, if that is all you can manage. Once a week sometimes seems to be too often. Once every two weeks generally works better.

How long you meet for can vary in the same way, but you should probably set aside an hour, knowing that you can get through the writing sandwich process in 50 minutes. Over time, with practice, you can probably develop your meetings:

- Try quick taking-stock meetings of 20 minutes over the phone, if you do not have time to meet face-to-face.
- Try using more of the 50-minute meeting to do writing, with very brief discussions of writing goals at the start and end of the meeting.
- Try building up to using the whole session for writing, starting where you left off at your previous meeting (at which you wrote yourself a writing instruction for your next task, so that you could start writing immediately).

You do not all/both have to do the same task at each session. The above list gives you some of the options that you might want to try at different times. You may also find that you come up with other options. As long as you stick to the time limit you have allocated yourselves, then you will be able to manage the writing, rather than letting it run away with you and, potentially, creating problems in other areas of your lives.

What can go wrong? What is most likely to happen to undermine your good intentions to use the writing sandwich is that you meet and decide that you do not really need to do any writing there and then, and that you will instead just talk about it. This means that your writing is postponed, rather than pro-gressed. To avoid this, you should arrive at any writing meeting feeling that you want to seize any opportunity, any time slot – however small – to write. Another problem might be that one of you has to cancel the meeting, meaning that you both lose out on the potential benefits of the interaction, at least, and, at worst, you fail to write. To avoid this, you have to have an alternative up your sleeve: if your colleague cancels, where will you go, what and how will you write, and is there anyone else with whom you can discuss it in the meantime, until your rescheduled meeting?

If this is all beginning to sound just a bit too 'scheduled', then you can reflect on why it is that stages in a writing project generally are not scheduled in this way, or, if they are, why no one talks about it. Other professional tasks are usually scheduled. This is not to say that we should bureaucratize writing, but that not to have some timetable for completing the task is one way of making sure it does not get done.

To sum up, there are many potential benefits of progressing your writing in this way:

Benefits of the 'writing sandwich'

- It's quick. It doesn't take up much of your time.
- You have a real audience who gives you a real response to your writing.
- You get immediate feedback, usually a positive reaction.
- You can respond to it immediately, in further writing for your paper.
- Each meeting constitutes a deadline.
- The meeting may be your only writing time, but at least you have that.
- The discussion usually stimulates more writing.

If you do find that you are tiring of this way of working, you can, of course, move on: build up to longer bouts of writing, work with other partners, bring together a writers' group, use the five-minute writing slot as a warm-up only, then move on to more academic writing. As your paper takes shape and as your structure becomes fixed, you can probably write straight from your outline, using it as a kind of agenda for writing.

It is perhaps worth pointing out an obvious feature of this strategy that is a key to its effectiveness, but that academic writers often struggle with both conceptually and behaviourally: the importance of keeping these interactions short and focused. Any time you sit down to write, you should try to design the writing slot in terms of time, content, using specific verbs – rather than the general verb 'writing' – and in terms of number of words required for the section.

As writers who have attended writers' groups or retreats begin to develop an incremental writing strategy, using the 'snacking' strategies, some report that they wrote regularly for three months after the retreat and then stopped. However, thanks to the strategies they learned on the retreat, they know how to get back on track. Sometimes they benefit from a refresher course or meeting, yet another argument for repeat retreats or regular departmental writing days away.

Remember that unless you have some way of dividing up the writing task, in terms of small sub-goals that are achievable in small amounts of time, then it is difficult, and at times impossible, to fit writing into smaller blocks of time. There may, at certain points in the working year, be no large chunks of time available for writing at all.

For new writers, the strategies in this chapter involve repositioning yourself as writer: for example, you can email an editor and say that you missed your end of the month deadline, but could have your paper in by the end of next week. In other words, create a new deadline and externalize it, rather than wasting any more time and energy worrying about whether or not they will still want it or feeling guilty about having missed the first – or second or third – deadline.

You can see yourself as actively solving writing problems. You get yourself to the position where you come up against a reason for not writing or another commitment that is getting in the way of your writing meeting and, instead of letting anger and frustration build up, you immediately start thinking about how you are going to make another time slot. Sometimes you do all this by yourself, sometimes in discussion with others, but you are always looking for solutions to, particularly, the problem of making time for writing and protecting it.

In any case, even as you solve that problem, another is coming along. There are still uncertainties. One of the stages of becoming a writer is to develop strategies that get you though this, that actually get writing done, and to be able to change strategies when the one you chose fails.

It may be time to do a bit of targeted reading. Perhaps there is an area where you now see you need to have a better grounding in the methodologies or approaches that others have used, so that you can measure yours against them and, if possible, make a stronger case for what you did, particularly if your piece of work is more modest than others'. This is not the end of the world – or your paper; it means that you might have to write more about methodology, or whatever that area is called in your target journal than you had originally planned. You might have to include some new topics, comparing your study to others in order to show that what you did, while contested and not as strong as others, was still sufficient to answer your research question.

This 'stop-and-read' moment may occur at any time. The trick is making sure that it does not stop you from writing altogether. It may be useful, for example, if you are writing about new reading, to rehearse how you will write about it, if at all, in your paper.

Writing can show up gaps in your thinking, and sometimes that prompts you to read more; yet, a gap in your writing does not necessarily represent or signal a gap in your reading. In fact, reading more can create new gaps – or the impression of them – in your writing. Any developing argument has gaps, gaps that require further writing, not just reading. The writing sandwich process can help you to develop further writing to fill the gap, through interaction with a peer rather than a pile of books and journal articles.

The school of thought that says you should not be writing until you know all the literature may make its voice heard at this time – either actually or internally – but writing as you read is one way of mastering the literature, and it is certainly possible to write without full 'mastery' of others' writing and research.

Knowing that dissatisfaction is part of the writing process, it might help to develop a sense of 'contingent satisfaction', meaning that you have defined what is 'good enough' to submit and can develop sufficient satisfaction to force yourself to let someone read it or to send it off to the journal. This is not to say that you send in a draft and use the reviewing process for feedback, but that you should not expect to feel completely happy with everything in your paper. Anyone who has written a PhD will recognize this feeling; it was meant to be your best work, but you know it has deficiencies. Yet you passed.

This feeling of the work not being good enough may have important origins in your lack of knowledge about what constitutes an/'the' acceptable standard of writing and research. Both your knowledge and your sense of the inadequacy of your work diminish somewhat as your papers begin to be published, because you begin to learn what that standard is. Moreover, this habit of questioning our work – by ourselves – is, of course, useful. We would not want to be complacent.

Finding readers: critic, mentor, buddy and others

A writing mentor is someone who actively wants you to develop and achieve as a writer. For the purposes of writers' groups, I have developed a note to guide those who are willing to take on this role. For writers, it might help them think through what they are looking for and to listen carefully to anyone who appears to be giving this kind of support. Clearly, you can deter-mine the role in a number of ways, or you may find that you have to take what you get.

This role might be formally or informally instituted in your department. You and your mentor might have to negotiate how you want to work together within certain parameters, such as the frequency of your meetings.

Notes for writing mentors

This note provides an initial guide to the role of writing mentor. Its purpose is to prompt discussion among those learning to play the role, those who are already mentors and those who are being mentored.

Remit

The remit of the writing mentor could be defined as follows:

- To support the development of specific, achievable goals and sub-goals and maintain the writer's focus on them
- To maintain contact with writers
- To provide support and specific advice to writers as required
- To monitor the writer's progress towards achieving specified goals
- To monitor 'study buddy' and other mentoring relationships
- To follow up on lapses, delays and failure in writing.

Experience suggests that writers may each require different forms of support; that is, all of these forms will not be required by all writers. Furthermore, the role can be customized by writers and mentors.

Tasks

The mentor's activities could include the following:

1 Weekly email contact with writers
2 Occasional one-to-one discussions as required
3 Occasional discussions with groups of writers, as appropriate

Time

One hour per week/month maximum, as agreed

In my staff development role I provide advice for mentors, who also need support, particularly if they are to find time to support writers and still have time for their own writing. Not everyone is a natural mentor. Many are willing to admit this and seek advice on how to play this role. Some do not feel that they are experts with sufficient authority, perhaps even lacking a credible body of publications themselves. Some mentors, therefore, will provide expert help; others might simply provide a more general form of support, which can be equally important. If you are writing your first paper and the resident experts seem intimidating, or simply will never make time to give you the benefit of their knowledge and experience as writers, then you will have to resort to some other form of mentoring, and for some that will suit them better in any case.

Finding a voice

The paper will achieve a far wider readership under my name than under the name of an unknown. Surely these considerations are more important than mere personal vanity?

(McCall Smith 2003: 31)

It is not simply 'personal vanity' that makes us want to have our say, in our own voices, and to be acknowledged for that.

Would voice-activated software or talking into a Dictaphone help you to find a writing voice? Some people wonder if this would help them to become more fluent in their writing, helping them to record ideas and rehearsals of text as they think of them; others find it a useful way to capture ideas quickly, particularly if they are engaged in another activity, like driving, for example.

If you do not have typing skills, speaking has obvious attractions. Perhaps in due course we will all use voice recognition software for many tasks, not just for writing. Without wanting to get into that debate – particularly on something that seems to be, for the moment, quite a personal choice – you could try these strategies and see what happens.

However, it may be that discussing your ideas and writing with others is a better, quicker way of developing your writing voice; doing regular writing, in a variety of modes, will help you, over time, develop your writing.

Finding an argument

There is nothing more to be said on this subject. Nothing.

(McCall Smith 2003: 11)

Writing about the connections and distinctions between your work and others' may reveal that you do not really know what they are, have not clearly worked out what precisely the main ones are and/or what exactly constitutes a viable argument in your field at the time of writing. Using this as a prompt for writing can help you to hone your own argument:

- What are the connections between your work and the work of other scholars and researchers?
- What are the distinctions between your work and theirs?
- What is the main connection between your paper and their publications?
- What is the main distinction between your paper and theirs?

Making a proposition:

> Propositions are interesting or uninteresting only in relation to the assumption-ground of some audience.
>
> (Davis 1971: 328)

Asserting a proposition is a legitimate way of writing for publication, but for it to work you will have to contextualize it thoroughly. You will also have to include the debate around your proposition in what, to borrow a term from Davis (1971), could be called an 'internal dialectic' (p. 331):

- What propositions have been generated about your subject?
- Which of these have become 'taken from granted' assumptions?
- What new proposition have you generated?
- How does your argument relate to established propositions?
- How does your argument relate to current assumptions?

This is not just a matter of including both sides of the debate, but about ensuring that your set of assumptions stands up against others' in a way that shows the sense of yours.

Formulating a hypothesis

> The role of hypotheses in research is an interesting one. Some writers on research methods treat hypotheses as a necessary part of research . . . However, this is an unnecessarily limited view of research. It fits well with a situation where there is an already well developed body of knowledge – that is, established theory from which hypotheses may be derived – but is less appropriate where the research is more concerned with developing our understanding of a relatively new field of study, that is, where the need is for theory building more than theory testing.
>
> (Burton and Steane 2004)

> Scientific research begins with a problem . . . Problems are tackled by the method or investigation, in an attempt to obtain evidence related to a hypothesis. If the problem is stated as a question, then each hypothesis is a possible answer to the question or a possible explanation.
>
> (Barrass 2002: 2–3)

A hypothesis is a general proposition. It is often taken as a principle on which an argument is based. It is a premise from which to draw a conclusion or, alternatively, the basis for action. The hypothesis tells us that certain things are known and that we can base future action and thought on these. In science it is used as a starting point for further investigation.

These definitions raise questions for your writing. If you are to include a hypothesis:

- Which type of research have you done – in a new field or in an established one?
- Were you testing or building theory?
- Are hypotheses used in journals in your field?
- If so, what do they look like?
- How exactly are they written – in what terms, using which words?

In other words, you can develop your understanding and use of hypotheses, if they are appropriate at all, by studying papers published in your target journal.

Constructing an argument

An argument starts by establishing a problematic, which is an argument in itself: how is this done in your target journal? List and analyse the published authors' ways of referring to the literature and/or to the published work of others.

How is the research gap defined? How is the literature defined?

- deficient
- open to debate
- incomplete
- missing certain components
- narrow

When you problematize – that is, when you make the case that you have an issue worth writing about – your issue in the literature, you do not have to problematize the literature itself.

A good technique for modulating the problematic is to refer to or quote someone in your field who has been even harsher or more radical than you want to be in his or her critique of a piece of research or a publication. This works particularly well if the harsh critic is an authority who is widely respected in your field.

The process of contextualizing your ideas in others' work – reviewing the literature – is not just a means to an end, going through the motions of mentioning the great, the good and the not-so-good-at-all; it is a way of honing your ideas and your thinking processes. You may feel that the end result is that you have blunted your original idea, when, in fact, you are likely to have sharpened it.

How you actually produce the type of sentences that are required, the type of academic writing you need, will be shaped by your target journal. Examples of academic arguments are analysed in Chapter 6 to demonstrate some of the key techniques.

The quality question

This chapter has introduced three strategies for generating text: freewriting, generative writing and writing to prompts. This gives you three ways to force yourself to write, even when you least feel like it and even when you are most uncertain about your topic and your ability in writing. All of them can be practised in very short amounts of time, a key feature for overloaded academics. Simply being able to produce text on demand is reassuring and builds confidence. These are important outcomes for academics who want to become regular, productive and successful writers.

For every research task, there can be a writing task. The writing strategies covered in this chapter are primarily about getting new writers started. At some point, you know you have to address the question of the quality of your writing, but, it has to be emphasized, this does not mean that you should stop using these generative strategies and move into a stage of revision.

The quality question means attending to the structure and style of your text, and your ability to do this may depend on how much effort you put into analysing articles in your target journal. Quality is defined in a particular way for that particular journal.

Calibrating your topic

Once you have (a) developed your topic, (b) started writing about it, (c) discussed it with your trusted peers, (d) topped up your reading and (e) had some pre-peer review – perhaps not exactly in that order – you need to check that your paper is still aligned with your target journal. If you have not already done so, write a working title to help you and your readers focus on the main point and your treatment of it. If you have, revise it now. Then compare your paper with a paper of a similar type published in your target journal within the past year. Assess the extent to which you are still doing what you set out to do:

- Are you doing what you said you would do in your email to the editor?
- Go back to your profile of the journal: does your paper fit it so far?
- Scan a couple of recent issues of the journal. Read a paper of the type that you are writing. Then review your own paper.
- Ask someone who reads the journal to read your writing so far and/or to discuss your ideas with you to assess how they 'fit'.
- Better still, if you know and trust someone who has been published in your target journal, and if they have time, ask them to read what you have written so far.

Use the feedback you get as prompts for further writing, developing your topic and perhaps even planning some of your sections. Write your development points in sentences – rather than notes – so that you think them through a bit more and, in the process, work out whether or not you need them in your paper at all.

It is perhaps worth repeating that this does not involve you in 'cloning' yourself to the journal; instead this is one of your focusing devices. This is another activity that you can bring to your writers' group.

Writing a working title

As you are thinking about writing or revising your working title, you might want to consider Sternberg's (2000) take on titles in academic publications ('Titles and abstracts: They only sound important'):

> Whether your article will be read by many people, few people, or virtually none at all . . . can be largely a function of the title and the abstract.
>
> (p. 37)

A working title can be a useful focusing device as you write. It can keep you from straying too far from your main line of argument. It gives your paper a name – distinguishing it from your other projects – with which you can refer to it over the weeks and months of planning, researching and writing.

You will already have identified your key words. How can you fit them into your title? Having scrutinized the journal, you know what types of titles they like to see:

- Is it the catchy buzz word?
- The contentious statement?
- The main catchy title – colon – then a more descriptive title?
- Is it a question?
- A question and an answer?

Your title can be an important starting point in catching the reader's interest, but since your first reader will be the editor, it is a good idea to model the style and content of your title closely on the limited range that appears in the journal. Remember also to put in the key words that will bring up your paper in literature searches.

Checklist

- Look for topics in what you already do, know or think.
- Use regular 'snacking' activities to produce text quickly.
- Defer the 'quality question' until later.
- Discuss your writing with others, show it to them at an early stage and get feedback.

4 Outlining

Level 3 outlining • Allocating word lengths • Writing an abstract – Brown's 8 questions • Outlining a paper – Murray's 10 prompts • Calibrating your outline • Checklist

It would be foolish to maintain that all writing must be planned. But it does not seem unreasonable to assert that good writers must be able to plan.

(Bereiter and Scardamalia 1987: 192)

... trying to follow a written plan can interfere with the generation of ideas through writing.

(Torrance et al. 1991: 46)

... planning encompasses more than the cognitive process of determining 'what to say' and 'what to do' in the text to be written.

(van der Geest 1996: 9)

The first quotation is itself a model of good academic writing: the authors use the device of starting with an overstatement and then distance themselves from it, not only making it clear that they do not intend to go that far, but also making their position in the to-plan-or-not-to-plan debate seem reasonable. They also make subtle, persuasive use of the double negative in the proposition that follows: how different is the effect of their chosen expression, 'it does not seem unreasonable to assert', from 'it seems reasonable to assert' – much more effective in the context of academic argument, much less likely to provoke instant refutation.

As a result, for all that every single academic will already have formed his or her own views on the value of planning in academic writing, the authors have eased themselves into the debate without immediately drawing too much fire – cleverly done. The authors must have thought carefully not only about the subject of their writing – how planning and writing interact – but also about how they could make their case persuasively in the context of on-going debates.

We can all agree with the authors that it is a good idea to plan writing or, for the purposes of this chapter, to produce an outline of your paper; the question is how to go about it when you are writing a paper for an academic journal: how much outlining should you do, in what form, what should an outline of this type of writing look like, and how will you use your outline as you write, if at all?

The second quotation – from a very different type of writing – questions whether planning serves any useful purpose at all; it may, instead, simply interrupt your writing process:

> Elbow [1973] and Wason [1985] both suggest that, as an alternative to constructing a plan, writers should simply start to compose in full text, allowing thought and inscription to run concurrently. This, they argue, may facilitate the generation of ideas in a way that is not possible when the writer is constrained by a pre-determined plan. Similarly, Scardamalia and Bereiter (1985) argue that writing strategies that permit an interaction between idea generation and inscription will produce text that is richer in both content and expression. However, they also observe that the skills required to manage such an interaction effectively are underdeveloped in many writers.
>
> (Torrance et al. 1991: 53)

While this study was conducted on undergraduates, it would be difficult to argue that it has no relevance whatsoever for academics who write, since the undergraduate years are, for many, the final opportunity for learning about writing. (At the doctoral level it is often assumed that writers already know what they need to know about writing.)

Perhaps the most contentious sentence in this quotation is the last one: 'writers' – which must include some academics, perhaps particularly new writers – will not necessarily have developed these skills. This is not to say that they cannot do so; if there is a barrier – to writing and development – it may exist among those who think they do not have to develop their skills.

The specific skills needed may not be what are often referred to as technical skills; it may be much more important that you develop the skills 'to manage [the] interaction of "idea generation" and "inscription" '. Planning, or outlining, can be a separate process, but it is not a good idea to stop writing while you plan. Nor should you expect your writing to flow once you have an outline. Nor will your best outline remain intact throughout the writing process.

Outlining – whatever that might mean in practice, in terms of specific activities – involves a range of very different thinking processes.

The purpose of outlining

- 'idea generation'
- forming a structure
- linking ideas
- clarifying a contribution
- creating coherence
- sifting and eliminating ideas
- finding direction
- contextualizing your work

Finding a way to do all of these at once may not be an achievable goal, or it may be a long-term goal, the by-product of multiple publications. What is feasible, even for new writers, is combining outlining and regular writing. Since this may be easier said than done – given the research referred to above – examples of frameworks and suggested writing activities are included in this chapter. The key point is that although the subject of outlining is treated here in a separate chapter, as if it were a discrete step, the activities described in other chapters are to be used here too.

The third quotation, drawing on earlier important work by Flower and Hayes (1981), identifies three different but related processes involved in the planning or outlining stage: 'setting goals for the execution of the writing task, generating ideas for the content of the text, and organising the ideas generated in a particular text structure' (van der Geest 1996: 14–15). This helpfully defines the different tasks: goal-setting, generating ideas and structuring, each of which might involve a different type of writing activity. Yet, if it is also true that 'separate tools for planning . . . and reviewing . . . will be experienced as drawing an artificial line between two activities that are intricately related' (van der Geest 1996: 21), then the collection of writing tasks that make up planning or outlining could be experienced, by the writer, as quite 'messy'. Perhaps this is a problem that writers who get bogged down fail to solve: yes, there are various different tasks to be done, but not in any linear order. Even when you have a linear outline, you may find yourself changing it and subsequently losing your way in your writing.

Analysis of the quotations from writing research shows how carefully you need to be thinking about your audience while you are outlining your paper – not just while you are writing it. Outlining is part of the writing process, after all. Your sense of other positions in the debate, as represented in the readership of your target journal, will, of course, shape what you write and how you write it. You can anticipate where opposition to your argument will come from. You can modulate your arguments accordingly.

In other words, the outlining stage may involve some writing, while the writing stages may include some revision of your outline. In fact, it may seem artificial to separate outlining from writing, but the point is to introduce in this chapter several strategies that have proved useful. Each is described in a separate section, but you can continue to use strategies for regular writing covered in other chapters, so that you can develop an integrated writing process. You can develop a set of techniques that you know work for you. This – together with your experience of submitting/publishing your first paper – will help to make production of your second and subsequent papers more fluent.

This chapter defines and illustrates strategies for outlining your paper in different ways: answers to lists of questions, headings, sentences, abstracts and graphics. All of these are important steps in the writing process; they all constitute 'writing' tasks that help you to maintain the focus of your paper as you write it.

You may be sceptical about some of these strategies: while some academics argue that they can only write an abstract once they have written the paper, writing an abstract is presented here as an important step in the process of designing your paper. There are also implications for your actual writing practices in this approach: the argument is that you also need a design for writing before you can allocate time slots to actually getting it done.

Moreover, a draft abstract or summary gives you text that you can email to an editor or give a colleague to read, in order to elicit early feedback. Feedback is crucial at this early stage, not just at later stages when you have a draft that you are relatively happy with. It can save you wasted time, stopping you, for example, from going off on a line of argument, or presenting what you think are all your significant results or detailing your specific methodology, when none of these is what the audience of your target journal will find most interesting in your work at this time, as judged by the editor, as expressed in his or her response to your 'initial enquiry' email. A further benefit is that discussion with subject experts and others at this stage can accelerate your writing/revision.

How much time should you spend outlining? It has been argued that you should spend 90 per cent of your time outlining and 10 per cent writing (Reif-Lehrer 2000). Whether or not you agree with this calculation, it does raise the question of how much is 'right' or 'enough'. Most of us probably spend less time outlining and more writing, or rather revising. This might be because, if we spend less time outlining, we still have many decisions to make as we write. That makes writing a more complex process than taking structural decisions before starting to write paragraphs and sentences.

This is a more complex process in the sense that you have to make several different levels of decision at once: deciding on content, sequence, style, level of detail, references to other work, coherence and so on – all at the same time. And all of these decisions have to be made 'in sync' with each other. This may be one of the reasons why academics rebel against the 'snack' writing mode: it is more difficult, perhaps impossible, to write in this way in short bursts, as such complex writing requires constant sustained concentration if you are to get it right.

Yet if that is how you learned to write, if that is how you see the outlining process, you may be wondering if it is really possible to do a kind of 'total design' for your paper. Certainly, the value of doing so is not difficult to understand, but it does require sustained concentration in the outlining stage and, if you remain sceptical, it can be difficult to put into practice. The frameworks suggested in this chapter are there to help you try this new type of outlining practice. They have been tried and tested in many writing workshops among academics and others, in various disciplines, in many parts of the world. This suggests that they are in a form that you can use as of now.

It is, therefore, a good idea to spend plenty of time in the outlining stage. This may save you an enormous amount of time later in the writing process, as you are able to write well, in a focused way, in your first draft. In fact, your first draft may be very good.

However, the route to being able to do that is, paradoxically, through regular writing; if you do not write regularly, your writing time may be just as long as it ever was no matter what you do at the outlining stage. In fact, if you increase your outlining time without decreasing your writing time, you may take even longer to write your paper.

As you develop an outline, therefore, keep writing in sentences. Use the regular writing strategies described in other chapters. You also have to 'calibrate' your writing at all these stages with your target journal. Targeting your writing continues to be critical.

There is another good reason for spending more time than you currently do on the outlining stage: 'Use the word processor to type the outline and then convert the outline to prose when you are completely satisfied with the content and logical flow' (Reif-Lehrer 2000). The important words here are 'completely satisfied': you may wonder whether you will ever use these words about your writing, but the point is that you have a chance, in your outline, to create a momentary satisfaction. Because the ultimate – and you might say 'real' – satisfaction of writing only comes when your paper is (a) accepted and (b) published, satisfaction can be deferred for a year or two. You therefore have to manage your level of satisfaction with work-in-progress by creating small satisfactions with what you have already done. The moment of satisfaction that comes with a completed outline derives from having a clear goal and a clear output: you either have an outline or you don't. Having an outline becomes a goal.

A more important question might be, what constitutes an outline that will drive your writing? This question is addressed in the next section, where 'level 3 outlining' is suggested as a mode of outlining a paper, one that takes up strategies for productive writing dealt with in earlier chapters, such as writing to prompts, and integrates them into this step in the writing process.

Do not wait for writing to 'come to you'; your outlining practices should still involve regular, short-burst writing, in which you continue actively to make yourself write regularly. This means that while the outlining stage is about making your writing linear, there are still non-linear – or perhaps parallel – processes going on. There is no need to attempt to stop this happening, and it may not be possible in any case, but you do need to have a way of capturing and filtering ideas and sentences as they pop up. This is not to say that they 'pop up' at random, since your brain will be working on your paper even when you are not actually writing it. Find a way to capture these sentences, since they do not always appear when you are sitting at your keyboard.

As you do all this outlining, you may find that whole sentences or paragraphs come to you, apparently at random. Write them down. If you know exactly where they fit in your paper, write them in under the appropriate heading, without worrying too much about how you will make the text around them 'fit'. If you are not sure where they go, or if they even belong in your paper at all, save them in a separate file and leave the decision about whether or not to include them at all in your paper until later.

The references quoted in this section show that scholars have been thinking about the planning process in writing for some time. There is a vast literature out there. Perhaps the most salient point, for the purposes of this chapter, is that juggling planning and writing is a difficult process that may itself have to be learned. Moreover, it supports the suggestion that you should be writing regularly during your planning stage.

Level 3 outlining

Everyone does outlines. Many people actually use them to shape their writing. Some use them most at the start of the writing process as a device for getting a sense of the paper as a whole, and then abandon them as they write. Others create an outline at the start and then modify it as they go along, making outlining part of the iterative process of writing, using the outline to document the changes they make as much as to structure the writing they do.

Everyone knows what an outline looks like:

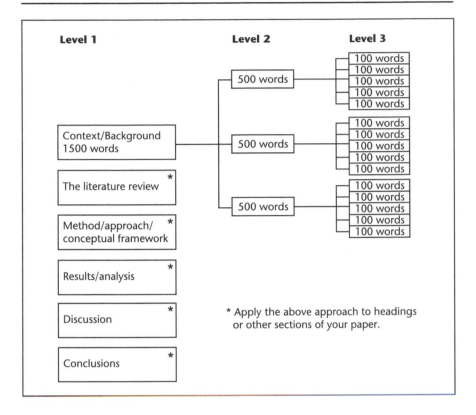

Every writer does a column 1 outline, going to the first level of outlining, some go into slightly more detail, moving into column 2, but, as far as I can tell, almost no one bothers to go as far as column 3.

There may be good reasons for this. Perhaps people feel that they will be wasting their time by doing so much outlining. Perhaps they have internalized the sub-structures that column 3 requires, although for new writers this may be less likely. Perhaps those who never go as far as column 3 are not aware of the benefits; they are not aware, for example, of how the columns can structure the essential thinking processes that are an important part of writing an academic paper. Producing column 3 may take hours of thinking, checking and rethinking.

Yet, each level has a purpose in the writing process. All of them can be used for different purposes, as you design your paper. In practice, you may find that while you favour one or other level – or perhaps you have some other way – of outlining, each has a distinct effect:

- **Level 1 outlining** is useful for setting out the proportions of your main sections. In this form it is easy to calibrate your outline with the target journal, checking that your sections are named in a way that is appropriate for that journal and that the proportions match.

- **Level 2 outlining** means making additional content and structure decisions. You can also do some checks on continuity: are the sub-sections in the right order? Do you really need them all? Can some section topics be compressed into a sentence or two? You can begin to think of the links and transitions you will need to use to make connections and changes of direction in your argument explicit.
- **Level 3 outlining** is a way of developing a detailed 'design' for your paper. You can decide exactly what is going into each section. At this level you can also check for internal continuity: are the content, proportions and connections coherent?

Each level can be seen as having its own purpose in the writing process, helping you to make different levels of decision. Staging the decisions in this way may be easier for new writers or for busy, experienced writers who can only work on their outlines in short time slots.

Of course, you will adapt your outline – even the level 3 outline – as you write, but you will more quickly and coherently be able to distinguish between what you should add and what you should cut from your paper if you have level 3 outlining; even with a detailed outline, you may find that you write a section that is not relevant to your paper. You can calibrate your writing with your outline: should you change one or the other? Will that still fit your target journal?

There may, of course, be a level 4 outline, which is even more detailed:

- **Level 4 outlining** means that you define the content of your sub-sub-sections, the points to which you have allocated 100 words. For example, if you decide you want to make three points, that could be three short sentences of about 30 words each, or a long one of 60 words plus a short one of 30 words.

This level of outlining raises recurring questions: are your points in the right order? Or should they be the other way round? Your choice of sentence length depends, of course, on how your points relate to each other: which ones will make sense handled in the same sentence, and which ones need separate sentences? Which of your points can be treated quickly, perhaps in general terms only, and which require a little bit more detail? How are they linked? Which link word will you use to make that link explicit?

This is where you may find that you have written 500 words before you know it. Will you then keep all of these words? Do they make the point that you set out to make in that sub-sub-section? Possibly not. You then have to cut out the sentences or part of sentences where you have gone off your point. Or you can change your outline, but you have to then check that your revision fits the rest of the section. If you lose sight of your main point, this is an ideal opportunity to do some freewriting or writing to prompts:

> **Writing activity to recover focus in the drafting stage**
>
> What is it I am trying to say in this section?
> What is the main point of this part?
> The main point of this section is . . .

Outlining is not about word-counting for its own sake; it is about you finding a way to prompt yourself to make the numerous decisions about content and order that will construct your argument. Each stage involves much more thinking than counting, but counting words as you go is a way of keeping a check on your writing. It is safe to assume that you will not always write exactly the number of words that you set out to write. You are likely to write more or less, in unpredictable patterns. In order to keep control and focus, you need to have some way of checking that what you are writing is relevant to your paper. An added benefit – and an important motivational tool – is that as you complete each section you see yourself achieving numerous sub-goals.

What are the implications of these approaches for your writing practice? If you only do level 1 outlining, you create a set of writing tasks that inevitably require large chunks of time. If you only do level 2 outlining, you still have decisions to make about content and continuity, and you will have to make these as you are writing. If, on the other hand, you have writing tasks as small as 100 words, you know that you can do these in short bursts. You can more easily fit them into your busy timetable. Your writing process is more easily and coherently 'fragmented', in a positive sense.

Once you have designed writing tasks, get them into your timetable, diary or electronic organizer. Establish writing slots for each task: how much time will you need for each task? When will you find it? This may involve some trial and error: how much time do you need, for example, to write one of those 100-word sub-sub-sections?

> **Scheduled short focused writing task**
>
> **Tuesday, 2 June, 9–9.30am**
>
> * Time allocation: 30 minutes for warm-up + writing
> * 5-minute warm-up: 'What I want to write about is . . .'
> * 25 minutes writing to prompt, taken from detailed outline: 100 words
> * If completed, write another 100 words for another sub-sub-section.

If you do not define your writing tasks precisely – perhaps even as precisely as this – you may struggle, and even fail, to establish how long you will need for each one.

In fact, you may not even see the point of doing so. You will fail to learn how long you need for each different writing task. This is not to say that there is one set pace of writing to which you should aspire, but if you note how long you take to produce each section you can begin to set yourself realistic goals, goals based on your actual experience of writing, rather than on someone else's output or some notional ideal rate. Setting specific, realistic goals is an important step in the process of becoming a productive writer.

Allocating word lengths

> I never approach writing thinking about quantity. I think about what it is I want to say.
>
> (hooks 1999: 16)

Many writers, like bell hooks, approach writing 'without thinking about quantity'; surely what you say matters much more than how many words you use to say it? Yet, just as your time for writing is not unlimited, so too your space – meaning the number of words – for writing it is limited. Clearly, it will depend on context; journals have stated word limits.

This is your starting point: take the total number of words available and divide them up according to what you think needs to be said. If this sounds too simplistic, you will soon find that it is far from simple, since it involves quite high-level decisions.

Academic writing involves a fair amount of thinking as you write, but you can think through some of the points you want to make – or know you have to make for the context in which you are writing – before you start to generate what you might call your first draft. Writing this way, with limits and limitations quite explicit at an early stage, means that your first draft will be good and may need less revision.

Writing an abstract – Brown's 8 questions

> Only by introducing formal procedures such as a list of questions to be answered – procedures that effectively disrupted the continuity of production – was it possible to get idea generation to take place apart from text production.
>
> (Bereiter and Scardamalia 1987: 202)

Devices such as lists of questions can help you to structure your ideas and move towards outlining and 'text production'. It could be that the various steps in writing – thinking, 'idea generation' and composition – can be progressed using different techniques or frameworks. It may even be that different stages require different frameworks. For many years scholars and researchers of writing have asked themselves these questions:

> There is a venerable tradition in rhetoric and composition which sees the composing process as a series of decisions and choices. However, it is no longer easy simply to assert this position, unless you are prepared to answer a number of questions, the most pressing of which probably is: 'What then are the criteria which govern that choice?'
>
> (Flower and Hayes 1981: 365)

This is all very interesting and rigorous, and this is one of the key papers in the development of cognitive approaches to writing, but for those not working in this field, the questions may not be that 'pressing'; you may be much more interested in frameworks that help you to make writing 'choices' and not at all interested in the criteria on which they are based. You need frameworks that help you think about writing, think as you write and write as you think. Most academic writers I have met have taken a passing interest in explanations of the thinking processes involved in writing, but they are primarily looking for ways of translating their thinking into writing. Whether they are right or wrong to do so is not really the issue. The point is that they need tools for getting started quickly, preferably tools that have been tried and tested in academic contexts.

One example is Brown's 8 questions. This has proved to be a useful tool for prompting those writing for academic journals, particularly new writers, to do some of the important thinking that is required for writing their paper. It gives you a framework for drafting the abstract or summary of your paper, considering such key questions as audience and the main purpose for that audience. This lets you see the paper as a whole, a perspective that helps you hold the paper together throughout the writing process.

An abstract is, in some ways, different from other forms of academic writing; you have to make a rhetorical adjustment. For example, while in the full paper, it is essential to provide a context for the work you have done, in the abstract you assert a reason why the work needed to be done, perhaps in no more than one sentence. This form of thinner contextualization liberates you from providing much in the way of definition and explanation. This again means that you can focus on the main points of your argument. At later stages in your writing process, you can use your abstract as a tool for maintaining that focus; it provides a kind of 'filter', helping you to decide what to put in and what to leave out as you write your paper.

This has advantages at this stage: writing on such a small scale, particularly at an early stage, means that it is easier to match up the different elements of your story; there are fewer distractions, fewer definitions and fewer explanations than will appear in your completed paper, so it is easier for the reader and, more importantly, for you the writer, to see and make explicit the connections between, for example, your aims and your methods. Nor do you have to represent the debate that has preceded your work in your abstract. If you have to refer to it at all – and that depends on the target journal – then you might need a sentence at most in your abstract or summary.

You have to write the abstract so well that the so-called 'general reader' can understand it. However, this does not mean that you should write it for someone who is not an expert in your area. When people tell you that a general reader should be able to read your paper or abstract, what they probably mean is that it should be extremely well written, with the connections between sentences crystal clear and the purpose and value of your paper explicitly defined.

For these reasons it can be useful to write your abstract at an early stage in the paper-writing process. In the past, you may have thought of it as the last writing task; many people do. But if you write it first you can use it as a touchstone as you write. In addition to revising it as you go along, you can revise it after your final revisions of the paper. In other words, write it first and revise it last.

Writing the abstract of your paper, therefore, forces you to capture the 'essence' of the whole: 'The word limits are arbitrary, but important for the discipline of getting down to the essence of what needs to be said' (Brown 1994/95).

Use Brown's 8 questions to draft your abstract:

How to use the questions

- Answer as many questions as you can in 30 minutes.
- If you get bogged down in one question, move on to another.
- Take all the questions literally, including the first one. Do not simply answer 'Those who are interested in my subject', since to assume that readers are inherently 'interested' in your writing is a mistake. People often object: how am I supposed to know who reads the journal? How indeed? How can I find that out anyway? The best excuse I ever heard was, 'How can I find that out? – I live in Fife'. The beauty of this question is that it makes you focus – for real – on a real audience. As soon as you do come up with two or three names, you will see that (a) your audience is more mixed than perhaps you thought it was and (b) what they are likely to find 'of benefit' (see question 7).
- Adapt your work to these questions, rather than vice versa.
- Do not be put off by the apparent focus on experimental research, which you might think is implied by the word 'results'.

- Stick to the word limits. Twenty-five words is one short sentence.
- If you are confused by questions 5 and 6, think of 5 as asking if your paper should make us *think* differently about anything and 6 as asking if your paper should make us *do* anything differently. If you find your answers overlap, you may not have really worked out the difference.
- Be sure to answer question 7, as it is the most important one. Revise it several times, if necessary. Once you have that sentence (25 words) you have the 'destination' of your paper. This is the answer to the 'so what' question, defining your contribution. In academic journals this is often the last sentence of the abstract/summary – check your target journal to see what forms this sentence can take.
- Discuss your answers – and emerging abstract/summary – with someone.

Remember that these questions can be and have been successfully used across a wide range of disciplines, including many non-scientific areas.

Write for 30 minutes on the subject of your journal article

1 Who are the intended readers? List three to five of them by name.
2 What did you do? (50 words)
3 Why did you do it? (50 words)
4 What happened [when you did that]? (50 words)
5 What do the results mean in theory? (50 words)
6 What do the results mean in practice? (50 words)
7 What is the key benefit for readers? (25 words)
8 What remains unresolved? (no word limit)

(Brown 1994/95)

In practice some writers, perhaps those with experience of reading and/or writing abstracts, get through all these questions in 20 minutes. Whether you take 20 or 30 minutes may also depend on your discipline. Some journals, of course, require very particular forms of abstract, and you will, at a later stage, have to adapt yours to that form, but the purpose of this activity, at this stage, is to set the limits for your whole paper.

If you want to analyse why Brown's questions work well at this stage of writing, note the proportion of the whole abstract that is allocated to each question. Specifically, note how much is allocated to writing that actually deals with your work – questions 2, 3 and 4 – as opposed to the proportion allocated to contextualizing and providing the rationale and explanations – questions 5 to 8. This allows you to concentrate on the main moves in your argument. If reading an abstract lets you see the paper as a whole, writing an abstract lets you work on it as a whole. The fixed limits for each sentence, moreover, ensure that you keep to appropriate proportions, not letting any one element of your argument overshadow any other.

Brown's statement that the 'word limits are arbitrary' should not be taken to undermine his strategy. In fact, I am not convinced that they are entirely arbitrary, since they have worked so well for so many writers and since they do help you to set appropriate limits. Yet, I do not want to give the impression that the number of words is more important than the choice of words. The word limits are, however, hugely important in making you get to the main point. This often involves thrashing through a number of other interesting – but not 'main' – points. In some disciplines the process of weeding out all the points that are not the main point is what reveals, for the writer, what the main point is. Working to these specific word limits is very hard work, but it is the type of hard work that produces a focused paper.

Whether or not your paper is ultimately, in its final version, preceded by your answers to these questions is not really the point. This may not, in fact, be the form your abstract will take. The point is that answering these questions will help you to sketch the whole paper and seeing it as a whole lets you check its internal logic. You can, of course, adapt the questions to suit your discipline – and many have been tempted to do so – although in practice they have worked well across a range of subjects. Alternatively, you can take your target journal's criteria and transform them into prompts for writing, if, and only if, you find that this works to generate focused text. If it does not, you may have to revert to Brown's questions.

What is it, in any case, that makes writers want to adapt the Brown framework? Is it that they already have a series of questions in mind? Is it that the discipline base, and being steeped in the journal's conventions – even if only as a reader – has given them an alternative set of questions? Or is it that they have never thought of writing for academic journals in this way? Many new writers have never broken the whole process down into stages like this. Naturally, therefore, this approach comes as a bit of a surprise, if not a challenge. The best response – surprise or no surprise – is to try the approach with your writing. Simply acknowledging that you understand what Brown's 8 questions are doing, or that you can see the sense in such an approach, is not enough; understanding does not necessarily lead to writing. Try this approach and then decide. Once you have spent 30 minutes answering these questions, you will have a sound basis for your argument. You can then use your answers to focus the sections of your paper.

As you adapt your abstract to your target journal's criteria and conventions, you may want to make use of some of the key words that seem to be dominant in your field at the time of writing. Alternatively, you may deliberately move away from this dominant set. Again, as discussed earlier, this may feel like you are cloning yourself to the values of the journal and its select group of editors and reviewers, but being rhetorical is about making sure you pitch your arguments in a way that is likely to be persuasive to the group who will actually hear or read them.

Which types does your target journal publish? Structured abstracts, with headings? The whole story in miniature, or just the background, leading up to the point where the introduction starts? Are they mostly background, outlining the problem, problematizing the issue, making the case that it is a problem, that it is where work needs to be done? Does it include no more than a general reference to or much more detail on methodology? Do your target journal's abstracts foreground results or outcomes? Or are these only alluded to, but not specified? Again, the point is to study, as if you were trying to become a scholar of, your target journal's abstracts.

Then there is the question of the extent to which the sentences – their order, proportion and level of generality or specificity – signal the structure of the papers that follow. To what extent, in other words, will you be able to shape your paper around what you have written in your abstract? This is an important question, as it affects the next step in developing your paper.

In any case, you can use these sentences – your answers to Brown's 8 questions – as prompts for your writing. You can take this suggestion quite literally: connect each sentence of your abstract directly to the corresponding section of your paper.

Building on your abstract

- Take the key words in each sentence of your abstract.
- Write them into section headings.
- Use them in the topic sentence and throughout the section.
- Define and explain the terms, as needed.

Each sentence in your abstract may itself appear, in an expanded or developed form, in your paper. You can develop your draft by using your abstract as a kind of key for your paper. Of course, this will not prevent you from changing your mind as you go along, but it may stop you from adding something that will require a complete rewrite, unless, on balance, you decide that a complete rewrite is unavoidable, once you have seen how the paper would look. However, if you do decide to keep your abstract as it is, for the moment, as you make changes in your paper, adjust the abstract to match.

Remember also that you may do too much 'smoothing' in your first paper, and certainly for the purposes of the abstract. Do not worry about this. You can always go back and write problems, glitches and unanswered questions back into your paper. They may, in fact, strengthen your argument, by showing that you overcame some difficulties, or acknowledge limitations, but nevertheless can make a claim to a modest contribution. For example, you might want to include things that did not go quite so well in your study, but are not so serious that they undermine your results, outcomes or conclusions – things that you will probably have excluded from your abstract.

Outlining a paper – Murray's 10 prompts

Working along the same lines, you could use these questions to capture the essence of your paper, forcing yourself to make decisions about the main points and establishing a strong logical flow at an early stage.

Note the proportions here that allow much more time, twice as much, for you to write about what you did, rather than why you did it or what you think it means. For the purposes of your paper, of course, you will be writing in the past tense, reporting on work done, which is why the 10 prompts are in the past tense.

As for Brown's questions, take 30 minutes to continue or complete these prompts within the word limits shown. If you find you have completed them in less than 30 minutes, go back and revise: for example, is there a logical flow between all of your completed prompts?

Murray's 10 prompts	
1 This work needed to be done because . . .	25 words
2 Those who will benefit from this include . . .	25 words
3 What I did was . . .	25 words
4 How I did that was by . . .	25 words
5 When I did that what happened was . . .	50 words
6 I worked out what that meant by . . .	50 words
7 I did what I set out to do to the extent that . . .	25 words
8 The implications for research are . . .	25 words
9 The implications for practice are . . .	25 words
10 What still needs to be done is . . .	25 words

If we compare Brown's 8 questions with these 10 prompts, we can see a shift in the proportions allocated to each element:

	Brown	Murray
1 Your work	150 words	175 words
2 Context, rationale, explanations, implications	125 words	125 words

The purpose of this comparison is not to show that one framework is better than the other, since they both have different purposes in any case; instead, it is to make concrete the point that you need to decide about the proportion of what might be considered writing about your own work and writing to support your writing about your work.

Clearly, what you decide to do will be affected by, or have to be calibrated with, your target journal, but it might be more effective simply to press on with this writing about your own work first, so that you generate ideas and text that are based on your work, rather than based on others'. Yes, you are joining an on-going conversation by targeting a journal, but you can use these frameworks to focus on developing your ideas in writing.

Calibrating your outline

The point has been made earlier in this chapter that you have to check that your paper is aligned with your target journal. This subject is given a final separate section here for emphasis. It may also work as a reminder. Even when you find that you are, finally, relatively happy with your outline, give it one final check: does it fit or challenge – as you intend – the norms and forms of your target journal at the time of writing?

Go back to your target journal and your initial analysis of it. As with any stage in the writing process, you may have become so engrossed in what you have to say in your paper that you have lost sight of what they want to hear.

Remember that the point of this exercise is not to compromise your research – though it may feel like that – but to be persuasive in your writing, fitting it to the rhetorical context you have selected: the journal.

What to check

- Cut and save in a new file any section that does not fit.
- Adapt the style of your headings and sub-headings.
- Do you have too many? – can you cut one or two?
- Check the relative length of your sections.

In fact, in this so-called 'outlining' stage, you could and perhaps should be doing several different activities at once.

Parallel writing tasks

1 Calibrating your outline with your target journal.
2 Putting your Brown/Murray sentences into your outline.
3 For each heading, writing sub- and sub-sub-headings in sentences.
4 Setting word limits for all sections.
5 Freewriting and generative writing on these headings.

Simply drawing up a graphical outline, even to level 3 or 4, will not necessarily produce writing. You do have to do some of these other activities, or at least some form of regular writing. These parallel activities, however, show how you can integrate the various types of writing and thinking to progress your paper.

Checklist

- Do various levels of outlining – they all have their purpose.
- Keep writing in sentences.
- Plan time for parallel tasks.

5   Drafting

What constitutes good writing in journals? • Shaping
sections • Streamlining • Turning headings into
prompts • Internal critique • Checklist

Drafting involves many different types of activity: writing to develop your idea
in paragraphs and sentences, outlining and revising your outline as you go
along and, finally, producing some of the features of academic writing.

The key point in this chapter, the secret that no one sees fit to tell us during
our undergraduate or even postgraduate years – perhaps, to be fair, because it is
not widely understood or acknowledged – is that when you actually do regular
'snack' writing about your paper and you have a detailed outline to guide your
writing, then your first draft is pretty good. You will have less revision to do,
and that saves you time and energy.

However, unless you do the regular writing, you will not be able to write 'on
demand'. You may find that you do not stick to the focus provided by your
outline. You may find yourself veering off onto other subjects. You may not
actually get any writing done, even though you have a great outline.

The short, sharp 'snacking' writing tasks do change how you write, not
just in letting you dribble on about whatever is on your mind, but in helping
you to develop an overlooked skill: focusing. Because such snack writings are
low stakes, academics often get the impression that they are no more than

therapeutic, but what you can learn to do is to focus immediately on the topic or prompt for your five or ten minutes. Over time, you will find, if you persevere for a few weeks, that you get better at this. Even when you are writing about a subject you do not know very well, where your confidence in what you have to say and how you are going to say it is low, your focusing skills will help you to develop your thinking.

Many projects falter at the drafting stage, as writers fail to use the work they have done so far in structuring the whole paper. They get a kick out of freewriting, or they kick against it, but fail to make regular time to write. They fail to keep up their promised writing buddy or writers' group meetings. They allow writing time in the diary to go to other priorities. They lose sight of what they were trying to do – and its value – and to get back on track begins to feel like starting the paper from scratch.

Just as writing without a detailed outline can leave you feeling that you are starting over, every time you sit down to write, not having a sense of your 'time outline' means that you are likely not to progress your paper. Just as having an image of the paper as a whole – in the form of your outline, your abstract and your analysis of the journal's framework – helps you to focus and, therefore, write, having a sense of the whole timeline for your paper means that you know where you are in the process at any given time and are more likely to stay on course, to resist distractions and to defer other 'priorities', even if only for 30 minutes.

This pattern suggests that there must be quite deep-seated reasons for not writing. Or, it may be that there are cognitive or behavioural gaps at this point, as there were, arguably, at earlier stages in the writing process. In other words, some writers, particularly new writers, simply do not have a process for progressing from outline to draft.

The structure of your whole paper can be designed using one or all of the range of strategies covered in this book so far: building on Brown's 8 questions, using generic structures or modes, or adapting one of the dominant structures in the target journal. Your key strategy here is to produce a detailed design for the whole paper, more detailed than new writers normally expect, before starting to write paragraphs and sentences.

If you do not do this, what you are doing is deferring the step of setting conceptual and word limits to each part of the paper and you will still be making structural decisions, still facing options and choices on several different levels: structure, content, focus, wording, style and so on. In practice, in order to manage these very different processes, you can continue to do different types of writing activity:

1 Outlining
2 Revising the outline
3 Writing-related tasks

What constitutes good writing in journals?

Every academic is familiar with the norms and forms of good academic writing in his or her discipline. Where academics' knowledge runs a bit thin is on the rhetorical strategies used in published papers. Only when you analyse papers in some detail do you see that there are effective – and recurring – strategies that you can use in your papers. This type and level of analysis prompts some academics to respond, 'Aren't we analysing this too much?'. But how else will you increase your understanding of what constitutes good writing at this level in your discipline?

The examples analysed in this section may not be in your own field, but they demonstrate the type of analysis you can do on papers in your field. This is one way of developing your expertise in academic writing. If you do not do this analysis, clearly you are going to be writing on the basis of your existing knowledge of academic writing, and that may simply not be sufficient.

The key strategies of academic writing in journals, it could be argued, are similar across the board: academic writing is highly signalled and signposted, there is usually a forecast of the whole paper in an introduction, and there is acknowledgement of other people's work.

Example 1

More has been written on *The Duchess of Malfi* **than on almost any other** non-Shakespearean tragedy of its time. **Yet the major** thematic **issues** with the play **remain in dispute: the question of** the Duchess' guilt, the motives of Bosola and Ferdinand, and the difficulties posed by the allegedly 'anti-climactic' final act **still invite contention**. While the emotions that the Duchess and her play inspire may be too heated for one more article to cool, **I nevertheless believe that a fresh approach** to the play – **an approach that investigates** the conflict between merit and degree – **can contribute to a resolution of these issues**. Indeed, **an assessment of** Webster's treatment of the tension between merit and degree not only helps **to vindicate** the Duchess' actions, **to explain** the actions of Ferdinand and Bosola, and **to justify** the play's final act, but it also **establishes** Webster's play as an unblinking assertion of the primacy of worth over inherited position.

(Selzer 1981: 70–1)

If you can get past your ignorance of the authors' subjects and can put aside your prejudice against a different referencing system than the one used in your discipline, then you can see that there are many skilful rhetorical features in this argument:

- uncontentious opening sentence, identifying the field for this paragraph and the paper;
- identification of the 'issues' that 'remain in dispute' and 'still invite contention';
- statement of the author's proposed contribution, 'I nevertheless believe' (alternative style could be 'It nevertheless could be argued');
- branding of the type of contribution, 'fresh approach' (alternatives could be 'new', 'different', 'innovative' and so on – which ones are used in your target journal?);
- claim that this paper 'can contribute to a resolution of these issues', not out to 'prove' anything, still open to further debate, writing in the language of debate;
- purpose of the paper identified in key verb, 'investigates', purposes of stages in the argument – or sections in the paper – also in verbs, 'assess . . . vindicate . . . explain . . . justify . . . establish'.

Example 2

A literature review demonstrates that since 1969, many authors have used variances of Verkoshanski's methodology in an attempt to establish the best stretch-shortening technique and training program (3, 6–8, 11, 32, 36). **There is agreement on** the benefits of basic stretch-shortening principles, **but controversy exists regarding** an optimal training routine (12, 16, 29, 38). Today, the chief proponents of the stretch-shortening approach are still found in the track and field society, since they continue to use Verko-shanskski's 'reactive neuromuscular apparatus' for reproducing and enhancing the reactive properties of the lower extremity musculature (1, 5, 32, 36). **Numerous authors have documented** lower quarter stretch-shortening exercise drills and programs, **but the literature is deficient in** upper extremity stretch-shortening exercise programs (16–18, 42–45).

Adaptations of the stretch-shortening principles can be used to enhance the specificity of training in other sports that require a maximum amount of muscular force in a minimal amount of time. All movements in competitive athletics involve a repeated series of stretch-shortening cycles (5, 13, 15). Specific functional exercise must be performed to prepare the individual for return to activity. **Perhaps in no other single athletic endeavor** is the use of elastic loading to produce a maximal explosive concentric contraction and the rapid decelerative eccentric contraction seen more than in the violent activity of throwing a baseball. To replicate these forces during rehabilitation is beyond the scope of every traditional exercise tool. **For example,** the isokinetic dynamometer that reaches maximal velocities of 450–500°/sec is not specific to the greater than 7,000°/sec of shoulder angular velocity seen during baseball pitch (20, 34). Consequently, specific exercise should be an intricate part of every upper extremity training program to facilitate a complete return to athletic participation. **The purpose of this paper is to explain** the theoretical basis of stretch-shortening exercise **and to present** a philosophy for utilizing the stretch reflex to produce an explosive reaction in the upper extremity.

(Wilk et al. 1993: 225–6)

The comparison of the Selzer (1981) and Wilk et al. (1993) papers shows that even in very different disciplines there can be striking similarities. Separated in time and discipline they clearly are, but there are several direct links. In two quite different journals the authors have set out their arguments in almost identical ways. This is not to say that you can write one way for all journals – quite the opposite is argued throughout this book – but that you can and perhaps should reveal the deep or generic structure underlying much research: context, rationale, problem, method, result, interpretation, implications. It depends on the journal.

Examples of articles published in journals in different fields show not only the generic features of academic writing but also the range of writing genres that can appear – and that you have to choose from if you are writing in this area – in journals within one field. Your choice of target journal may not be an entirely free one; it may depend on the type of work you are doing and the stage that your work has reached.

The range of publications within one discipline, in terms of length, depth of treatment and balance of theory and other content, can be demonstrated in the field of organic chemistry. The next example comes from a quick-turn-around journal that does not require the detail of the others: in the journal *Chemical Communication* the priority is to get the information out quickly, while *Tetrahedron* requires more complex and detailed papers. These journals, therefore, range from concise to complex, with some combining the two. All may require careful communication of the methods, but in quite different forms.

Example 3

Optically pure lithium amide bases **have proven to be versatile tools** in modern asymmetric synthesis. *Indeed*, highly enantio-selective deprotonation reactions **have been accomplished** for several sets of substrates, including conformationally locked ketones . . . *In turn*, **many of the more recent advances in this area have been accomplished by** the development of new homochiral ligands and the tuning of reaction conditions to improve the selectivity of *these* lithium-mediated deprotonations. *In contrast* to the Li-based strategies, magnesium reagents **have received relatively little attention** for use in asymmetric synthesis . . .

More recently, **studies** within our laboratory **have shown how** . . . magnesium amides can be employed as alternatives to their more widely used lithium counterparts . . . *Consequently*, **with a view to developing** asymmetric Mg-based protocols **we considered that these observations . . . would allow** good levels of stereoselectivity in organic transformations **to be achieved**. Herein, **we report the first use of** homochiral magnesium amide bases as reagents . . .

(Henderson et al. 2000: 479)

Even if all this sounds very foreign to you, you can track the stages in the argument in the usual way: the words in bold signal the movement from existing work and what it has shown, to the area that has received less attention to date, and finally to the proposed new work and its specific aim.

Note also the use of link words between and within sentences (in italics), and that many of the link words are positioned at the start of the sentence. Note the popular academic sentence that tells us, in a verb, the purpose of this paper: 'report the first use of'. Not everyone likes this sentence type – some find it annoying – but it does still appear in many published papers, and when it is not there, academic readers, in discussion, often say that they miss it. So it must serve some useful purpose.

The chemistry journal *Tetrahedron* allows – or requires – authors to go into much more detail. In order to preserve the unity of the more complex paper the authors maintain focus on the aims of the study by pointing out how each successive phase of the experimental work moved them forwards:

Example 4

In an effort to further establish and, moreover, **widen the scope of our novel** Mg-amide mediated enantioselective depronotation process, our attention was turned to consider the desymmetrisation reactions of alternative prochiral cyclic ketones and, more specifically, 2,6-disubstituted cyclohexanones.

(Henderson et al. 2000: 479)

This sentence works well to make a coherent and explicit link not only between one stage of the work and the next, but between the stage being discussed and the 'big picture' of the research aims. Further links between stages in the work are created throughout the section reporting on results at the beginning of each paragraph:

Based on these promising results and to further explore the potential of this reaction system . . .

Returning to our Mg-amide base (*R*)-**3**, we remained unsatisfied at the length of time required to achieve an acceptable level of conversion of *cis*-**6** to **7** . . .

Moving on to consider reaction of *trans*-2,6-dimethylcyclo-hexanone . . .

Following on from these encouraging results, we then decided to investigate the behaviour of . . .

(Henderson et al. 2000: 479)

A fifth example, first published in 1985, was republished by the journal editor in 2000, to represent the editor's years in office. It is worth noting the editor's reasons for positioning this one paper in this way, since it gives some insight not only into this particular editor's perspective but also, perhaps, into the characteristics of good academic journal writing:

Val Belton described a project which, as she took great pains to point out, was very simple and did not even solve a problem. It merely helped the decision-makers to understand the problem before taking the decision. I have to take issue with the '*merely*'. It is a well-researched fact that the majority of 'bad' decisions stem not from a poor selection from available options but from the mis-identification of the real problem. Providing a better understanding of problems is generally what I have hoped to achieve.

(Hough 2000: 896)

Example 5

INTRODUCTION

This paper describes the use of a simple multi-criteria model as a decision aid in a large service company, which will be called Financial Information Services Ltd (F.I.S.L.) engaged in the process of choosing a company with which to place a contract for the development of a computer system. The computer system, a financial management aid, was to be provided to clients as a chargeable service. [66 words]

F.I.S.L. did not have expertise in-house to develop a proven and reliable system of the type it wished to market sufficiently quickly to respond to pressure from competitors. By involving an outside organization, it hoped to be able to overcome these difficulties whilst meeting the objective of educating its own staff in this type of system. A further possible objective was to bring the system in-house at some time in the future. The system is a large-scale one involving the extraction and collation of data from world-wide sources and the formatting of the data into reports for use by clients anywhere in the world. [104 words]

Evaluation

. . . **No formal checks were made of** the independence assumptions necessary for an additive model of this type to be valid, **but we were aware of these** in the specification of the model and throughout the analysis. **It is generally accepted that** the additive model is a robust one,[2,3] **and it was felt that greater insight would be gained** in the time available from the use of a simple model than to attempt to construct a more complex representation of the decision. [82 words]

The next stage was to weight the criteria at level-2 in line with their contribution to the overall objective. The weights at this level represent the cumulative weight of all level-3 criteria which are sub-criteria of a particular level-2 criterion. **These** weights can be assessed either by direct comparison of the criteria at level-2 or by selective comparisons of criteria at level-3. **It was decided to adopt** the former, more direct approach and to supplement this by consistency checks using the implied level-3 weight. **Initially** the persons responsible for each section of the analysis were asked to give their personal opinion on the weights to be used at level-2. **This information was used as the basis for** sensitivity analysis before the group came together to discuss this issue. **This approach avoided** the possibility of long discussions about these weights when the disagreements may have been inconsequential. [146 words]

Thus it seemed that the real decision was to be made between Company A and Company B. The overall weighted score emerging from the multiple-criteria analysis indicated a preference for Company B. The scores were 59 and 68 for Company A and B respectively; Company C had scored only 27. **However, too much emphasis should not be placed on these numbers. Further inspection** of Figure 2, the graph of results aggregated to level-2 of the hierarchy, **shows** that there are criteria of greater and lesser importance on which each company is ranked more highly. A thorough sensitivity analysis was carried out to identify those changes in inputs to the model which would significantly affect the outcome – i.e. which would reverse the ordering of companies A and B in the overall evaluation. **The working group was confident about** the evaluation of the companies on the majority of the criteria, **although there were a few areas for which information was lacking** which were considered in detail in the sensitivity analysis. [167 words]

We were aware that such an analysis is necessarily simplistic and that if more than one weight or score were to be changed simultaneously, the outcome may be more marked. . . .

Thus, at this stage of the evaluation, it appeared that Company C was emerging as preferred, with Company A a close second and Company C a distant third. This was in accord with the feelings of the working group [short paragraph] . . . .

The decision to recommend Company B was not shaken by further recourse to the negative review of each company. [one-sentence paragraph]

Certain features of this paper work very well:

- purpose of paper stated in opening sentence;
- little background/context – focus on the 'project';
- analysis criteria defined and numbered;
- pros and cons addressed, showing knowledge of research method;
- effective use of mini-arguments;
- 'model' is constructed from research data (p. 269);
- links at start of paragraphs.

The author makes a clear case not only for the contribution the study makes, but, perhaps more importantly, for the scale of that contribution; as the editor said, this study will not solve all problems – in fact, potential weaknesses in the study itself were identified in the work and are addressed in the paper – but will provide a means of understanding them.

All of the examples of published academic writing show similarities and differences across the disciplines. Within disciplines there can also be wide variations in published papers. This type of analysis reveals the rhetorical modes, the norms and forms, the dominant conventions operating at a particular time in a particular journal. The question for new writers is which ones are operating in your journals at this time and how can you incorporate your work within that format?

Shaping sections

Use the work you have done already in outlining and 'abstracting' to develop your draft.

Building on the abstract

- Take each sentence of your abstract – drafted using Brown's 8 questions or Murray's 10 prompts.
- Copy and paste them into your draft file.
- Write for five minutes on each.

Write topic sentences that express the main idea of each step in your argument, soon to be, or already emerging paragraphs, and then develop the point that follows each one. In this way, you can use the writing of topic sentences as a bridge between the outline and a first draft text: you are moving towards prose step by step.

Take a look at your target journal, particularly the type of paper that you are aiming to write. Are there any changes you should make to the shape, such as:

- making mini-arguments;
- including internal critique;
- anticipating refutation;
- writing the debate into your paper?

Even if someone has just published a paper that is close to yours, say so. Include it in your debate. Say how yours differs, what yours adds.

From this point on, you may think that there are endless revisions, when, in fact, you are probably responding to some set of internal prompts, assumptions and understandings of what is expected in writing for a particular journal. Yet, if your revisions are focused in this way, you will have less of that sense of uncertainty about the direction of your writing; you will know that the revision is part of the plan for the paper. You have a perspective that lets you see that your revisions are all moving in the right direction – the direction you set and fixed, as far as possible, in your outline.

Streamlining

This is where you own up and realize that you may have more than one paper in your paper. Many new writers do. They try to put all their eggs in one basket, thinking that it will make for a stronger paper, when, in reality, it weakens the paper by making it unfocused. Cut out anything that does not seem to be part of it, saving it in a new file, possibly for future papers.

At a certain point you have to finish it off and acknowledge that you will not be including all the points you thought you would because you have run out of time, ideas or energy or, more importantly, because you realize that those points are no longer relevant. However, you may not realize this last point until you have submitted your paper or perhaps until after it is published, when you realize that someone else has judged it to be sufficient, even when you yourself were not sure that it was.

Drafting may be more about getting your paper finished and submitted by your, perhaps self-imposed, deadline than about taking as much time as you need to include all that you have. Be prepared to abandon material, notes, ideas that you think are excellent. Save them for another paper.

Turning headings into prompts

It is all very well having a detailed outline, but that is no guarantee that you will do the writing. Designing an outline is, after all, a very different type of activity from writing in paragraphs and sentences.

Yet the two are so closely bound together – and both are important for progressing a writing project – that you have to find a way to keep both going. Perhaps most importantly, you have to persevere with regular writing while still working on the outline, so that you can stay in the writing 'habit'. If you do not write regularly, getting started can be much more laborious and this, in turn, can undermine your confidence, taking you back to where you started, or at least leaving you with the feeling that you are starting over. This is possibly where those who have tried to write and failed lost momentum or motivation; their writing process would not see them through this stage.

You can bridge the activities of outlining and drafting by using prompts, using your outline as a driver for writing. If you re-write your headings and sub-headings in the form of sentences, you can turn them into prompts for writing, even for writing in short bursts. This is an important way of integrating the strategies covered in this book: combining the 'simply start writing . . . just do it' approaches with the rigorous academic thinking and structured writing needed for a journal paper.

In order to use headings as prompts, they have to be written as prompts. The characteristics of good prompts are, to recap: written in simple language, using personal pronouns and, at this stage, perhaps using verbs. There are, of course, other styles of prompts; in fact, you may feel that you want to use prompts written in a more academic style.

For example, instead of having section headings that are, normally, one or two words or a short string of words, write a sentence that describes the writing task for each section in more detail, using, if possible, a verb:

Comparison of a heading and a sentence

Heading   *Cardiac Rehabilitation*

Sentence   *Define the form of cardiac rehabilitation that involves exercise, as developed in the west of Scotland over the past ten years, in 200 words (30 minutes).*

The heading tells us what the subject of the section will be, while the sentence gives us a writing instruction. Your outline can now be a set of sentences like this, each an instruction to write. In fact, the verb 'write' is now too vague; a more precise verb, describing the task, is more useful, and makes it easier to manage the set of tasks as you write them. This also means that you will be able to go back to your outline and know what it means – what would 'cardiac rehabilitation' mean to you after a day or two, in terms of a writing task? This means that your outline will work as an outline.

You can use verbs to write headings for your paper, in order to decide what the main point is and how you are going to build up to that point:

Choosing the verb for your paper   The aim of this paper is to . . . [verb].

You can also select verbs to articulate the stages in your argument:

Choosing verbs for your sections   This paper analyses . . .
It argues that . . .
It also illustrates . . .
It goes on to argue . . .
Using . . . the paper analyses . . .
    to illustrate . . .
The paper concludes by
    suggesting . . .

(Kitson 2001: 86)

Once you have written your string of verbs, you can check that your sequence is coherent, logical and sufficient to add up to your main argument verb. In other words, before/as you start writing pages of paragraphs and sentences you have a checking mechanism, so that you do not waste time and give yourself extra revision work to do that could be avoided. This is how you can develop a progressively more and more detailed design for your paper, and the more detailed it is, in theory, with practice, the less time you will need for revision.

Verbs can help in this way because they make you define the function of your argument – what is your paper trying to *do*? – and the function of the stages in your argument – how is each section moving your argument forward – what is each section *doing*? Even if, in your completed paper, you do not use verbs in exactly this way, it can still be a useful outlining tool.

For further examples to add to your repertoire of verbs for academic writing, see Ballenger's (2004) list of 138 'Active Verbs for Discussing Ideas'. The first ten in this wide-ranging list signify different lines of argument and/or types of paper that, for example, the main verb will promise to the reader:

informs
reviews
argues
states
synthesizes
asserts
claims
answers
responds
critiques

(Ballenger 2004: 238)

These are all possible lines of argument, each requiring a particular type of writing. Some will be more relevant to your discipline than others. Analyse the use of verbs in your target journal. There is probably a limited set of verbs, not an infinite list of possibilities, that are acceptable in that journal at any particular time. Think about what each verb signals in terms of type of argument and structure.

For example, a paper that 'narrates' will move through a set of time stages, with those stages marked out by time words, like 'Firstly . . . secondly . . . next . . . further . . . following . . . subsequent' and so on towards 'finally'. If you write a 'narration' paper, you will have to think about how much time you want to cover – and why – and how much detail you need to allocate to each stage – and why. Do you really need to write about all the stages? Or will you select some and leave out others – probably and why? Which will you include, and why; which will you not include, and why not? How many words will you need – according to the journal's style – for these mini-arguments? Are they even there at all in recent issues of your target journal?

Alternatively, if you are writing a 'categorizes' paper you will have to decide which categories to put items into and why this might constitute a 'contribution' to the literature or to knowledge. Does this bring a new perspective to your subject? That might be sufficient in some disciplines, in some journals.

How would you organize a 'contrast' argument, perhaps contrasting your work or idea with others'? First deal with one subject or approach, then the other? Treating each separately? Describing their pros and cons as you go along. Then dealing with their main similarities and differences in a third main section? Or focusing on the main difference? Or the main similarity? Would that be the main point of such an argument?

While this discussion of three types of argument, signalled by three different verbs, handles each separately, you can, of course, combine these – and many others – in your paper. With one eye on 'what you want to say' and another on 'how they want to hear it', you are trying to decide how to focus and pace your argument. These crucial structural decisions are quite difficult to make as you go along. It is not impossible to make structural decisions as you write – and you will make changes as you go anyway – but it is a more complex process and much more demanding for new writers.

There will, of course, be other ways of signalling the main line of argument and its articulation, other than using verbs. You may find that your journal uses a different style. Even if this is the case, using verbs at the outlining stage can help you during the writing process to work out the stages in your argument, even if you finally change the style of writing before you submit it. This is a useful tool for structuring your points and making sure all your writing focuses on your main point.

Even if you do not particularly like this style, with its predominance of verbs, personifying the paper and its sections, as if sections – rather than the author – were doing the analysis, as in the Kitson paper quoted above, there are two points to be borne in mind: firstly, Kitson's paper was published, which we can take to mean that such a style was acceptable for that journal at that time (2001); and, secondly, our own preferences in style and structure should not – but often do – limit our stylistic choices. If you were to target this journal, this would be an appropriate style to use. This is not to say that you should plagiarize, but that you should carefully consider the extent to which you should observe and (re-)produce features of the style endorsed by your target journal, rather than simply acting on your preferences. While this may seem to be common sense, it does not, from discussions with writers, appear to be common practice: they frequently resist the very idea of writing in a style they 'don't like'.

Here is the whole abstract with the verbs highlighted:

This paper analyses the relationship between government and nurse education policy using the current changes in England as a case study. **It argues that** there are times when ideologies of governments and professions coalesce, signifying the most opportune times for advancement. **It also illustrates** times when policy shifts are made because nursing is perceived as relatively insignificant in the order of health policies and politics. **It goes on to argue** that nursing leaders need to be aware of the political and policy context in order to select the most effective methods of moving the agenda forward. Using UK reforms, particularly the English strategy document Making a Difference (Department of Health 1999d) as a case study, **the paper analyses** recent events in nurse education **to**

illustrate key points. **The paper concludes by suggesting** that the nursing profession must recognize promoters and barriers for change and commit itself to the transformation of nursing practice through the realization of a new educational agenda that embraces the principles of new democracy. Namely, these are equality, mutual responsibility, autonomy, negotiated decision-making, inclusivity, collaboration and celebrating diversity.

(Kitson 2001: 86)

Another example of an abstract shows similar techniques:

This article seeks **to explore** the complex underpinnings and dynamics of the act of forgery, compared with instances of copying witnessed in art therapy sessions involving people with learning disabilities. The argument **focuses on** two theoretical frameworks: the first **concerns** the concept of joint attention behaviours; whilst the second **focuses on** psychoanalytic concepts which underlie both the infant's early visual experiences and the nature of the art object for the perceiving individual and its relevance to the broader culture. The central intent is **to establish** an equitable confluence of both developmental and psycho-analytical concepts – the product of which can usefully inform the art therapeutic process.

It is **proposed** that forgery and copying, although separate in essence, share similar factors, insofar as both seek to adopt a false and acceptable image for the spectator. This is traced to, and **given meaning** by, Winnicott's concepts of the mirror-role and the false self.

The text also **concerns itself with** the biographical interpretation of three well-known forgers, whose lives appear to indicate causal reasons for their eventual act of deception. This is **juxtaposed with** the learning disabled client's need to employ the work of 'recognised artists' **to present** an acceptable and valued self-image.

(Damarell 1999: 44)

Further examples of abstracts in different disciplines show further uses of verbs, including nominalization, turning verbs into nouns, such as 'overview' and 'analysis', and the passive voice:

This paper **seeks to identify** whether the slow progress in transition experienced by the countries of the former Soviet Union (FSU) arises from weaknesses in implementing effective corporate governance or from weaknesses in the broader economic environment. **An overview** of progress in transition in the FSU **is presented** followed by **analysis** of developments in enterprise ownership and governance. Problems in measuring the link between governance and performance and alternative mechanisms for enhancing the efficiency of enterprise in the FSU **are discussed**. The paper **concludes that** the problems of transition in the FSU concern delays both in introducing corporate governance mechanisms and in introducing an appropriate competitive market environment.

(Estrin and Wright 1999: 398)

Personalized Web applications automatically adapted for different clients and user preferences gain more importance. Still, there are barely technologies to compensate the additional effort of creating, maintaining and publishing such Web content. **To address this problem**, this paper **introduces** a declarative, component-based approach for adaptive, dynamic Web documents on the basis of XML-technology. Adaptive Web components on different abstraction levels **are defined** in order **to support** effective Web page authoring and generation. ... Finally, hierarchical document components playing a specific semantic role **are defined**. The hyperlink view for defining typed links **is spanned over** all component layers. Beside the reuse of both implementation artifacts and higher level concepts, the model also **allows to define** [sic] adaptive behavior of components in a fine-granular way. As a further benefit the support for ubiquitous collaboration via component annotations **is introduced**. Finally, the stepwise pipeline-based process of document generation **is introduced** and performance issues **are sketched**.

(Fiala et al. 2003: 58)

There are clearly other ways of signalling structure here, along with the verbs, such as the combination of problem and solution, cause and effect, and verbs that refer to the work done, rather than to sections of the paper:

Optically pure lithium amide bases **have proven to be versatile tools** in modern asymmetric synthesis. Indeed, highly enantio-selective deprotonation reactions **have been accomplished** for several sets of substrates, including conformationally locked ketones ... In turn, many of the more recent advances in this area **have been accomplished by** the development of new homochiral ligands and the **tuning** of reaction conditions **to improve** the selectivity of these lithium-mediated deprotonations. In contrast to the LI-based strategies, magnesium reagents **have received** relatively little attention for use in asymmetric synthesis.

(Henderson et al. 2000: 479)

More recently, studies within our laboratory **have shown how** ... magnesium amides **can be employed** as alternatives to their more **widely used** lithium counterparts ... Consequently, with a view to **developing** asymmetric Mg-based protocols we **considered** that these observations ... would **allow** good levels of stereoselectivity in organic transformations **to be achieved**. Herein, we **report** the first use of homochiral magnesium amide bases as reagents.

(Henderson et al. 2000: 479)

There are also 'Verbs That Help You Integrate Quotations' (Rozakis 1999: 110).

It is probably obvious that as writers we have to be ready to vary our style for each audience. What examples of published papers show us is how stylistic variation, or any other form of variation, can challenge our sense of what constitutes 'good writing'.

At this point, it might help to refocus on your goal: is it to write what you like as you like, or is it to get published? This may sound cynical, but it is not intended to be; instead, it is about being rhetorical, making writing choices that are 'right' not for your own taste but for your audience and the discourse in which they perceive themselves currently to be engaged.

The benefit of taking time to write sentences rather than headings in this way is that you now have a set of writing instructions for yourself. You know what your writing tasks are. Whereas your headings told you no more than the subjects of your writing, your sentences tell you what type of writing to do, in a certain number of words, to a certain level of detail and in a number of minutes or hours. This writing instruction sets useful limits to the writing task. This is not a matter of counting words until you have enough; it is about making tough decisions about how much, or how little, to say about each subject or, when you review your collection of sentences, to check whether you need to write about the subject at all.

This process requires you to do a lot of hard thinking; in fact, this can be one way of structuring that thinking. It is also a means of stopping yourself from running off after interesting tangents.

People often ask me where, in all my writing activities for just 'getting on with it', all the thinking that writing requires is going to happen. They imply that I am somehow misrepresenting the labour of academic writing, drawing an idealized process. They point out my apparent assumption that everyone has the material, knowledge and intellectual capacity required to write for academic journals. Not at all. You may find, in the course of doing the writing activities I suggest, that you do not have enough knowledge, that you do need to check references or that you have a limited understanding of what constitutes a publishable argument.

My point is that this is the very agony and ecstasy of writing. It is not a reason to stop, but a point at which to persevere. My argument is that these writing activities will expose such limitations, not hide them. Your task is not to try to fill all your knowledge gaps before you write, but to use writing to develop your understanding. In some fields, this statement will seem plainly absurd, but even in chemistry, writing about an experimental process with all the required precision and accuracy can reveal limitations in the new writer's knowledge. Putting your knowledge down in writing is, literally, a testing – you could even say almost 'experimental' – process in itself. In fact, because the approaches suggested here are new they may seem strange in other fields too, but if you wait until you have 'done all your thinking' before you write, you may find, it has to be emphasized, that you do not write at all, or, at least, you do not publish as much as you set out to.

Ultimately, of course, it is up to you to find a way to connect up the stages in your writing-thinking process. Clearly, this may be a very individual matter. It may be related to discipline base, learning style and other factors. Or it may not be. But you can use these outlining strategies to keep your thinking focused and to keep yourself writing. Remember that people in many disciplines have done so. Of course, it goes without saying that you will only realize these benefits if you try the strategies.

You can also use freewriting to produce draft text. How does freewriting progress a paper? How does it progress to draft? If you have practised it enough, then you will find that you can write on demand, as if you were simply freewriting, to the headings or sentences in your outline. Again, it is not sufficient to think about these writing practices in the abstract; you have to develop actual practices that produce writing.

Since you will be no less busy at this stage in your writing process than you were when you started writing your paper, it is important to continue the 'snack and binge' strategy. The strategies for generating text covered in Chapter 3 will help you to work out what you want to say, to focus on actually saying it in writing and to dispense with procrastination. Equally important, they can help you work out what you do not want to say in your paper.

As you write, keep checking your word count – easy to do, if you are writing straight on to the laptop – so that you can see when you achieve, or exceed, your word limit. As the words mount up, it can help to keep your motivation going. As you meet one target – 200 words in this section already – set yourself a new target – 200 more words to complete this section (given that I know that I have two more topics of 100 words to cover). Again, when you reach that target, set another one. Keep checking the total word count. At the very least, this will help you to calibrate your writing with your outline and its word limits per section.

Internal critique

Many new writers assume that they have to 'smooth' out any weaknesses in their research and ignore potential refutations in their paper, but building critique into your paper, writing the debate into it, will strengthen your argument.

You can do this either early on in your paper, as you review both pros and cons of your method or approach to your subject, for example, or at the end of your paper, where you anticipate refutations of your conclusions, or both.

Anticipating refutation

- What are the pros and cons of your approach?
- Why did you reject the very good reasons for doing it differently?
- Have you built a strong enough case for your methodology?
- Have you made a strong case for any adaptations of standard methods?

These are not just intended to be prompts for your thinking; you can write explicitly about these questions, checking whether or not they appear at all, and if they do in what form(s), in your target journal. How much you should write about them will depend on the context, but you could write a sentence or two now, acknowledging that there are other ways of doing what you did and of making sense of it; and also that there are different interpretations others could make. It would not hurt to include this even as a kind of aside. It does not require a whole section, unless, of course, some aspect of your paper is highly contested or controversial, in which case you might even have to write a section on it, perhaps as much as 500 words, perhaps even more. Clearly, you would have to balance such a word allocation with other parts of your paper.

If you really have to write so much justification for this section, then perhaps that could be a paper in itself, in which you really go into detail on the pros and cons. You could consider more of the complexities of research choices and interpretations, such as pros in certain contexts being cons in another.

As you weigh the pros and cons of this type of internal critique, it is a good idea to go back to your outline: where and how does this phase in your argument fit? This is where you can start revising your outline in ways that add detail and strengthen your argument. Your outline, however detailed, is still changing as you write, but if you have already put some detail in it, it will not completely change shape. You may find that you want to make sweeping changes in light of a new insight or something you read recently, but it may be a better idea to save that for future papers. You will have to weigh it all in the balance. If you have already had good feedback on your discussions, scribblings and outlinings from trusted colleagues, then it might be a mistake to pull your paper into a new shape. Likewise, if you have sounded out an editor and he or she has shown interest in your paper as outlined, you might find that they lose interest if you change it radically. Go with what you have.

Checklist

- Use both structuring and generative strategies.
- Write from your outline.
- Write regularly, using freewriting and generative writing to get into the habit.

6   Revising the draft

Foregrounding generic aspects of academic style
• Revising the outline • Revising drafts • Generative
writing • Using the writers' group • The critical friend
and the 'tame' subject expert • Revision processes
• Iterative processes • Developing a concise style
• Polishing • The final revision • Checklist

Even after all your work on structuring, there may still be work to do in revealing the plan of your paper. In reality, what this means is that you probably did not produce, in paragraphs and sentences, an exact replica of your outline. And even if you had, you would still be revising it at this stage. In other words, in revising your draft, you will be looking to make the structures clearer and more explicit, but you will also be thinking about and rethinking that structure at the same time.

You used the outlining process – your graphic, list of sentence or series of verbs – to decide in advance what you were going to write about – and that is crucial for stimulating focused writing – but the revising process still involves discovery of the structure in the course of writing. If this sounds contradictory, that may be because this stage of writing is contradictory: writing involves both deciding in advance what to say and discovering what you want to say as you make choices about how to say it. It is not, therefore, a weakness to make changes to your text that are not based on your outline; quite the reverse, this shows that you are thinking about your subject, perhaps refining your ideas. You can, of course, still use your outline as a point of reference, to check whether you are sure that you want to add a point that has just occurred to you. As you make changes, you have to go through certain steps in the revision process again, and this is where the iteration comes in.

Moreover, at this late stage in your paper-writing process, you are not simply looking to complete your outline, you are aiming to invent a form of closure for your paper, whether or not that involves replicating, or even completing, your outline. It may not even mean retaining all of your draft.

At this stage, when you are most acutely aware of your potential audience(s), therefore, you have to concentrate on the coherence of your text – its internal coherence. Whether or not it will be seen to be coherent by those judging your paper is another matter. Their impending judgement can interfere with the essential revision processes, sometimes leading writers to work too hard at buttressing their arguments:

> The specter of . . . judgment . . . has created problems for the woman writer: problems of contact with herself, problems of language and style, problems of energy and survival.
>
> (Rich 2001: 13)

Assuming this to be as true for male writers seeking to enter the select group of published writers for the first time, as it is for females, this presents a whole new set of potential barriers to writers. This analysis might also explain why writers' energy for writing threatens to seep away in this last stage, even when they have done so much and have relatively little left to do. Revising is still writing, with all the same decisions and, perhaps, uncertainties of the earlier stages.

There may be more to the revision step, therefore, than simply honing academic writing style. It comes as a shock to many postgraduates and staff that so much revision is required, but lengthy revision may be the result of inadequate planning and feedback. For academic staff, the tendency is to see the need for multiple revisions as a weakness in their thinking: 'I thought I had finished that bit . . . How did I miss *that*?' You may, therefore, learn something about the strengths and weaknesses of your outlining process during the revision stage. There may be things you did that you would do differently for your next paper.

Finally, whether your outline works well or not, revision involves many iterative steps, as you make smaller and smaller changes to your text, and this iteration is reflected in the sections of this chapter: an initial long list of revision steps is gradually whittled down to a smaller list of minor refinements. As the list of revisions reduces, the revisions are themselves scaled down.

Foregrounding generic aspects of academic style

Academic writing is highly signalled and signposted. Readers are generally supplied with a route map for the whole paper at the start, assisted by signposts along the way and signals to take a turn here or make a connection there. This should mean that readers never get lost in your paper. They never have to retrace their steps. They always know where they are, how far they have travelled along the road, and how long they have to go to reach the end of your paper. They know how everything fits in and, most importantly, they do not have to read your mind to work out how sections or paragraphs are connected to each other or to the 'big picture' of your on-going argument.

Consequently, the most important revision – and one that new writers often forget or simply do not know – may be signalling your structure explicitly. It is one thing to have a logical structure and another to make it transparent in your writing. This may mean making it more explicit than you think it needs to be. Even if you feel you have done this already, check it.

Reveal the plan

- Do you have a forecasting paragraph at the start of your paper, saying what each section does?
- Do you need to state how each section progresses your argument?
- Do you end each section with a sentence, or two, on how it has progressed your argument?
- Do you start each section with a reminder of what it is going to do?
- Does your key term appear regularly throughout the paper? Have you used different terms, in the interests of variation – if so, will they be clear and unambiguous to your readers?
- Have you built the case that your research makes a contribution throughout your paper, and not just at the end?
- Is there an exact match between the aim, at the start of your paper, and your claim, at the end of your paper? Do the same terms, that is the same words, appear in both places?
- Have you put link words at the start of paragraphs and, where necessary, at the start of sentences? Run your eye down each page of your paper: is the logical flow obvious? If you feel there is a jump in the story line, put link words at the start of paragraphs.

If all this seems just too, too deliberate, then you may want to do a couple of these revisions, not all. It might be a good idea to have one last look at a recent paper from your target journal, just to see how the line of argument is signalled throughout.

Work hard at getting a few sentences to be very clear, particularly those that mark key steps or turning points in your paper, as in the following examples from papers published in different academic disciplines, illustrating concise writing, link words at the start of sentences, sentence length variation and even a one-word sentence.

Ten clear sentences

1 In conclusion, we have been successful in developing a straightforward preparative route to a novel homochiral Mg-bisamide reagent, from a structurally simple, readily available, and relatively inexpensive chiral amine. (Henderson et al. 2002: 479)

2 The model was never viewed as prescriptive or normative by the decision-making group; neither was it a descriptive model, nor a requisite model, as described by Phillips[1] – 'a model whose form and content are sufficient to solve a problem'. (Belton 1985: 273)

3 I do not mean to overstate the positive resolution of the conclusion of *The Duchess of Malfi*. (Selzer 1981: 79)

4 Are we arguing that facts are useless, or that the discourses of expository intent, such as the modernist research paper, be abandoned? No. We are suggesting, however, that facts and expository writing have limits; they allow only certain types of inquiry to take place. (Davis and Shadle 2000: 440)

5 Other factors must be considered in order to answer the question as to why the nanomechanical properties of the treated samples (cryosectioned and time-varying etched UHMWPE samples) were higher than the untreated samples. (Ho et al. 2003: 364)

6 Furthermore, this short study demonstrates that, depending on the nature and demands of the cyclisation substrates, mild modification of the initially established DSA protocols can lead to further improvements in reaction efficiency. (Caldwell et al. 2001: 1429)

7 Although the existence of the slow component has been demonstrated, the putative mechanisms have not been clearly established. (Carra et al. 2003: 2448)

8 Prima donnas seldom write great scholarly books. (Pasco 2002: 82)

9 But these survey data have a limitation: They only show what people are willing or able to tell us about themselves in regard to writing; awareness of inhibitions about writing, as teachers or writers, is probably incomplete at best. (Boice 1990: 14)

10 Thus, this study aimed to extend the study of Bethell et al. [6] by defining the grade and involvement of physiotherapists in the United Kingdom in delivery of cardiac rehabilitation. (Thow et al. 2004: 99)

What is it that each of these sentences does well? What can we learn from looking at them in isolation, out of context? There are features of good writing in each that you can adopt in your papers. These authors demonstrate how important steps in academic arguments can be taken in a single sentence.

Key steps in your argument – in one sentence

1 Not claiming too much, while using the word 'successful'.
  Choosing words that precisely define your contribution.
  'Straightforward . . . simple, readily available, and relatively inexpensive'.
  Sentence starts with link word.
  Patterning: three points on what they developed and three more about the amine.

2 Similarly, Belton takes great care to clarify that her contribution is not to provide a solution to a problem but a means of understanding the problem better. In this sentence she leaves no room for doubt: three negatives – 'never . . . neither . . . nor' – tell us what *not* to think about her work. Perhaps forestalls refutation too.

3 Making explicit what you are and are not claiming in your paper.
  Avoiding overstating by specifying that that is what you do not want to do.
  Building potential (mis-)interpretations of your writing into your writing.
  Addressing them directly.

4 Rehearsing decisions made in analysis or interpretation.
  Using a rhetorical question to focus.
  Writing about 'what you are arguing' explicitly.
  A one-word sentence, unusual in academic writing, but very clear.
  Using 'arguing' for what they do not do and 'suggesting' for what they do.
  Semi-colon to make a point concisely and follow it up with elaboration.

5 Managing the transition between one phase of discussion and the next.
  Distinguishing stages in your answer to your research question.
  Showing how stages in the research relate to each other.
  Showing how these stages, taken together, build up the answer.

6 Starting key sentences with link words.
  Clarification of factors/conditions in which interpretation will stand up.
  But still claiming the result loud and clear.
  Specifying the scale of the result: 'short study'.
  Modulating the claim: 'can lead to'.

7 Distinguishing, in one sentence, what has and has not been done.
Frequently, there is evidence of an effect, but not of the mechanism that creates it.

8 Using a short sentence to assert a view.
Summing up the point to be made, using colourful language.

9 Using short opening sentence, linked to elaboration by colon.
Distinguishing what you can and cannot evidence in your analysis.
Saying explicitly what your data can show, using exactly those words.

10 Linking your work to the literature.
Moving from previous research to your new work, reported in one short sentence.
Linking with a specific, named piece of published work.

Each of these stages in your argument could, of course, be allocated more than one sentence in your paper. The point is to be sure, on the one hand, not to omit such important statements entirely and, on the other, that you do not spend too long on them, either in terms of words or time; one sentence may be enough.

You have to judge whether these steps can be handled in a long complex sentence, for example, linking the paper to the literature, or in one simple sentence, followed by amplification, or in one sentence divided into two parts. There are, of course, disciplinary differences between these examples, but they display some of the same characteristics of good written debate across the disciplines.

In practice, you may end up with a much longer version of your point, perhaps a string of sentences, and then have to prune them back to one sentence. Or the reverse may happen; having written one sentence, you then feel that you need to elaborate. You will, surely, choose to do both these types of revision, for different purposes, perhaps at different points in your paper, with the overall 'design' and intended structure of your paper shaping your revision decisions.

Revising the outline

Your outline can also be a useful part of the iterative process of revision: all along you have used it as a kind of touchstone for your writing, providing focus at every stage. But it too may still be evolving. There may be a point that requires, on reflection, more words than you had allocated for it in your outline. Go back to your outline and use it to judge whether or not you need to add anything. You will, of course, also have to circle back to your abstract and introduction, whether or not you decide to make the change you are considering.

Probably the best way to make sure that you do not go off on a tangent and lose the coherence you worked so hard to create at the outlining stage is to force yourself to revise your outline before you write the extra section you think you now need:

- What is the subject of the new section?
- Write a one-sentence prompt.
- Set a word limit.
- Insert this into your outline: what is the effect?
- Where will you take the extra words you need from?
- What does that do to the overall balance/sense of your paper?
- Are you sure you *have* to add this to your paper?
- Or can you save it for another paper?

There may, of course, also be sections or sentences that you now see should be cut. Again, check your outline first: will the paper still be coherent if you make that change, and will other changes need to be made in order to smooth over what might now be a 'jump' in your argument?

These questions merely make explicit the decision-making process, creating a pause in your rush to revise. Consider the possibility that your paper may be good enough – although it could always be improved – as it is.

Revising drafts

Topic sentences are important; they clarify what the topic of your paragraphs are, in the first sentence of each paragraph. In a well-written paper it is often possible to scan the topic sentences and form an immediate impression of the whole argument. This has the effect not of making your argument seem obvious and your articulation of it laboured – as new writers sometimes fear – but of showing your reader that you have a logical structure and giving them an overview of what it is. In this way, topic sentences can function like headings and sub-headings; in fact, topic sentences, used well, will develop the key words of your headings.

In practice, it may take several revisions to achieve this effect. Drafts can move some way towards it, but there may be further honing to do, and topic sentences should be on your checklist for revision.

For example, you may have put two points in your topic sentence, without indicating, through punctuation, which is the more important:

Example

It has only been since the early 1960s that isokinetic devices i.e. devices that allow for movements to be performed at controlled velocities, have been available on the commercial market. These devices such as the Cybex II Isokinetic Dynamometer (Lummex Inc.) measure the torque produced throughout the range of voluntary limb movements held at constant pre-set velocities. It has been suggested that these devices provide an ideal means of measuring an individual's torque generating capacities and that the measures given provide greater information on the expression of strength in maximal voluntary limb movements relative to other methods traditionally used.

You could improve this paragraph – as a step in an argument – by making three simple changes:

- Put one point in the topic sentence, not two.
- 'It has been suggested' is ambiguous; clarify who 'suggested'.
- Cut the long last sentence; state the main point at the end of the paragraph.

If you decide to keep two points in a topic sentence, use parentheses: two commas show which is more important:

Either

It has only been since the early 1960s that isokinetic devices, which allow for movements to be performed at controlled velocities, **have been available on the commercial market**.

Or

Isokinetic devices, which have only been available on the commercial market since the early 1960s, **allow for movements to be performed at controlled velocities**.

The words in bold mark the main point; the point between the commas is secondary. The first option means that the main point of the paragraph is the commercial availability of the devices; the second option means that the main point is what these devices do.

Once you have made the first change in the topic sentence, it becomes clear what you should do to improve the rest of the paragraph, since the rest of the paragraph should develop the point made in your topic sentence.

Revision

Isokinetic devices, which have only been available on the commercial market since the early 1960s, allow for movements to be performed at controlled velocities. **These** devices, such as the Cybex II Isokinetic Dynamometer (Lummex Inc.), measure the torque produced throughout the range of voluntary limb movements held at constant pre-set velocities. **They** provide an ideal means of measuring an individual's torque generating capacities (Reference), and thereby greater information on the expression of strength in maximal voluntary limb movements. **This** is what traditional methods could not do.

For the purposes of illustration, link words have been added and emphasized in this revision in bold. If they are placed at the start of the sentence, then it is clear how the reader has to connect your sentences. If the link words appear later in the sentence, the reader has to hold some information in his or her head until the link word arrives.

Again, you may be thinking that this is just too much linking, but over the course of several thousand words, and at certain points in your argument, you really have to ask yourself if there is any such thing as 'too much linking' and what negative consequences could realistically result if you did overdose the reader on link words. Futhermore, at certain points in your argument, even what you might see as 'over-linking' might, in fact, be essential, if you are to take the reader through every step of your procedure, your justification or your interpretation, for example.

You can also use topic sentences to place your main theme or key words regularly before the reader, unifying your paper. You can also refer back to your study's aims or your paper's purpose – using these as key, unifying words. You may wonder whether this, too, is a repetition too far – many new writers worry about repetition, when, in fact, it is a useful device – but if a key word is not repeated, it may not emerge as a key word.

Links within paragraphs and links between paragraphs do not, of course, all tumble out in all the right places in your drafts. These are further items for your revision checklist. Checking, by scanning, your topic sentences, without reading the paragraphs, is another way of checking the coherence of your paper in these final stages.

Generative writing

What purpose can five-minute bursts of writing serve at this stage?:

- You can write about uncertainties in or about your paper.
- Develop a few answers to anticipated critiques.
- Continue writing practice.
- Maintain confidence in your ability to put words on paper.
- Write about any part of your paper you are not, even at this stage, completely satisfied with and try to find a better way of saying it.
- If it gets too complicated, start with the prompt, 'What I am really trying to say here is'.
- Write to focus on how much – or how little – you still have to do.
- Write about your sense of audience for this paper, how they will read it.
- Rehearse ways to build uncertainties into your paper, as appropriate, without undermining your whole argument.

Generative writing is perhaps most useful at this stage for keeping you focused on the task in hand.

Using the writers' group

At this late stage the writers' group can serve a number of purposes:

- providing general support;
- readings of and feedback on your final draft;
- objective assessment of your paper;
- hints and tips on effective targeting and writing;
- acknowledgement of how much you have achieved;
- affirmation of the purpose of writing for academic journals;
- reminder of your personal writing goals.

Perhaps the most useful purpose, as you are forcing yourself to complete your paper, is helping you to make time for the many final revisions.

The critical friend and the 'tame' subject expert

Recruiting a critical friend, who knows the aims and plan of your paper, and a 'tame' subject expert, who will not rip your paper to shreds, can help at this stage. The former can help you maintain focus within a series of drafts; the latter can provoke the sharpness and accuracy needed for your final draft. Both can help the writing project along if they are aware of what it involves: realizing the planned structure.

This is when you need 'hard' feedback. Although it may not be comfortable, if this is your first paper, you are likely to have made some mistakes, either in the technical work or in your writing or both, and you can safely assume that some of them will not be apparent to you. The purpose of getting hard feedback at this stage is to make sure that you correct these errors before sending the paper in. Do not look to the journal editors to provide that feedback for you – they will not appreciate your using them in this way.

You just have to acknowledge that no matter how much time you have put into revising, there will be more to do. It might help, also, if you can acknowlege that you are still, even at this late stage in the writing process, learning about writing for academic journals.

If you feel some of the feedback your subject expert gives you is more savage than 'tame', then you can, of course, go back and discuss this with them. But first check that there is not some purpose to their apparently over-critical comment.

Tell your critical friend what your deadline is – when you want to send your paper off to the journal – and, if you can, give him or her a deadline for getting feedback to you.

Revision processes

Rather than thinking that everything has to be revised, to infinity, shift your focus to key points in your text:

- Forecasting: have you written a short summary of your whole argument at the start of your paper, including the paper's purpose and stating how each section will move towards achieving it?
- Signposting: do you provide references to the main argument throughout your paper, stating, possibly at the end of each section, how it has advanced your argument?
- Signalling: do you provide links and transitions – when you change direction – at each stage in your argument?

If this seems like overkill, remember that if you do not provide these signs, the reader will have to work out how your paper holds together as they go along. In many cases, of course, they will manage this; but you are asking them to do all the thinking, and to do it along the lines that you did. They will already find things to challenge in your paper without you feeding them further opportunities to question what you wrote. In other words, assume that however well argued your paper is, it is still going to be subject to debate; it is still contested. This is why you need to make the logic of your argument explicit.

Iterative processes

Move from abstract, to draft and back to abstract again, as you verify that what you said you would say is, in fact, what you do say in your paper.

Notice how you circle back and forth, making smaller and smaller changes. See this as a process of refining, and spare yourself the misconception that you should have spotted a required revision earlier. Recast what you might previously have seen as errors or lapses in concentration as necessary steps in a thorough academic writing process.

You can take this a step further and establish a systematic iterative sequence:

1 Abstract: which words are used to describe the aims/purpose of your paper?
2 Introduction: are these same words used here? If you have used different words, should you revise them to match?
3 Abstract: does your revision match the terms you use in your abstract? Are you making the same point?

This may seem a bit tortuous – more irritation than iteration – as if you are simply making more work for yourself: one change surely leads to another. There may be some truth in this: you may be adding rather than matching, and, if this is your first paper, you will have to watch out for that, or get your readers to watch out for it. Expect it to happen and have some way of noticing it: go back to your outline, for example.

This is iteration with a purpose. You should find that you make smaller and smaller changes, as you consolidate and reveal your outline. This is not to say that major changes are forbidden, but to acknowledge that they may not always be as important as you think they are.

Your continuing uncertainty about how your paper will be received by reviewers may lead you, at this late stage as at earlier stages, to feel that you have to add 'extra-strength' arguments, as if that would, in any case, forestall further debate.

Developing a concise style

The first principle of developing a concise style must surely be accepting that you can cut words, sentences and even whole sections of your hard-earned writing.

What to cut

- Words you know you use, that have no particular effect and are sometimes just vague, like 'some' or, as in this sentence, 'sometimes'.

    Instead of saying 'some', why not just say how many? It is good technique to hedge your statements, so as to write debate rather than dogmatism, but this is just pointless. Cut it.

    Once you have cut one of these words, develop the habit of asking yourself if you really need that word whenever you see it from now on.

    Make a list of words you know you will regularly have to cut.

- Adjectives and adverbs – are they really making your point or your emphasis clear? Sometimes a sentence is stronger and clearer when an adjective has been cut, like the word 'really' in that first sentence.

- Using bullet points?

    Make them one-liners.

    Use verbs to start them.

    Work at pruning them until you can fit your point on one line.

- If your word count is over the journal's limit, cut all of these – it is amazing how much is non-essential when you have to cut 1000 words.

You can cut whole sentences, where there is elaboration – is it really needed? – or repetition, even if for emphasis. Consider cutting whole paragraphs, particularly in the conceptual/theoretical sections – is there too much of that? Are there too many definitions? Too much going back to first principles? Do you need them all? Finally, re-read your conclusions – are there too many? Could you sharpen the focus by cutting one or more?

Polishing

'Polishing' implies minor, surface revisions:

- Check the format against the journal's instructions for authors.
- Remove any unnecessary words: adverbs and adjectives?
- Check your references carefully: punctuation and so on.
- Check them against the references in your paper.
- Check the word count. Note it at the end of your paper.
- Check that you have the current editor's address.
- When submitting electronically, tell the editor which operating system and word-processing package you used.

These are far from superficial in the sense that editors report, informally, that they do not read papers that have not been submitted in the required format. With the quantity and quality of submissions, they can afford to do so.

These final polishings are also not superficial in the sense that they require your close attention, and that may be difficult if you are approaching your deadline, desperate to send your paper off, or just tired and demoralized:

> I am having such trouble this week – it is a sloppy slippery week. My work does not coagulate. It is as unmanageable as a raw egg on the kitchen floor. It makes me crazy. I am really going to try now and I'm afraid that the very force of the trying will take all the life out of the work.
>
> (Steinbeck 1970: 130)

Sometimes you just lose sight of what still needs to be done, of whether any polishing is needed, of whether it is good enough yet for the polishing stage. Ask someone to read your paper and to answer the question, 'Is this ready to submit?'.

You may feel that by doing any more revision at all you will be squeezing the life out of your writing. You may not recognize when you have done enough. Or your paper may cease to make sense or to have value. You are too close to it.

There is no definitive answer to the question of when you know that it is time to stop revising, let it go and send it off. This is where an agreed deadline will be extremely useful, forcing you to get rid of your paper in spite of your array of dissatisfactions. At some point the iterative process, going back and forth between text, outline and abstract until you get them to match, has to stop. The list of polishing steps may help you to move to that point.

The final revision

No more, the text is foolish

King Lear, IV, ii, 37

Read the whole paper, from start to finish, one more time, going through all the sections in order.

Check that you have made it crystal clear what you are – and are not – claiming to contribute in your paper. Can you refer to that quality when you submit the paper to the editor?

Checklist

- Find someone to read your complete draft.
- Keep up the regular writing.
- Revise key points in your paper very carefully.

7   Finding time to write

Incremental writing • 'Binge' or 'snack'? • A writing plan • Goal setting • 30-minute slots • Monitoring progress • Creating a place for writing in your life • Becoming a regular writer • A six-month writing programme • Checklist

> If you set a short term deadline (even of five minutes) you *will* write something/produce something and more often than not, it's as good as what you would have done with double the time!
>
> (writers' group participant)

There is a popular misconception that we need to wait for mood, ideas or inspiration before we can write and that once we have started we have to keep going. This is what people often call 'flow'. In their accounts, it does not occur very often, but many new academic writers seem to aspire to it.

Along with this conception, there is the popular belief that even once you have decided to write, you have to 'work yourself into writing again each time' (Blaxter et al. 1998a: 141). Since both assumptions make writers delay in actually getting started, particularly if they do not have much time, they are worth challenging. How often do you have any time to write, let alone a time slot that coincides with your mood or inspiration? If your answer is 'not very often', or even 'not often enough', then waiting for a writing 'mood' to come along is going to be a mistake. Some new writers may never even have had the experience of being in the mood to write, in any case: 'It isn't a question of mood. It's a question of concentration' (Coward 1999 [1941]).

Disappointingly, to some, Boice has argued, based on his empirical research, that if you had more time, you would not necessarily write more. This finding makes some heads of department very happy, as they take it to mean that they can immediately cancel all sabbaticals. This is not what it means. Boice has shown that if you had more time, you would be likely to persist with the writing habits you already have, and this would not necessarily lead to increased productivity.

This suggests that we need to consider changing our writing habits and that the nature of that change should be regular writing in short bursts. Rather than waiting for inspiration or mood, you can get into the writing habit through regular writing. This will seem crashingly obvious to some, but writing for academic journals does not seem to be done in this way. There may be a good reason for this: academic writing requires the highest standards of content and writing; this cannot be achieved in small increments. In addition, the really intricate and difficult thinking work cannot be done in 15-minute bursts. This is true. And if you do have large amounts of time to write – and if you find you write plenty in the time you have – there is no need for you to change. However, if you find that you are not achieving much – or anything, in terms of publications – in the limited time that you have, you may have to change your writing habits.

An even more obvious way to capture this idea is 'If you are not writing regularly, you are not writing regularly', and one student in a workshop improved on this further by saying 'If you're not writing regularly, you're not writing'.

This chapter presents the argument that combining 'binge' writing, writing in large chunks of time, and 'snack' writing – writing a little often, for example in 30-minute slots – is a productive strategy for making time for writing in a professional schedule, and still having a life. This topic – changing personal writing practices in order to increase productivity and enjoyment – could fill a whole book in itself.

Then there is the question of 'selfishness', putting yourself, and your desire to write more, first, more frequently, which is often cited – among new writers – as one of the main reasons those who publish a lot manage to do so. The new writer, by contrast, invests value in teaching, sometimes in over-teaching. This is a contentious issue: am I going to go as far as to suggest that you should spend less time on your teaching in order to make time for your writing? Well, it is certainly worth looking at how you spend your time. You are probably far too busy already. Where is writing time going to come from? Something has to change.

What this range of issues indicates is that you have to find a way to fit writing into your life; this may mean making changes to other areas of your life and getting the support of others in your life as you make such changes. Or as others have put it – although they were referring to thesis writing rather than writing for journals – you can see finding time for writing as a 'lifestyle change' (Burton and Steane 2004: 98). This may lead you to think of writing in new ways:

> First, it helps you recognize the level of effort and the intensity of effort needed, and second it helps you to reflect realistically on how you spend your time now, and on ways that you can integrate the tasks associated with the thesis into your existing lifestyle.
>
> (Burton and Steane 2004: 99)

The same could be said of writing for journals.

There are, therefore, many sound strategies you can use in your writing for journals, but if you are still hung up on the question of protecting time for writing – to the extent of failing to do it – you will not write. If you are determined to persist with your old habits, you may not write. Until you make time regularly to put words on paper or screen, you will not know that you can write.

Incremental writing

> I'm too busy to publish! This is like the excuse of the manager who is too swamped with brush fires to take a time management course. Time management isn't the problem. Change is the problem. Unless people are ready to alter their lifestyle, they will always be too busy. People like to pretend that they are using all their time wisely. But if you watch them, you quickly become convinced that they are not as productive as they could be. For example, I am missing lunch with my friends to write this article. I don't want to skip too many lunches with the gang because that's fun, but so is publishing.
>
> (Matejka 1990: 9)

A sensible way to become a regular writer is to make small demands on yourself, at any one time. This is easier than it sounds, since it may require you to plan your papers in different ways.

Incremental writing is the approach advocated throughout this book, involving treating the writing of an academic paper as a design project: think about audience, purpose, scope and structure before you worry about paragraphs and sentences. Chapter 4 showed how you can produce the total design of your paper. Once you have this, you can write in short bursts. You can even write with a certain amount of confidence since you have already decided what you want to say and how you have to say it. You can be confident to the extent that not only have you found something to say but you have also thought it through and tested it against your reading.

If you divide the writing into small tasks, small increments, you can fit writing into your busy life:

> To overcome fears about writing, I began to write every day. My process was not to write a lot but to work in small increments, writing and rewriting.
>
> (hooks 1999: 15)

Regular writing can have the effect of removing the fear. Each increment is small enough to be manageable, rather than daunting. On the other hand, if you do not have an incremental model, you do not experience that sense of gradually, little by little, making progress. In fact, you may not make any progress.

This is one of the 'soft' outcomes that this book is driving towards: the 'hard' outcomes are the outputs, the numbers of papers readers of this book publish in academic journals, while the 'soft' outcomes are the writing habits they develop along the way, the confidence they feel in their ability to write and the barriers to writing they remove.

'Binge' or 'snack'?

> All of them did it by making time to write rather than waiting to 'find' time.
>
> (Cameron 1998: 14)

You might as well wait for time to find you as wait to find time. Making time for writing – for anything – is an active process. One of the most challenging transitions is moving from 'binge' writing – 'I can only do my best work in large chunks of time' – to 'snack' writing – you can write almost anywhere and almost any time. So many new writers resist this suggestion that I have come to assert that the most productive model is 'snack and binge', with the proviso that all binges should be structured, perhaps not as 'three-course meals', but along those lines. Some have taken issue with the word 'binge', suggesting, instead, the word 'feast', so as to capture the enjoyment that comes with the headlong, seemingly unstoppable, magical 'flow' of writing that does sometimes happen.

'Flow' is a word that crops up again and again. It is part of how people define good writing practices and good text. The downside is that it seems to come unbidden and, even when 'bidden', does not come often enough. It is possible to induce this flow state by a combination of regular writing and joining up the writing sessions.

This seems counter-intuitive to many new writers, yet, again, it has to be said that their discomfort with the idea of writing this way is based on no more than thinking about it; in practice, in other words, it might prove less radical than they think.

Even if you feel that you will be sacrificing what you feel are your most 'creative' moments (large chunks of time) by carving your thinking and writing into such small 'snacks', your brain will be working on your writing project while you are not writing; be ready to note ideas, headings or questions as they come to you at unpredictable moments. Capture these in sentences – rather than notes, bullets or fragments – so that they will be more meaningful when you come back to them later and so that you develop the point a fraction further.

A writing plan

The key point of this section is that while there are general principles for making writing time, you have to create real time slots in your diary. This means 'matching' your outline to your diary, literally using the detailed outline you have created of your paper-in-progress to map out the writing slots you now need to produce text.

Many authors have quite rightly addressed this question of planning for writing, offering useful general advice:

Planning time to write: general advice

1 Decide to do it.
2 Decide on your focus.
3 Plan your work.
4 Remember how many things, in real life, get done in the last 10 per cent of available time.
5 Think in terms of small blocks at a time.
6 Open your daily planner.
7 Commit to the schedule.
8 Unplug the phone, close the door . . .
9 Try not to exceed your allotted time.
10 Plan to edit later.
11 Schedule time for peer review.
12 Plan time to celebrate!

(Black et al. 1998: 20–1)

However, an effective writing plan has to be more specific than this, and it has to fit into the time that you actually have. I still think that if writing is not in your diary, it is not in real time. Of course, there are people who can carry this information – tasks, times, priorities – in their heads, and if you are one of them, then this may all seem a bit too programmed. Yet this is a model for changing your behaviour and this may mean changing some aspects of how you normally think about and do writing, particularly for your first few papers.

What would a more specific writing plan look like? It would define writing tasks and place them in the diary. It would include the full range of writing tasks, not just drafting sections of the paper. More importantly, it would show the results of breaking your writing goal into sub-goals:

Writing plan: general			
Week beginning	**Goal**	**Sub-goals**	**Activity**
Monday 1 Oct	Choose target journal	Analyse papers	Copy and read
	Contact editor	Email (follow up?)	Three sentences
Monday 8 Oct	Literature review	Classify readings	Write overview
Monday 15 Oct	Review articles	Critique Smith paper	Write summary
Monday 25 Oct	Outline paper	Summary	Brown's 8 questions

You can do one of these plans for the coming week, or month, or year.

Yet is this really going to work? Does this tell you when you are going to do your writing? To a certain extent it does, of course, but there is no definition of two key features: time and length. How many words is each task to produce – what is the scale and scope of each? How long is each slot to be, in terms, literally, of minutes or hours?

While the plan illustrated is a good start – and it looks like what new writers present when they first draw up writing plans – I would argue that an effective plan has to be more specific than this, at least for your first few papers, as you are actively seeking to establish your routine of regular writing for publication.

What would a more specific plan look like? – it would look and function more like a programme for your writing. How you produce it is by going back to your outline:

1 Take each heading, sub-heading and sub-sub-heading separately.
2 Allocate each one a time slot of its own.
3 Go through your whole outline if you have time.
4 If not, just do what you can in the time you have.

For example, the prompt for a short burst of writing used in Chapter 4 defines the writing task. It specifies one element of the outline as a writing instruction, using a verb to define the type of writing required, 'Define', and allocating a word limit:

Define the form of cardiac rehabilitation that involves exercise, as developed in the west of Scotland, over the past ten years (200 words).

This could fit into a 30-minute slot in the writer's diary. The same approach could be used with other sections and sub-sections, if you have done the 'level 3 outlining' described in Chapter 4. These have to go into the diary, alongside all your other tasks. If you do not use a diary, it may be time to start.

Writing plan: specific

Monday	8.30–9am	*Define the form of cardiac rehabilitation that involves exercise, as developed in the west of Scotland, over the past ten years (200 words).*
Tuesday	11.30am–12	*Overview the different professionals involved in this development (150 words).*
Wednesday	12.30–1pm	*Describe the role of physiotherapy (100 words).*
Thursday	8.30–9pm	*Summarize Newton and Thow papers and state how present study takes this work forward (200 words).*
Friday	6–6.30pm	*Define and justify aims of the study (200 words).*

You may wonder at these as headings for an academic paper. You may wonder if the word allocations are right. You may even have started to question the purpose of the research. However, the point of this illustration is to show how you can map your level 3 outline on to real time slots. If each of your writing tasks does not have a time slot, how will you know when you will be able to do it? By not allocating a time slot are you not more or less planning not to do it? More importantly, if you do not produce something along these lines, how will you do the task of working out when – realistically – you will be able to write?

If, in practice, you find, for example, that you fail to write your 200 words on Monday, then move on. You certainly know what your next writing task is: to do that task in your next designated slot. You may also find that you cannot do one of these slots every single day. You can, of course, do a longer slot, as long as it is structured around your outline. At the end of the week, take stock: to what extent have you been able to write to plan? Can you already tell that certain slots will never work, while some always work? Or is it too soon to say;

should you give this approach another week or two? Are you able to note – in a separate file – emerging ideas for future papers, using your outline to mark what to leave out of the one you are working on now?

If this seems like just too much planning – time spent planning that could more usefully be spent writing – then, again, remind yourself that what you are doing here is trying to change the habits of a lifetime and to make sure that they stay changed. When do you have time to do all this planning? Well, if the outlining is already done, all you really have to do is sit down with your diary and be realistic: resist the temptation to do too much in a short time slot or to run over the end of your dedicated time slot, perhaps creating a new 'catch up' problem, unless that too is part of your plan, and you can see a way to streamlining the task that you are currently ignoring.

There will, of course, be times when you have to interrupt your writing programme, perhaps dropping a time slot for other professional or personal reasons; it is not the end of the world, but in some situations it might point to a weakness in your planning process. For example, maybe it is not a good idea to allocate too many writing slots to Friday afternoon, if you are usually exhausted by then. Or, you might surprise yourself, and find that the sudden onset of euphoria that the prospect of the weekend brings gives you a brief – 30 minutes will not exhaust you – burst of energy. It is possible, for example, to do one of those 30-minute time slots between getting home and going back out again, settling down to relax or taking over the caring for the evening.

This step – planning your writing slots – has to be integrated with all of the other work you are doing on your paper; it has to include the many different types of writing activity that are proposed in this book: freewriting/generative writing, or some version of it, some form of regular focused and unfocused scribbling in short bursts as well as the more structured 'writing-to-the-outline' time slots.

Goal setting

Probably one of the most serious and motivating activities is to set goals. How many articles or books could you realistically expect to get published in the next five years? Add another one, or two, to that total. (Remember you are always capable of much more than you think.)

(Drake and Jones 1997: 52)

This is good advice, if it makes you think ahead and develop a plan for a body of work. It might help you to see your work in 'units', rather than trying to fit too much of your work into your first paper.

However, it could be bad advice if it makes you overreach, as many academics do in their writing, trying to do too much in the time available, or rather in the that is not available. The error that many new writers make is thinking that they can, for example, write a paper over a weekend or a month – then they become depressed and guilty when they find that they cannot. When I suggest that they should take six months, many object. Of course, if you do write a paper in a weekend, that is excellent. Some people can write that way. Some find that they can write about some subjects that way, subjects that they know and have been thinking of writing about for some time, for example. But most of us need more time.

The following examples illustrate how learning to set writing goals and sub-goals may itself take time. Three writers, from a group of about 30, wrote out their goals, after an initial discussion of the range of strategies that, I suggested, they needed to be thinking about and adopting over the longer term. The point is not to show weaknesses in their planning strategies, since, for many, this was their first formal discussion of writing in a professional context; instead, the aim is to show that while each writer picked up on my suggestions, they still had some work to do to bring definition to their goals. Otherwise, they would, experience suggests, be unlikely to achieve them.

New writers' over-reaching goals

Writer 1

- Review articles in several journals.
- Decide on target journal.
- Email editors.
- Do some freewriting sessions about ideas for article.

Writer 2

- Clarify topic.
- Identify journal – determine style and preferred article type.
- Request 'notes for authors'.
- Five minutes freewriting per day.

Writer 3

- Identify a journal.
- Consider what type of paper.
- Do five minutes writing practice daily.
- Organize meeting with someone else for feedback.

They are all picking up on the 'right' tasks, but are in danger of trying to do too much in the time they will have, and it is not even clear from these goals how they will be using that time. No matter how small the goal, there still has to be a real – and realistic – allocation of time to do it.

What these examples show is that even when we have discussed what constitutes 'good goals', and even when the group is very experienced and knowledgable in goal setting, having helped patients, for example, set goals for recovery, rehabilitation or health promotion, there is still a lack of definition of writing goals. This suggests that good goal-setting skills are not automatically transferred to writing tasks, as if writing were a completely different task – different from all others – for which goal setting were not appropriate for some reason.

This might be an overstatement, but the 'over-reaching' tendency seems to be strong among academics. What happens is that they set goals that are far too large, even when they think they are setting sub-goals. For example, they set a goal of 'writing the literature review section' by the end of the week. This goal is nowhere near specific enough.

Contrary to the quotation at the start of this section, therefore, the best advice might be to do *less* than you think you can. If you admit that you are still learning about setting writing goals that will work, then you can start by changing your perception of what is 'enough'. Do less. Do much less than you think you 'should' achieve in the small amounts of time available for writing. Make the sub-goals as small as possible, so that they are genuinely feasible. Be prepared to fail, to revert to your old habits or to feel uncomfortable with the new regime even if it does work. But persist with your specific sub-goals.

Realistic goals: do less than you think you can	
How long is that section to be?	800 words
What is the content?	Literature from 2000 to 2004, UK and US
How is it structured?	Options:
	As a debate/two schools of thought/ three main approaches/as a narrative/ chronology/two main groups of researchers
How many sub-sections?	4
What is the length of each section?	Section 1 100 words
	Section 2 200 words
	Section 3 200 words
	Section 4 400 words
What is the story of each?	Section 1 Overview of . . .
	Section 2 Summarize work of X, Y and Z
	Section 3 Evaluate . . .
	Section 4 Demonstrate need for . . .
When will you write it?	Monday 3–4pm and Wednesday 7–8pm

Unless the writing goal is defined to something like this level of detail, there will be problems achieving it. If the sub-goals are not small, then they cannot be achieved in small amounts of time. Only large amounts of time will do, and if large amounts of time for writing are not available, then you have a model of writing that is dysfunctional.

This method will work if you find a way to join up your small sub-goals, that is, if you can connect the work of one session, Monday 3–4pm in the above example, with Wednesday 7–8 pm. At the end of each writing slot, write yourself a writing instruction:

Write yourself a writing instruction

- My next writing task is to define . . .
- The next section will summarize . . .
- My next 30 minutes will be for describing . . .

The purpose of these is to make sure that you know exactly what you have to do when, after a gap of a day, a week or a month or more, you come back to your writing project with no more than a vague memory of where you were when you left it. Instead of re-reading what you wrote last time, you can get straight on with the next bit. Instead of getting bogged down in revision, you can take your paper a stage further. Most importantly, instead of feeling that you are, in a sense, starting from scratch every time you go back to your paper, you will feel that you are always moving it forward. This is crucial for your motivation, as much as for actual progress with the paper.

So much thinking is still to be done; thinking and writing will have to occur simultaneously. No wonder people report that it takes them so long to get started. No wonder they feel that they must have time to think before they write. If they have not designed the task, then, of course they need thinking time. Thinking and designing time will also have to be timetabled.

I sometimes get the feeling that academics denigrate goal setting as a bit too simplistic, behaviourist, not entirely appropriate for academic work, and con-straining their creativity and cramping their style. I wonder if some of them see goal setting as a kind of lower-order skill that they feel they should have moved beyond, even though many have not yet developed effective practices or alternatives.

Yet this may be exactly the problem with academic writing: it is positioned apart from other forms of writing – when, in fact, it has much in common with other forms. Perhaps part of the problem is that there is a knowledge gap: academics do not learn the literature on academic writing.

30-minute slots

If, after reading the previous chapters and sections, you are still not convinced that this short burst approach works, then it is time to try it for yourself. If you have tried it once or twice, then I would suggest that you persevere, since this 'snacking' approach constitutes significant behavioural change.

Write for 15 minutes. Do it twice. Count the number of words written.

Write for four sets of 15 minutes. Prove to yourself that you can write 1000 words in one hour. The aim is to generate text – try to forget/delay the question of quality. You can use any topic at all, but it might make more sense if you used some of your prompts. To really make this work, you need to top-and-tail your writing sessions: as you end one session, define your task for the next one.

Remember that the word 'write' may no longer be adequate in defining your writing tasks and sub-goals: what kind of writing do you want to do? Reviewing? Summarizing? Analysing? Reporting? See other examples in other chapters.

Monitoring progress

You can monitor your progress, in terms of output, as you go along, looking back to take stock and looking forward to set new goals. This could be a further variation on your 30-minute meet-to-write session:

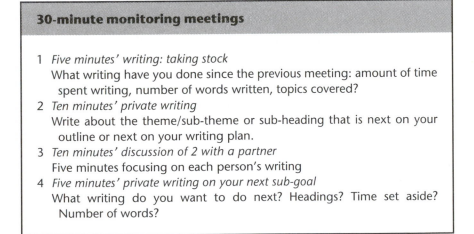

30-minute monitoring meetings

1 *Five minutes' writing: taking stock*
   What writing have you done since the previous meeting: amount of time spent writing, number of words written, topics covered?
2 *Ten minutes' private writing*
   Write about the theme/sub-theme or sub-heading that is next on your outline or next on your writing plan.
3 *Ten minutes' discussion of 2 with a partner*
   Five minutes focusing on each person's writing
4 *Five minutes' private writing on your next sub-goal*
   What writing do you want to do next? Headings? Time set aside? Number of words?

This can be useful for calibrating your motivation, checking that you are not trying to do too much and acknowledging that you – sometimes – have done more than you thought you had.

In practice, again and again writers turn up to such meetings and, after reporting that they have not done much since the previous meeting, then reveal that they have, in fact, done more than they set out to do. They have completed more than they set out to do, by the deadline of the meeting, and yet feel that they have not done 'enough'. What is that about? Over-reaching? Setting unrealistic goals? The frenzy of academic life that causes them to lose sight of what is 'enough'? The answer to this question is probably quite individual, but it is as well to look out for this pattern and to have some way – if not this, then what? – of reorienting yourself towards your sense of progress.

Creating a place for writing in your life

Although some writers feel that they need to write in the same space, the same physical space, it may be more productive, and worth trying, to write any time, any where:

> . . . in your dentist's office, on an airplane, at the train station waiting for someone else's commuter train, between appointments at the office, at lunch, on a coffee break, at the hairdresser's, at the kitchen table while the onions sauté.
>
> (Cameron 1998: 14)

Over the past ten years, finding time and space have come up so often as the absolute barriers to academics who want to write more for journals. Is it that there is a connection between creating space in your life and finding space for yourself in the published world? Is it impossible to create space for writing while you still see no space for yourself in writing? Is it that we have to invent a writing self before we have actually published? Or is it that we are trying to invent a published self when what we really need is a writing self?

Perhaps it is not until you are finally part of the published world that you can legitimize your time and space for writing, to yourself and to others. Perhaps this is because, as new writers, we are not yet in an environment to write and perceive the writing environment as 'other' or 'out there'. Perhaps there are just too many other demands on your time and space: 'Rare is the woman writer of any race who is free (from domestic chores or caring for others – children, parents, companions) to focus solely on her writing' (hooks 1999: 167) is a statement that may be true for male writers too.

Limiting the time for each writing activity often brings sharper focus to writing, and having limited time in one place, for example when you are travelling, can sit well with these short bursts of writing. The trick is to 'make writing time in the life you've already got' (Cameron 1998: 16).

Becoming a regular writer

> Habit . . . functions in human life as a flywheel functions in a machine, to overcome temporary opposing forces, to keep us behaving for a time in a particular way, according to a predetermined pattern, a general rule . . . habits function to help us avoid making decisions on a case-by-case basis, to commit us to decisions made earlier, and to reap the benefits of following abstract rules rather than particular impulses.
>
> (Rachlin 2000: 7–8)

Rachlin (2000) argues that this is not – in spite of popular belief – an internal battle only; external factors, particularly social environment, play their part. This raises the question of why we need to develop 'harmonious patterns' (Rachlin 2000: 8), harmonious with what? With our ambitions? Aspirations? Family? Friends? Colleagues? Our personalities? How are these patterns created? – by developing good habits specific to writing? Do we know enough about the literature on self-control to do this? We think we do, then we fail, then we blame ourselves. Alternatively, we could learn more about how to establish 'harmonious patterns', have more likelihood of success, and achieve what we want to in writing.

> . . . the more I write the easier and more joyous a labor it becomes. The less I write the harder it is for me to write and the more it appears to be so arduous a task that I seek to avoid it.
>
> (hooks 1999: 168)

For academics, the answer is that you just have to find ways to write – preferably some of the time in private writing – if you are to become a regular writer. There is no mystique to it, and there are numerous strategies for forcing yourself to try it. The key might lie in the social dimension: can you find others who are trying to become regular writers with whom you can work as you move towards this goal?

A six-month writing programme

For new writers particularly, it might be helpful to think about the whole process of writing your first paper in real time. If you are not only aiming to write a draft of your paper, but also develop your academic writing practices, you should be careful to pace the different activities over a realistic period, such as six months.

Writing for publication

Structured programme for productive writing

Six months

Phase 1   Months 1 and 2

1 Getting started: freewriting, generative writing, prompts
2 Personal writing goal: targeting one journal
3 Developing an outline

Phase 2   Months 3 and 4

4 Detailed outline: themes, sub-themes and prompts
5 Draft abstract/summary
6 Regular writing: freewriting and generative writing

Phase 3   Months 5 and 6 . . .

7 Draft introduction and revise
8 Draft review of literature and revise
9 Draft all sections and revise
10 Feedback from journals and resubmitting . . .

This programme does not actually state that you should include feedback cycles at each stage, but it is assumed that you will be either writing with others – in the sense of meeting to write and discuss writing – or having others read your writing. It will also help to have milestones along the way, for taking stock, calibrating goals and generally coordinating your efforts to write your paper by your deadline. There are certain stages in such a six-month programme where such coordination could occur, and there are certain topics that you might find it useful to focus on in such meetings.

Coordinating meetings

Start-up   Day 1

Barriers to writing, strategies for productive writing, personal goals, sub-goals, study buddy, incremental writing

Set-up   @ 2 weeks

More sub-goal definition, targeting journals, contact with editors, getting into the writing habit, demystifying academic writing, routines of writing, structures, soft and hard outcomes, diary time, monitoring

Check-up   @ 3 months

Outlines, productive writing habits, resetting goals

Round-up   @ end

Successful strategies and processes, making time for writing and protecting it, sharing achievements, setting new writing goals, non-academic writing

At the end of one such six-month programme, one group of participants were asked about the persistent 'time' problem – it had come up again and again in discussions throughout the six months. It would not go away. For some, the problem persisted, but as a group they had begun to generate new analyses of the problem and, at last, and to their immense relief, some solutions. Some of these involved a change in their priorities, or at least beginning to think about such a change. This is one advantage of such long-term programmes: participants have time to work through recurring complaints, which can become boring or just frustrating if repeated over several discussions. It was possible to discuss solutions that had failed, in an instructive way, and attitudes that were holding them back, which became obvious once they were externalized. The group finally came up with their own list of solutions, some of which are ambiguous, because there are no easy answers. They were intending to be positive, while describing ways of making time as an on-going challenge:

Making time for writing?

- 'Research is not a residual . . . But it can become that.'
- 'Maybe other things should become residual?'
- 'Put a notice on your office door.'
- 'Being selfish is not a bad thing.'
- 'Don't feel guilty about doing research.'
- 'Even when I have a half-day for research, I don't use it; something else comes up, like marking.'
- 'Any time we have for research is just by chance.'

- 'Technology makes it easier for people to find us.'
- 'Students always find you.'
- 'At certain times, students must take priority, for example at times of course work submissions.'
- 'You can't protect the half-day for research.'
- 'There is no space for research/writing at work.'

One person had come up with a more devious approach: putting a notice on her office door that said 'Please use other door', when there was no other door. Whether or not she put this into practice remains a mystery, but what is clearer from the other comments about how to make time to write is that there are blocks. It is difficult. There are people who will stand in your way. Even though there is a research imperative – I have heard it called 'research myopia', calling into question the potential for neglect of teaching – in all our institutions, there may be no facilities or 'permission' to take writing time. Making writing time is almost bound to feel like you are going against the grain. It can even feel wrong, but this does not mean that you will never solve the problem. Many already have.

Checklist

- Put writing time in your diary: specific tasks at specific times.
- Expect this system to break down initially – persevere.
- Monitor your progress in terms of your sub-goals, not your goals.

8   Dialogue and feedback

A writers' group • Writers' retreat • Dialogue • More
freewriting and generative writing • Checklist

This chapter argues that writers can use or build a network of contacts – people engaged in writing – meeting regularly to write and for support and feedback. New writers may benefit from having access to different audiences at different stages in the writing process. The value of the writers' group is as a forum that allows you to rehearse your arguments orally among other academics. The key point is to get as much feedback as you can, but also to engage in dialogue about your work.

Such networks of writers may exist already in your institution or in your department, but if not, you can set one up yourself. In the midst of what is often a completely competitive culture, it is possible to build collegiality. In the midst of fragmented days, it is possible to meet to write. It may seem paradoxical to be taking individual responsibility for creating a new collegial-ity, but it may be your only option. Otherwise, you will have to go it alone, and that can take much longer.

You may have to choose your colleagues carefully. If this sounds overly cautious and more than a bit paranoid, then count yourself lucky that you have not yet encountered academics who set out to undermine each other. Just when writing becomes the first thing you want to do – rather than the last thing you want to do – other people may start to put up new barriers.

Of course, if your department is already collegial, and you are surrounded by mentors and positive peers, then this will be less of an issue, as long as you are able to get the type of feedback on your writing that actually moves your paper towards publication and helps you develop your understanding of what writing for academic journals involves.

A writers' group

There is no point in waiting for the culture around you to change; you can, instead, create a micro-culture that supports you as a writer. This micro-culture need not only include people in your own area. There may be someone in your institution who can set up and/or run a writers' group of people across the institution but, if not, you can do it yourself.

While the idea of a writer's group will seem a new departure to some, it is similar to other activities routinely used to support research in some disciplines, such as reading or journal groups. The difference is that in a writers' group you focus on writing for journals rather than reading them. A writers' group can provide a range of readers. It can also create a more positive, cooperative environment for writing than seems possible in many departments, where there appear to be so many other agendas running.

Clearly, there are many ways of using such interactions, but having a source of positive – yet critical – responses to writing-in-progress can help writers to keep writing. The knowledge that someone values your writing and sees you as a writer can be motivating. Writers – even new writers – can facilitate each other's writing. 'Buddy' relationships often spring up in this context, and two writers working together can share the load of researching the journals, pool information on editors and put their heads together to develop productive writing strategies to overcome blocks and barriers.

This book draws on academic writers' experiences, and in this chapter they illustrate how writers' group discussions of writing can normalize barriers to writing and neutralize some of the guilt and 'baggage' that new writers often carry with them about their writing, since they know full well that they could have done more to make sure that they got more done.

Why set up a writers' group? Why not just get on with your writing? You may want to think through the potential purposes of a group, particularly if you are going to be the one to set it up. This need not be a huge task; a writers' group can involve as little as four or five people, as long as you all want to write. With such a small number, it should be easier to focus on one main purpose that suits everyone. Frequently, the most motivating purpose is simply making time for writing. Making even a small amount of time for writing – such as two or three hours per month – can be an extremely effective starting point, since it is a small and therefore achievable goal.

Trying to make more time, on your own, without support, would be more likely to fail.

Purpose of a writers' group

- Making time for writing
- Getting feedback on writing
- Discussing writing practices
- Developing productive practices
- Sharing information about journals, editors and reviewers

This is not a hierarchy of tasks, nor is any one of these exclusive of the others. It is up to the group to establish its primary purpose. In fact, there is no need to fix one purpose and then try and limit the group's discussions and activities to that; there probably has to be some flexibility. Each member of the group may well be looking for something different, and while no group can accommodate everyone's needs, there has to be some agreement on the broad purpose, so that it can become a collective purpose. Since the problem of making time for writing – and protecting it once you have made it – seems to be so prevalent for academics, and not just new ones, this should probably be a kind of 'bottom line': whatever the level of productivity, and it might be slow at first, at least the group will have made real time to write. This is why it is so important that meeting time is not taken up entirely with talking about writing; the writers' group involves participants doing writing at each meeting.

For some academics, this will be the only time they have for writing, at least initially. It may be that they have no control over the allocation of their workload, but if they can secure agreement that they can attend a writers' group, they have started to make professional time for writing, in, admittedly – but perhaps cleverly – a small way. Once they are in the group and discussing ways to write, they may well find other strategies for making other time slots available for writing. If this leads to outputs then the case is made that a writers' group has benefit for the institution and the department, and not just for the individual.

Some new writers have felt the need to 'cloak' their writing time as 'meetings', since meeting time is easier to protect than writing time. It is easier to decline another meeting if you already have one in your diary. It is already established practice to have meetings; it is not a practice the writer has to 'invent'. This strategy demonstrates how difficult it is to establish time to write and to legitimize it. This strategy may seem dishonest to some, since it involves what some see as an element of deception. An alternative is, of course, to arrange a real meeting with other writers in the writers' group and to establish that this is a regular and legitimate use of your time – your professional time, not just your personal time.

Once you have started writing, every group has an important choice to make: are you going to read, and comment on, each other's writing, or not? It is legitimate and useful to discuss writing practices, including writing goals and progress towards them, and that may be enough for your group – talking about your writing. Or, you could agree to review each other's work:

> To improve your writing you don't need advice about what changes to make; you don't need theories of what is good and bad writing. You need movies of people's minds while they read your words. But you need this for a sustained period of time – at least two or three months. And you need to get the experience of not just a couple of people but of at least six or seven. And you need to keep getting it from the same people so that they get better at transmitting their experience and you get better at hearing them.
>
> (Elbow 1973: 77)

'You don't need advice about what changes you need to make' – this is an interesting statement, since it does not represent even a new writer as a complete novice. New writers already have knowledge of what does and does not work in academic writing. More importantly, Elbow defines the learning that is needed: developing a sense of audience. This most important of lessons, in Elbow's view, is one that can be developed in writers' groups.

Elbow's representation is of a sustained development period, more sustained than a one-day workshop or a couple of discussions with your head of department at review or appraisal time. An initial commitment to two or three months is helpful, since it provides a framework for the first stage of a writers' group. In fact, some people make such speedy progress, in terms of acquiring skills and strategies, that two or three months may be all that they need.

Elbow's advice is novel, given the practice in many educational contexts of single readings of a piece of writing, and given the secrecy and reticence that often surround academic writing, and given the workshop practice of working with different partners. It makes sense to develop such reading knowledge, so as to be able to provide informed help, informed in the sense of someone else becoming familiar with the developing argument of your paper and aware of what you are trying to achieve in it. There is also the frequently neglected and underdeveloped skill of listening to feedback. This too might take two or three months, if you are only meeting once or twice a month.

As the purpose and membership of a group are established, it might be useful to discuss and agree on more specific aims.

Aims of the writers' group

- To progress a writing project
- To make real time at work for writing
- To provide a forum for discussion of writing
- To provide a framework for the writing process
- To develop and exchange effective strategies
- To complete and submit a paper to a journal/chapter for a book or whatever.

Each writer needs a specific writing project, and a specific aim to achieve within the first three months. Aims will change over time, and you can review them after the first phase, after two or three months. Everyone in the group should know each other's writing goals.

As each group meets for the first time, there may be all sorts of potential talking points on the agenda. Some people will simply want to sound off about how hard writing is, about how unfair it is that there is no support and about the absurdity of academic journals themselves. This is an important discussion, but it can only go on for so long. The first development phase may well be moving yourself beyond this point – if this is where you are at – and if you have one or more of these voices in your group, you, or someone, is going to have to facilitate a 'moving on' discussion. Simply talking about these problems is not the only way to resolve them; you can also write about writing problems and solutions. However, you can also write about potential topics at this stage, in ways described in Chapter 3.

The very plurality of the group can, of course, be a strength, even if it takes some getting used to: 'Very few of us have a reasonably filled-in vision of the world. We tend to develop only those areas we are interested in' (Mailer 2003). Naturally, as an academic, you have to develop the area you are interested in, but your development can be accelerated by interactions. Their unpredictability can be both refreshing and frustrating.

There may be dominant characters in your group. That can be a strength or a weakness, depending on how you all manage each other. There may be too many agendas running. There may be uncertainty about the writers' group as a mechanism to increase productivity. There may be confusion about what you are actually meeting for or about what useful purpose the group is likely to serve. You may lose sight of what you set out to do and you may not realize that you are already beginning to achieve your appropriately modest goals.

Keep it simple

- We all want to publish in academic journals.
- We can give each other feedback on writing practices.
- Our writers' group will make time for writing during the working week.
- We can support each other in our writing.
- We can develop more productive writing habits in this group.

It is easy to over-complicate the writers' group, but all you are doing is prioritizing writing through a group process. You therefore all have to bring your group work skills to this initiative and you have to be comfortable with the others in your group fairly early on. If you have hand-picked your own group – not a bad idea – you should be off to a strong start in this respect. However, remember that you are all in this for yourselves, and participants – not the group – are responsible for their progress.

Activities

- Analysing journals you are targeting
- Discussing your writing plans
- Doing writing: writing about writing or writing your paper
- Setting goals for writing and monitoring each other's progress
- Giving and receiving feedback on writing
- Identifying strategies that work: making time and getting published

---

For the structure of your group's meetings, you can opt for a loose or tight set-up, but the key elements are discussion and writing, and for these you can use activities described in earlier chapters.

'Presenteeism' – the pressure to simply be present and visible in your department – can be a problem, but as long as your head of department has not actually said you must be in the department at all times – and even if he or she does, is that non-negotiable? – then you have the option of working else-where. You cannot allow others' petty reactions to shape your writing. There have even been situations where the head of department has agreed to writing time away from the department, as long as no one else knows about it. This is, by design or otherwise, likely to divide you from your colleagues – which may, of course, be the intention – but if it is your only option, and if it gives you what you want – time to write – then you might want to jump at it regard-less. You are never going to be able to keep everyone happy, nor are you responsible if everyone is unhappy because you are writing. As long as you achieve the necessary outputs, this is good for the institution and the department. This may be yet another motivation for working with writers in other departments.

There are pros and cons to working across disciplinary boundaries. Some of the pros are: (1) you are not so likely to get caught up in discussing primarily the content of a paper; (2) you can concentrate on the flow of each other's argument, spotting gaps or inconsistencies; and (3) you can leave behind the 'baggage' of the department, including, if your group is going to work, its internal competitions. Some of the cons are: (1) you will not get expert feedback on the content of your paper from your writers' group – you will have to get that from someone else; (2) this may create uncertainty that you feel you cannot resolve and that, in turn, may inhibit your writing; and (3) you may not 'test' your idea sufficiently at an early stage.

For new writers, the pros should outweigh the cons for one main reason: the group will help you get started and help you keep going. It is, of course, important to have input from published people in your field and you will, of course, be hugely grateful if you can find someone who is prepared to give up their time to give you feedback on your paper. But it is equally important that you have feedback along the way, as you are drafting your paper, that is not too critical and that focuses on developing the argument. If that sounds too soft – or even unwise – then clearly you can combine the two; this does not have to be an either/or proposition.

You may not be looking for 'profound insights about' yourself, and since the learning that people do in such groups is difficult to measure, you may not be persuaded that it actually occurs as claimed. However, there is more to writing well, at the top of your profession, than grammar and punctuation. It is difficult to disentangle thinking and writing abilities; they may develop in tandem. For example, as you improve your skills of articulating your ideas to others, you may find that this improves your ability to articulate your ideas to yourself, that is, your thinking.

Finally, perhaps the greatest benefit of attending writers' group meetings is that people often report that they arrive at the meeting 'in a frenzy, but leave on a high'. Some turn up with very low feelings about their writing and about academic life in general, and leave with a sense of satisfaction at having, in spite of everything, progressed their writing project. This facility for turning around very negative feelings is perhaps one of the healthiest outcomes of a professional activity.

Writers' retreat

One way to kick-start a writers' group is to have a writers' retreat, taking writers off-campus. Of course, there may be permissions to seek in order to do this, and even when you do have permission, there will be those who think you are mowing the lawn, putting up shelves, going to the gym, or whatever it is that these people think – it need not have any basis in reality – when they cannot actually see you in the workplace, while they are slaving away on the treadmill.

This mode of protecting time for writing is very effective. While you might think that getting completely away to do nothing but write is a luxury that you simply cannot afford, there are ways in which you can adapt the retreat mode to your environment. The idea is to protect some time – however short – for nothing but writing and talking about your writing with others who are prepared to do so too.

One of the potential benefits is that in a retreat environment you can make swift changes to your writing behaviours. A vast literature tells us that changing our behaviours takes a long time, that there are numerous 'steps' that we have to follow to achieve long-term change and that we need social support to make it work. Clearly, there is so much evidence across such a wide range of human behaviour that we would not want to challenge this.

Yet, when you take people out of their normal environments, change comes quite quickly: at a writers' retreat you can make significant progress with your project. The difficulty is when you go back to your normal working environment: there is no protected time for writing and your momentum runs into the sand. What you can do is adapt some of the features of the complete retreat to your working environment, making quite short 'meetings' to write, ideally with a colleague or two, at least in the first instance. This means in practice bringing the activities of retreat into your working environment, or finding some other place where you can do so. In other words, you can create a mini-retreat for yourself in a variety of different places and at different times.

There are several modes of retreat, each suited to different goals and each making different demands on your resources: the week-long retreat, the two-day mini-retreat, the 'day away' and the one-hour retreat meeting. They all share the same key features:

- Get off campus and, if you have more than one day, make it residential.
- Get away from distractions, email, phone, other responsibilities.
- Focus on your writing and actually do some.

The key is to get away from the office, since many find that they can do no writing whatsoever there. A few people do find it possible to write in their offices, as long as they can quit email, turn on the answering machine and have an office where they can shut the door, put up a notice saying 'Meeting in progress – do not disturb' and know that they will not be interrupted.

Some people find that they can 'retreat' to write at home; but others find this impossible, as they are distracted by tasks that need to be done there, or there are potential interruptions there too. Where you go to retreat to write is clearly a personal choice, and if you go with someone else, or several others, you have to find a space that suits you all or, more realistically, make it suit most of you most of the time.

The longest of these modes, the complete retreat, involves a week off campus. This can be organized with a self-selecting group from work, perhaps by your staff development unit or teaching and learning centre. One of the best examples of this mode has been run for several years at the University of Limerick (Ireland) (Moore 2003). Briefing sessions before the retreat help to establish the retreat concept, prompt participants to prepare and focus and test commitment to the full week's work.

The programme for the week's retreat starts with an orientation session on the first night, followed by social time over dinner. Every morning participants attend 'springboard' sessions for the first hour each morning, if they wish, and then have the rest of the day, from 10.30 am until 8 pm, to write. These sessions help participants to get started, to set goals for the day's writing and, after the first day, to take stock of progress since the previous day. Private writing, freewriting and pair-share discussions seem to work well to trigger focused writing during these sessions. Some of the strategies for regular writing are new to participants, and therefore time is allocated for discussions of the strategies themselves, their immediate impact and their long-term use. Other subjects covered in brief presentations include finding your voice, responding to reviewers' feedback and behaviour change. The writers can also have discussions with each other in the course of the day, and one-to-one discussions with a reader in residence, who reads and comments on drafts of papers.

The pros of this model are that writers have plenty of real time and space to write. The cons are that they have to be ready to confront their writing targets head-on and are under pressure to make real progress with their project. You might be thinking that having so much time and space would take the pressure of, and that does seem to happen to begin with. By the middle of the week, however, participants begin to feel that they should have achieved much more than they have, and often feel under even more pressure to produce precisely because they have so much uninterrupted time. Even though there is no 'account' taken of people's written output at the end of the retreat, departments who have contributed to the cost of participation are going to want to see some 'return' for their money in terms of publications or other outputs. This is yet another very good reason for setting clear, explicit goals and letting others know what they are. Almost all the participants are highly productive during this week, achieving their goal and, often, making progress towards other goals and defining new goals for future outputs.

There are additional challenges for writers with families, particularly if they have young children. Some single parents find it a struggle to get sufficient childcare. Anyone with any caring role might simply find that this is not a model that works practically for them, in spite of its obvious attractions. But there have been participants with these responsibilities on previous retreats, which suggests that it is not impossible.

Participants' evaluations show that this is a very positive experience, but there is always the 'return to reality' factor: will they be able to continue to be productive writers, or to do any writing at all, when they return to their departments, where their first task will be to catch up with everything they let drop in order to attend the retreat? This is such an important question that it is directly addressed as part of the retreat experience, on the last day. This is where the writers' group comes in, since it is one way of sustaining the impact of a retreat over the longer term and transferring some of its features to the work environment.

A retreat of this type obviously comes with a cost; in fact, it can be quite expensive to run, although the argument can be made that the return to your institution – in terms of research culture and outputs – is worth the investment. It is possible to include external participants and to use their fees to subsidize internal participants. This might be beyond your own organizational remit, but you might suggest this strategy to someone who can make it happen. You may have to push for this, or find someone who is prepared to do so, since even when funding has been secured, it is not always possible to find someone who is prepared to take on this new and substantial task.

You also need staff: the person who does the 'springboard' sessions probably has to be someone who is an enabler, who knows a bit about writing and is not too focused on any one discipline to the exclusion of others. This is someone who can look across the disciplines and can stimulate discussion of writing across disciplinary boundaries. They can use the activities described in this book for the important 'getting started' and 'warm-up' writing sessions.

If the week-long retreat is simply not feasible, there are other shorter modes of retreat: the two-day mini-retreat, the 'day away' or, at the very least, the one-hour retreat meeting.

The two-day retreat, whether residential or not, allows you to focus on your writing without worrying too much about the work you have left behind. Unlike the week-long retreat, which is ideally held far enough away from campus that participants are not able to get home, the two-day retreat allows participants to meet domestic responsibilities. It has the added advantage of being cheaper. Because time is short, it is probably as well to include only those who have specific papers or other projects in mind.

The programme should probably be more structured than the week-long model. The writing day should probably be timetabled with a progressive series of writing tasks that build the paper, combining generative writing activities and structuring activities with discussions and mutual reviewing of outlines and drafts. Individuals may have their own way of structuring such a writing day, and people will be at different stages, so some flexibility will need to be built in.

For the purpose of building, or building on, long-term writing relationships and on-going discussions, it is probably important to intersperse writing time with discussion. The proportion of writing time to other activities can be as much as one third; that is, 20 minutes in any one hour can be spent doing some form of writing towards the paper. Using or developing a detailed outline is probably a key task for the second half of the first day, since that can then drive focused writing on day two.

Some participants will doubtless respond that they have not yet chosen their topic, but this should be the work of the first half of the first day; until the topic has been fixed, it is very difficult to make progress in writing. Of course, the topic can be selected and focused through writing, and writing tasks that do this should therefore probably feature in the first half of day one:

Two-day retreat			
		Programme	
Day 1	**Morning**	Choosing topic	*Writing prompt and 'sandwich'*
		Developing topic Discussion	*Freewriting*
		Focusing topic Discussion	*Generative writing*
	Afternoon	Developing abstract Discussion	*Brown's 8 questions*
		Detailed outline Discussion Writing	*'Level 3' outlining*
Day 2	**Morning**	Targeting a journal	*Discussing extracts from published papers*
		Reasons for rejection Writing prompts Writing Discussion	*Using the outline*
	Afternoon	Writing Discussion Planning Goal-setting	*Writers' group*

You can, of course, vary the order of these activities. For example, it might make more sense, in some groups, to start a retreat with 'targeting a journal', rather than leaving it until day two. It depends on the group: what stage are they at?; will they find the analysis of published examples intimidating if it comes first?; do they already have topics to write about, such as conference presentations to convert into publications?; are some of them writing a thesis, with publications a secondary goal? As long as both text-generating and structuring strategies are in the programme, as long as there is time for both writing and discussion, and as long as the participants are actually willing to write there and then, it will work. Since most academics report that writing by hand is not their normal practice, it helps if participants have laptops for the retreat.

A further alternative is the quick retreat: a day away. There is more of a tradition – if that is the right word – of departmental away days at some institutions, but the one-day retreat for writing would be a new approach, and a new case might have to be made for it. It may be that only some members of the department will choose to participate, and it is probably as well to establish who wants to and to work with them. Others will find their own ways to write.

Keeping it in the department is not the only way to run a one-day retreat. Mixed groups can work just as well, sometimes better. It could be more difficult to organize, you might think, but if all the writers are self-selecting, and you start with the people you already know, and if they are all keen to write, then it might be easier than you think.

The value of the one-day retreat is that you do not have to drop everything else for longer than one day. The value of the departmental retreat is that you are establishing a culture of writing in the department; the department has acknowledged that writing is sufficiently important to attract dedicated time.

The format alternates writing and discussion: writing for different periods of time – 5, 20, 30 and 60 minutes at a time – discussing in pairs and in the whole group. Discussion provides peer review, support and encouragement, as required. The specific writing activities maintain focus while prompting structured development of the paper. All these techniques are described in this book.

One-day retreat

Programme

Morning	Decide on topic and type of writing	*Write to prompt*	10 mins
	Set goals for the day in pairs	*Writing sandwich*	10 mins
	Introduction to Brown's 8 questions		20 mins
	Draft abstract/summary	*Brown's 8 questions*	20 mins
	Break		15 mins
	Discussion in pairs		15 mins
	Writing		30 mins

Afternoon	Outlining/writing to outline		30 mins
	Peer review discussion	*Whole group*	30 mins
	Break		15 mins
	Writing		60 mins
	Goal-setting: long- and short-term in pairs		20 mins

Once you have run one department programme, the argument for dedicated time for writing, while not quite won, has moved on a step from leaving individuals to take responsibility for changing their time-management strategies. If the day has been even partially successful, then you can consider when you want to repeat it: could there be regular writing days? Could there be one per month? Or one per year, always in the same month? Could it be held in the department? As with other interventions described in this chapter, such days might constitute some people's only writing time.

Meet to retreat: some writers find it useful and productive to get out of the office to write for as little as an hour. We should, of course, have such things as lunch hours, but in the present culture, there seem to be few of those. The one-hour writers' meeting involves meeting not simply to talk about writing, but also to do some. This means finding a place where you can both/all talk and write, where there is a surface, as much space and peace and quiet as you can get by with, and where you can open a laptop without disturbing anyone's sense of decorum and without getting robbed of it on the way back to the office. Ideally, this should be in a place where you are unlikely to meet colleagues from work, unless, of course, you want to make your writing visible in that way. Some people have managed to fit such meetings into visits they have to make to other campuses or to students on placement. If your writing partner is some way away, you can meet half-way. There were two writers who met at a supermarket café for this reason. The key factor in this strategy might be that you have disguised writing as a 'meeting', making it easier to protect the time slot. You do not even have to tell everyone what the purpose of your 'meeting' is.

There are benefits to simply getting off-campus. This can immediately change a person's feelings about the subject of their writing. In some cases, what seemed like a chore and a bore suddenly becomes interesting again. Writers recover their interest in writing by, perhaps ironically, taking it away from the work environment. Many academics report that they cannot write in their offices, and there is no 'writing room' in any organization. Nor is there any timetabled 'writing period'. In a sense, writing does not exist in real time and space in a university. You have to invent the time and space for yourself. At least initially, it may be easier to start writing somewhere else.

This does suggest that some work environments are not only not conducive to writing but positively working against it, not just in the sense of not providing time or support, but, perhaps more importantly, in the sense of creating a context where writers lose sight of their motivations. Without wanting to get too deeply into this analysis, it must be said that getting away from the work-place for a week, a day, or even an hour – with the express purpose of meeting to write – can have benefits. Any form of writers' retreat can lead to a surge of momentum and enthusiasm for writing, overcoming many of the barriers – real and imagined – to writing. I have seen people get stuck into a pile of old data, that they have been meaning to write up for months or years, with new enthusiasm and commitment.

Getting completely away from the workplace may seem like an impossible luxury; some may not even have that option. Yet it can be positioned as a legitimate staff development activity. It is an important activity, if you can demonstrate outputs, for the university or organization, not just for the individual writer.

Another model for writers working in groups is Brown's 'learning set for writers':

> A learning set is a group that meets regularly to talk about common prob-lems and to look for solutions. A learning set of authors provides face-to-face reviewing by friends, most of whom lack preconceptions about the content of a paper or its context. This approach has strengths that blind refereeing can never provide. It provides an immediacy and support that allows authors to get deeper into their papers than they would otherwise do . . . there is less defensiveness and this makes it easier to see the grains of truth that lie in most criticisms. After a few meetings, it can also bring authors to profound insights about themselves and their work.
>
> (Brown 1994/95: 3)

This model emphasizes the value of finding participants who 'lack pre-conceptions' about your paper, or about your writing or writing in your discip-line. This can interfere with the developing articulation of your ideas. This again suggests that there is more value in inter-departmental groupings than many academics would anticipate. Brown even goes as far as arguing that this process can do things that the alleged 'gold standard' of blind reviewing can-not do. What he seems to be saying here is that the instant feedback – and the additional interactions – with real readers can help writers more.

The word 'friends' rather than, for example, 'peers' or 'colleagues' suggests a different type of relationship can develop in such learning sets. Identifying common problems and generating solutions is where genuine learning can occur. Perhaps this terminology will appeal to some more than others, but it does, interestingly, open up more possibilities. It also goes directly against the competitive culture that dominates in some departments.

None of these activities – writers' groups, retreats and learning sets – is seen as 'remedial' in any sense – though they might be perceived as such in some parts of your institution. The popular misconception that all you have to do is write, and that as long as you are not actually writing you are wasting your time, is, unfortunately, persistent. Instead, the retreats and writers' groups are

about creating new structures that support writing, establishing collegial relationships and bringing writing – and discussion of writing – into the working
day. Because becoming a regular writer, to the standard required, takes considerable time and effort, it makes sense to have some developmental – rather
than remedial – activities in place. If writers are actually to change their
behaviours, they surely have to have some support. This may not be available
within departments.

How much time you put into making the case for such interventions, or
getting someone else to take up the case, is up to you. But you do not need a
full-blown institutionally funded system to initiate some of the more small-
scale versions of them. How exactly you begin to set it all up is quite simply to
get together a few colleagues and run the first and all subsequent sessions
with a fairly loose agenda. The following starter prompt can be used to start
numerous meetings, not just the first one:

Writers' group: getting started

1 Warm-up for writing (five minutes, in sentences, private)
   What writing have you done and what do you want to do?
   OR
   What part of your paper/outline are you going to write today?
2 Writing on chosen topic (20–30 minutes, private or for peer review)
3 Discussion of writing done, progress made and/or exchange of papers for
   review

This type of structure will help you take stock and look forward, maintaining
your goal-setting skills. More importantly, you will produce writing. While
stopping the discussion for a session of writing is unusual – it's not how we
normally work – it does create writing time. Defer the 'quality question' for the
moment. If you are writing to your outline, which you should be as soon as
possible, the goal is not to produce 'quality' academic writing, but to generate
rough draft. You may have to keep telling yourselves that.

I am not sure that every writers' group has to spend time and expend energy
thrashing out its aims or objectives before participants can start writing. I am
not even convinced that you really need an agenda, in the normal sense of the
word. It seems to me that you can focus the whole session – 60 or 90 minutes –
on writing and talking about the writing you have done, are about to do and
have just done. If this seems simplistic, I should add that this structure seems
to work quite well with quite diverse groups, and on that basis is worth a try. In
the course of trying, you will quickly learn what works and what does not:
going round the group asking, 'Who has completed the task they set themselves at the last meeting?', may not be conducive to sharing and collegial

discussion. But we can all learn from our mistakes. If you find something does not work, or seems to work against writing and sharing, then you can all agree not to do that again.

Dialogue

Dialogue – meaning genuine, engaged, two-way discussion of writing; discussion of the content with someone who has read your writing and doing the same for them – has real value. It can help you to clarify a point in your argument; in fact, it can persuade you to clarify a point that you thought you had already stated sufficiently clearly. Thanks to the response of a real reader you see your writing in a new light. You can even begin to write in a more positively dialogic way, taking more account of the different perspectives in current debates in your area. You may end up worrying less about what your intended readers might think and more immediately getting on with the task of addressing their needs and interests.

You can use dialogue with peers to grow your sense of audience: by addressing real audiences' responses to your writing – in a writers' group, for example – you can develop a sense of where your academic writing needs revision. If you do this regularly and if your discussion goes into some depth, you can develop your skills of written argument and, sometimes, be prompted to develop alternative lines of argument. You can also become much more sensitized to the value – rather than feeling that you are going through the motions – of making a strong case for your work, perhaps stronger than you thought you needed to. You can become much more skilled at addressing refutations, and you can include this within your paper. This helps you with the important task of writing the debate into your paper.

The face-to-face nature of the discussions, the potential for instant feedback and the opportunity immediately to engage with feedback, mean that you cannot just note the feedback, thank your reader and head off to mull it over on your own. Although that is always an option, you have an opportunity to go into more depth and to rehearse one or two options for revising what you have written. If the writing your reader was looking at was, in any case, a rough draft, then this is extremely valuable revision time: you can actually get some revision done, or at least started, immediately. Leaving it until later, when the clarity, purpose and usefulness of your reader's comments may have evaporated, will mean that you have to start from scratch: you have to take time to recall what your readers said, you have to try and place their particular comments, and you have no one to rehearse your revisions with and no immediate feedback on your proposed revisions.

Dialogue is, therefore, very much a part of the writing process. For this to work in reality, there probably has to be both talking and writing time, so that you can capture some of the revisions you know you have to make, some that your reader suggests and other points that occur to you in the course of the discussion.

More freewriting and generative writing

The stakes are higher at this stage in the writing process, as you are now committed to delivering a certain line of argument, having moved well beyond the exploratory stage, the planning stage and even the research stage. The stakes are also higher because you have contacted journal editors and one of them is now perhaps if not exactly 'waiting' for your paper, then at least expecting it to arrive some time soon.

Yet there is still value in low stakes writing. The original uses of these activities, such as doing freewriting as a warm-up for academic writing, are still there, but they may have different purposes at this time, or you may use them in different ways. This is not to say that you should move on from the earlier uses; quite the reverse: the writing habit is always supported by low stakes writing. Both high and low stakes writing can run in tandem from now on.

Continuing uses of freewriting and generative writing

- To work out your responses to your readers' feedback
- To work out a step in your argument that is still not clear
- To clarify a complex section in your argument that is not yet clear
- To fill a gap in your argument that has just been pointed out
- To begin to articulate why you disagree with some of the feedback

---

As with earlier uses of freewriting, deferring the 'quality question' will help you to focus on developing the idea. The aim is to work out your writing problem in writing. The result of these activities may be that you clarify your thinking or that you produce writing you can insert – as it is or with some revision – into your paper, with one eye on the total word length, in relation to your target journal's maximum. A missing step between you choosing one of the purposes in the above box and generating text might be that you do not yet have a prompt. You could, for example, use a question posed by your reader as a prompt. Or you could use the prompt 'What I am trying to say here is' to start your writing. You can then compare it with the text that you have already written to see if there are any major or minor differences, any sentences or fragments that will clarify your point in your paper. Freewriting, generative writing and writing to prompts can, therefore, still be useful at this late stage in the writing process in this way. This is when you can see the full range of writing strategies combining to make up a productive academic writing practice.

Checklist

- Working with a writing 'buddy' or writers' group can help you make time to write.
- If you can't go on a writers' retreat, bring features of retreat into your workplace.
- Keep up the regular scribbling, using it to solve writing problems, as required.

9 Responding to reviewers' feedback

The 'grim reader' • Examples of reviewers' comments
• Destructive feedback • What to do with hostile
reviews • Contradictory comments • Rejection
• Resubmission • Responding to feedback from editors
and reviewers • What now? • Acceptance • Proofs
• Offprints • Marketing your writing • What next?
• Recycling and 'salami-slicing' • Writing a book
• Developing a programme for writing • Checklist

It would be easier for them to reject your paper outright.

(Day 1996: 120)

Start by assuming that you're fully entitled to applause if you have: . . .

• Gotten bad reviews with good lines in them.

(Appelbaum 1998: 241)

Even famous novelists have had their share of bad reviews: '*Catch-22* has much
passion, comic and fervent,' said *The New York Times*, 'but it gasps for want of

craft and sensibility' (Appelbaum 1998: 241). You should expect to get some bad reviews in your time, and there is no reason, when you think about it, that you should not learn something from some of them.

This chapter covers the critical final step in writing a paper: what to do when your paper is returned for revision. Reasons for rejection are covered first: anecdotally, we are told that the most common reason given is that the paper was sent to the wrong journal, although this may just be the editor's way of saying your paper has not met the journal's standard in some way, without taking the time to tell you why.

Insights into why papers are rejected are provided in, for example, a *British Medical Journal* publication listing methodological weaknesses that lead to rejection; and the argument is made that inadequate targeting might be a more common problem that you would think. Targeting a journal is not, it seems, simply a matter of common sense. It seems that people frequently get it wrong.

However, it may be that your paper has not been rejected, and that you have revisions to do. A process for working through your reviewers' comments is described in this chapter, along with discussion of examples of real reviewers' feedback. A strategy for focusing on what revision actions you might want to take is provided, along with hints and tips for writing an effective cover letter or email.

Above all, be content that you have received feedback, since it is much worse when a paper goes missing for months or more. Then you have to start pursuing the editor for feedback, and this can be time-consuming and frustrating. You may not always like the feedback you get, but it is better than not hearing anything.

The 'grim reader'

When you were writing your paper you naturally had to have a sense of your reader in mind. That imagined reader may be quite different from the actual readers. Reviewers do generally give papers a thorough critique. This may well be the toughest critique you will ever receive on your writing, until you submit your next paper for publication.

Sometimes reviewers appear to be unnecessarily 'grim'; they seem to take too hard a line, to miss points you felt you had made thoroughly in your paper or to want you to write a completely different paper. After all the work that you have put in to get to this point, you feel that you simply cannot be bothered to revise it again. This is a big mistake. If the editor invites you to resubmit, the best thing you can do is to get on with the revisions right away and you will have a good chance of being published if you can respond positively to the reviewers' comments. There are no guarantees even at this stage, but you will have a good chance if you can make the revisions they are looking for.

Feedback is not always fun. Sometimes it seems plain wrong. But you can always learn from it – perhaps an overstatement to say 'always', but when you look at the paper in its published form, you will probably, from that secure position, be more able to admit that, yes, the reviewers' comments did improve your paper. If you never got any negative feedback, how would you learn?

It can almost be said that you should expect to have revisions to do when the reviewers' comments come back. For whatever reason, this has become the norm. Expect there to be differences of opinion among the reviewers; this is not that unusual, across the disciplines. Expect them not to have seen what you see as the elegant symmetry of your sentences or the robustness of your conceptual framework.

Expect them even to take issue with your literature review and, particularly, with your definition of the 'problem' you set out to solve in your work. This is a sensitive area: you are by definition critiquing a situation, perhaps even people who have worked in that context, perhaps also people who have researched it before you, including some quite noted names. Your statement of the problematic that you set out at the start of your paper, however carefully you crafted that section, is itself open to debate and may draw fire.

Sometimes it is just one word that has pressed the reviewer's button. You may have been just too challenging or raised a challenge that the reviewer was not comfortable with, or in terms that he or she would not use. Modulating an assertion by beginning with the words 'It could be argued that' may help lessen the dramatic effect that some of these statements seem to have on some reviewers. You can also align yourself with an authority in the field or, even better, quote an established figure in the field whose critique of the way things are is even more vituperative than yours. This will make yours seem quite moderate by comparison.

This is not to say that you have to comb through every single word of your paper looking for triggers that have set the reviewer off, but you do have to bear in mind that reviewers will bring not only a different perspective, but also, potentially, a different vocabulary and a different sense of what constitutes publishable work than you have, particularly if you are submitting your first paper. Their feedback will tell you a lot about where they are coming from, much of which, it has to be said, you will not be able to anticipate.

Examples of reviewers' comments

The purpose of this section is to show how bad reviews can be. My intention is to take the shock – though perhaps not the sting – out of any negative, verging on hostile, reviews you might receive.

The following two reviews are reproduced here, word-for-word as I received them, including the italics, but with the paper's and journal's titles removed.

This was a co-authored paper, although only I was singled out by the reviewers by name. The paper has since been published, with revisions.

Reviewers' comments

Reviewer 1

My impression on the paper by Dr R. Murray entitled [title] is *very negative*. A short, 2-printed-pages statement would be useful as an invitation for discussion. The authors make many superficial statements, often clearly not based on any direct experience of curricular developments.

I am convinced that our Journal of [title] would not benefit from such a lengthy manuscript whose content is very limited.

Reviewer 2

Cet article aborde la question de l'interactivité dans l'enseignement. C'est un problème important et l'exposé est très intéressant.

Même si on n'y trouve pas d'éléments nouveaux ni de recette miracle, il me semble que le problème est bien posé et les considérations énumerées me semblent constituer un bon point de la situation.

Ainsi par exemple, je trouve que pour organiser un débat sur la question, la lecture préalable de ce texte constituerait un excéllent point de départ et éviterait de recommencer une analyse classique des avantages, inconvenients et difficultés de l'enseignement interactif.

J'ai toutefois quelques interrogations (concernant plutôt la forme): . . .

Moyennant ces quelques remarques, je crois que, par sa bonne synthèse d'une importante problèmatique, cet article mériterait une publication dans l'[title of journal].

While the key message we take from reviewer 1 has to be those two words 'very negative', for reviewer 2, even if you do not speak or read French, you can probably make out such key words as 'problème **important** . . . très **intéressant** . . . **bien** posé . . . **excellent** . . . **bonne** synthèse' and, strikingly, 'mériterait une publication'. Reviewer 1 wants the paper rejected; reviewer 2 thinks it should be published.

When I show these two reviews to new writers, their first reaction is shock: 'that must have hurt'. Well, yes, it did. New writers make a number of interesting observations:

1 The reviews are contradictory.
2 They don't really say what is wrong with the paper and what you can do about it.
3 This is unprofessional. It's just too destructive. Unnecessarily so.

My co-author and I shared made similar observations, when these reviews arrived, but we were greatly helped and reassured by the editor's letter, which helped us to put the reviews in perspective. Interestingly, his opening sentences confirm both the new writers' observations and our own:

Editor's letter

Two experts on the Editorial Board of [journal title] examined your paper . . . One is very opposed to the publication of your paper in its present form. Another considers your paper interesting but suggests a re-writing of the document. You will find, attached, their comments. . . . Here are the most important points to take into account:

- Introduce the problem of interactivity within the title of the paper;
- Avoid superficial statements not consolidated by results;
- Reduce the length of the paper, limiting your text to the main points;
- Avoid, in the body of the text, the use of dialogue;
- Avoid also the use of 'I' if the paper is written by more than one author.

You will understand the need of such rewriting of your paper and I am pleased to invite you to submit your new document as soon as possible.

Yet, this letter comes as a surprise to new writers: how can the editor have decided to go ahead with the paper after even one hostile review? This raises other questions: who decides on whether a paper is to be rejected or revised for resubmission? How can we find out the answers to these questions; is there any data?

In spite of everything, and for obvious reasons, the authors' reply to the editor can always begin with the words 'Thank you'. We kept the email short, in order to save the editor time and effort, and given that we were not really going to say very much at this time, apart from signalling the crucial point that we did intend to resubmit:

Authors' reply to the editor

Thank you for your feedback on our paper [title] which we found very useful. As suggested, we will change the title.

We are revising the paper now and will resubmit later this month, or, at the latest, early next month.

If there is a particular deadline you would like us to meet, can you let me know now?

Starting with 'Thank you' provides a positive start to our letter/email. What else were we saying in this reply?: we signalled that we intended to be responsive to the critique by our immediate action on one of the reviewers' suggestions, changing the title. We tell the editor our deadline, in order to motivate us to get the revisions done by then. Without a deadline, or if we were the only ones who knew when it was, revisions would fall behind a long list of other priorities. By inviting the editor to give us a deadline, we are both trying to be accommodating and prompting the editor to think about which issue of the journal we will be published in. We then got on with our revisions, resubmitted our paper and had it published in due course.

What we learned from this experience and, it must be said, from these reviewers' comments, is that we had overstated our critique of the status quo. We had not provided evidence for all of our critique. We realized that much of this problem was located in one section, so we cut it all out. This is another important lesson: you do not need to keep every word, or even every section, in for your paper to work.

There are, therefore, potential lessons for writers in reviewers' feedback. The challenge is to work your way through what can seem harsh, even overstated, critiques, from reviewers who seem to be implying – and sometimes stating – that the author does not know what he or she is writing about. Some reviewers appear to want to undermine – rather than assist – writers, while others take a more 'instructional' approach, though sometimes in a dogmatic tone:

Reviewer 1

Problem Number 8
Location – Page/Para: 21, last paragraph
The focus of the paper is on the quality assessment of research. The final paragraph makes no reference to research. It reflects an issue of the paper warranting attention: this initial focus is on quality, but as one moves through the paper the focus increasingly moves toward assessment and evaluation. They are similar; quality is achieved through assessment and evaluation. But the paper is on research quality. **Keep to that topic**.

Reviewer 2

The general case made in this paper is clearly stated and given quite good general support both from the literature cited and from arguments within the paper. However, I have several serious reservations, which can be summarised as follows:

1 I think that the paper reveals **a lack of comprehension** about TQM and furthermore it **merely asserts** its central influence in UK Higher Education **without citing evidence**. The result is that some of its criticisms are not necessarily aimed at the most appropriate target.

2 A number of assertions are made, especially in the central part of the paper, **without adequate referencing or supporting evidence**.

3 The recommendations in the final part of the paper are **rather sketchy** and **lacking in both detail and justification**.

The reference to 'several serious reservations' naturally rang alarm bells, but, again, as long as the paper was not actually rejected, there was still work to be done and a chance of publication.

We could critique the critiques: there are, of course, certain principles in any field that we can legitimately 'merely assert', since they are not open to question, or, you may have judged, not as open to debate as other statements in your paper. Yet, clearly, in our resubmission, we would have to distinguish more carefully and perhaps explicitly between what can and cannot be merely asserted. Comment number 2 makes this point again, locating the flaw more precisely in the paper. Comment number 3 may be making the point a third time, though it would be worth thinking about this carefully.

As for the comment about recommendations: is it not the nature of recommendations to be 'sketchy'? We obviously thought so, and judged that, whatever we thought, this was appropriate for this journal. Nevertheless, something required further development in this case. This comment is a reminder that even conclusions should be mini-arguments, with the case made for them, and the link between evidence and conclusions made quite clear: what is it that you can – and cannot – evidence?

By contrast, some reviewers can be quite positive, even encouraging:

The encouraging review

Thank you for asking me to review this paper. This a **comprehensive and well-written** paper about the use of medical humanities in occupational therapy. While I **enjoyed reading it**, I am not sure it is ready for publication as yet. Essentially it describes 3 courses in which medical humanities are used. Although the courses do have outcomes, there are assumptions made within the article that the outcomes have been met without any evidence or data to support this.

In addition, the article is unduly long at 8,000 words.

I do feel it would be very helpful to have a contribution on how medical humanities could be taught in the journal. I wonder if these authors would be prepared to redraft this as a much shorter version on how a medical humanities course could be constructed and the possible benefits.

It is difficult to predict what kind of feedback you are going to get. The point is to be prepared for the worst, to try to treat any feedback analytically – rather than emotionally – and to work out the extent to which you can deliver what they have asked for and how you are going to produce it. If there are issues raised by the reviewers with which you disagree, you can, of course, go back to the editor for further discussion.

Destructive feedback

It does sometimes seem that there are reviewers out there who like nothing better than to tear a paper – and its author – to shreds. New writers sometimes feel that they are being held back for no good reason, that the reviewers are simply protecting their power base and the narrow concerns of a small group.

Reviewers, given the chance, might reply to that accusation by asserting that they are responsible for upholding the standards of the journal specifically and the discipline generally. They might complain that this is quite an arduous job, when they are already very busy people, for which they receive no reward or recompense in cash or time. In fact, many reviewers report that they are frustrated by the falling standard of papers they receive to review and are impatient when they feel that authors have simply not done enough work, have not bothered to present their papers in the appropriate format, or are using peer review as a development process.

All of this speculation does nothing to take the sting out of destructive feedback. Nor is it entirely acceptable to be destructive when we all know they can write their comments in a different way. You have to wonder, if reviews were not anonymized, would reviewers be so destructive? Some journals distribute written guidelines for reviewers, encouraging them to provide constructive criticism, reminding them that their comments are sent to authors.

However, there is another way of reading destructive reviews: what seems 'destructive', when you first set eyes on it, may not, in fact, be as serious as you think. The comments may be very negative, yet the editor may only request 'minor revisions'. Even comments that seem to destroy your structure and style – carefully considered and targeted though they were – can still be translated into revision action points, as long as the editor has not used the word 'rejected'. The editor is not out to undermine or contradict reviewers, but they do often work at softening the blow. For example, the following reviewers' comments did not stop the editor from using the word 'positive' in his or her cover letter, inviting the authors to resubmit:

The title is a bit **weak, long-winded, and descriptive**. A more direct title is suggested.

The text uses a **plodding and subject-indeterminate passive form**, and some **awkward construction**, such as, 'The results identified . . . to be . . .'. Sentences tend to be **long and over-structured**, '. . . the epidemiology of . . . on . . . may be influenced by . . . of . . . and . . . at . . . during'.

. . . Results and Discussion: The authors proceed to analyze different factors and conclude that some are more important and others not. They proceed to discuss in great length various factors, explaining why some intuitive ones, such as water temperature, did not turn up as significant, while others did . . .

Overall, I found the paper meritorious, but **difficult to read**. The study is of practical value and consequence in the industry, and may be applicable in other organizations. I do not have specific scientific changes (the authors appear to be careful researchers), but it would help the authors' case if they **tightened up their writing style a bit**, especially in the Discussion, which is **much too long**.

What can we learn from this example of reviewers' feedback?: that reviewers have their own idiosyncratic view of what constitutes good academic writing?; that there are no general rules in writing for publication at all?; or that the authors of the paper can still improve their style and, more importantly, targeting?

- Some of the comments seem to go against good practice: for example, the reviewer is not a fan of descriptive titles, although for many of us, keeping titles descriptive is a key goal.
- The passive form seems to be so heavily endorsed in some disciplines that some writers will be surprised to see this critique of its use; but is it a problem with specifically how these authors used it, rather than with passive in general?
- Is there an implied negative in 'at great length' – and does it matter? As long as the editor has requested 'minor revisions', all the authors have to do is work out how these comments translate into revisions and, it would seem, how much to cut from the 'much too long' Discussion section.

What to do with hostile reviews

Once we lose our sense of grievance everything, including physical pain, becomes easier to bear.

(Greer 1991: 428)

Taking the subject of negative or destructive reviews one step further brings us to what seem to be openly hostile reviews. Any of the above reviews could be seen as hostile, at least in parts, by new writers. The point is that you have to learn from all the reviews, even if your paper is rejected.

Having a sense of grievance is very different from taking out a 'grievance', formalizing your complaint. A sense of personal grievance about a hostile review can inhibit revision and resubmission. Yet, if your paper has not been rejected, and if you have a good chance of getting published, why not just follow the reviewers' suggestions? Will they really change it all that much?

If your paper is rejected, you can revise it for submission to another journal. There is no point in a hostile response to a hostile review. What, after all, is your goal: to get your paper published or to improve the standard of reviewing in academic journals?

Remember the recurring weaknesses, reasons for rejection and common problems covered in this book – have you committed one or more of these errors? Even if you worked hard to avoid them, you may have made a minor slip that has irritated the reviewer. For example, remember how easy it is to overstate a critique of others' work. There may be one part of the paper that has triggered the hostility, and if you can work out which part it is, cut it. As a first step, take a good look at your contextualizing section(s), where new writers are at most risk of overstating a criticism of someone else's work, or of education in a certain field or professional practice, giving the impression that nothing is right. That may be where you have drawn fire. Sometimes all you need is a 'perhaps' or a 'potential' to modulate your argument where it is overstated. The key point is not to take it personally.

You also have to own up and admit that you can still improve your paper. Even though when you sent it in it was in a form you thought was as close to 'perfect' as you could get it, others will not see it that way. Some of this you can anticipate; some of it will take you by surprise.

Contradictory comments

It seemed that reviewers did not overtly disagree on particular points; instead, they wrote about different topics, each making points that were appropriate and accurate. As a consequence, their recommendations about editorial decisions showed hardly any agreement.

(Fiske and Fogg 1990: 591)

It is not unusual for reviewers to disagree – not that they know this themselves – in their comments on a paper. This can be disconcerting, but, once again, if the editor has not used the word 'rejection', then you still have a chance to do some revisions.

There is no need, therefore, to be thrown by such disagreements. Perhaps they merely reflect on-going debates in your field. Perhaps there are shades in this debate of which you were not aware, and this is what has come out in your reviewers' responses.

Whatever the cause – and it might be more interesting than productive to ponder this at any great length – your task is still to work out what the responses mean, not how they came to be so divergent. There may, of course, be lessons to be learned from this, but you should not be too shocked if it happens.

Rejection

. . . perseverance and the ability not to get downcast by rejection, which is certain and ongoing, is just part of the game – even when you're published.

(Messud quoted in Roberts et al. 2002: 50)

You need to be able to transform rejection – and what feels like rejection, but is only a request for changes – into learning.

There is a useful and thought-provoking list of reasons why papers are rejected in Greenhalgh (2001). Some would argue that papers are rejected because the work is simply not good enough, but the number of contradict-ory reviews – even in scientific disciplines – suggest that it is not as simple as that.

Your paper may be rejected if there are weaknesses in your work; but there may also be weaknesses in how you have explained your work or, more importantly, in the case you have made for doing the work in the way that you did. The following adaptation of Greenhalgh is designed to show what you might be able to learn from common reasons for rejection about the skills of written argument:

Common reasons why papers are rejected for publication

(adapted from Greenhalgh 2001)

- *Your study did not examine an issue considered important by the journal's editor/reviewers.* Spell out why it might be important to the journal's readers. Make a stronger case for its importance.
- *Your study was not original,* or you did not make a strong enough case for its originality. If you cannot make the case for 'originality', try another term, one that suits your work better.
- *Your study did not test your hypothesis,* or you did not make the connection between the two sufficiently clear, strong or explicit.
- *You should have conducted your study in a different way,* or your argument for your method in the context in which you were working is weak. Were your research procedures sufficiently defined and argued for? Were you careful to make the case against logical and widely accepted alternatives that you did not use?
- *You compromised on your research design.* Can you make a stronger case for this? Even if this was the result of practical difficulties or resource deficiencies, can you still learn lessons from this? Is a smaller-scale report in order?
- *If your sample was judged too small,* should you be presenting and analysing your data in different terms: as a pilot study or a case study? Are there limited lessons you can learn? Can you make the limits to generalizability more explicit? Did you acknowledge the potential limitations of a small sample?
- *If your study is judged to be 'uncontrolled',* then perhaps you have submitted your paper to the wrong journal. Or perhaps you have to be more selective in what you are calling 'data'.
- *If your statistical analysis is found to be incorrect,* then you have some work to do before you submit your paper elsewhere, if it was found to be inappropriate here.
- *The conclusions you drew from your data were not justified.* Is this, again, a case for strengthening your argument for your conclusions, perhaps even going through them one by one?
- *The reviewers judged that you had a conflict of interest,* for example financial gain from publication. Did you make a sufficient case for your safeguards against bias?
- *If the reviewers tell you that your paper was so badly written that it was difficult or impossible to understand,* then you may have some work to do to improve your writing style – but you probably knew that anyway. Alternatively, you may be a very good writer, but might have to make more of a stylistic compromise between your preferred style of writing and the dominant style in the journal at this time.

When new writers see this list they are either incredulous that authors would submit papers with such serious weaknesses or unclear as to the relevance of these criteria: 'What does this have to do with our writing?' Presumably, the many authors who were rejected for these reasons had worked hard to avoid these weaknesses and knew full well how high reviewers' standards would be. Surely these are all common sense? Or perhaps the authors still have work to do, not necessarily on their research, but on their writing.

Of course, this list only provides insight into one set of academic disciplines – medicine and the health professions – but it also shows the range of reasons for rejection, and we should remember that this list is offered as 'common' reasons. There are other such lists and perhaps the best use of them is to consider how you can strengthen your arguments so as to avoid these weaknesses. Some writers who address common weaknesses take the more positive line of suggesting how you might avoid them:

Solutions to common problems

1 Following publication guidelines
2 Using appropriate terminology
3 Informing the reader of sources of information
4 Providing sufficient background literature
5 Analysing and synthesizing the literature adequately
6 Providing continuity of content

(Hayes 1996: 25–7)

These suggestions seem to be about solving problems in the text, rather than the methodology. Each problem may have its origins in insufficient argument for, to take point number 4, the literature that is referenced. In other words, you could argue that the literature you have referenced is sufficient, and that to reference other literature would be to lose focus on your topic and, potentially, in your argument. Yet, some reviewers do want you to acknowledge a wide range of research. Whether that is because you have left their work out of your review, or whether adding other references will genuinely strengthen your review – and thereby the impact of your argument – is for you to judge.

What revision actions could you take: could you simply add one sentence on all the other sources, or one on each, without doing too much harm to the continuity and focus of your paper? Or could you add a sentence that makes a more explicit case for the literature you have referenced as sufficient for the purpose of this paper? Or should you really have stated, explicitly, why you have not dealt with certain literature that some will think does belong in any discussion of your topic; since you have a sound reason for doing so, should you perhaps go ahead and say what it is? You may be putting your head above the parapet unnecessarily – and for no particular benefit to your paper – since what you most want your reader to notice and think about is, surely, other aspects of your paper.

The point is you will probably have to have this mini-debate with yourself about how to respond to reviewers' comments. This debate may be easier or quicker if conducted with someone else, particularly if this is the first paper you have submitted to an academic journal.

As with the previous list, the context is the health professions, but there are points here that could be helpful to new writers in other disciplines. As with the previous list, you may think that these are pretty basic errors for authors to make. You wonder if that is because the discipline context – occupational therapy – is not as mature, in terms of published research, as, say, medicine. Yet the previous list was taken from the medical context, suggesting that such errors are not just oversights on the part of inexperienced authors, since even experienced authors have had such 'basic' feedback from time to time. Remember how 'basic' some of the reviews quoted earlier in this chapter were, commenting on the authors' writing skills, accusing them of not knowing about the subject and of not writing a paper about what they said they would. These critiques may still seem overstated, but this is the one remaining hurdle between you and publication.

At the end of the day, whatever the reason for the reviewer's comment, be it bias or genuine sense of weakness in your paper, you just have to get on with revising it, unless, of course, you feel that the comment is inappropriate or takes you beyond the scope of your paper. One thing is sure: you will learn more about your target journal from reviewers' comments on your writing.

Resubmission

If your paper has not been rejected, get on with the revisions and resubmit as quickly as you can. Acknowledge that you may have overstated a point here or lacked clarity in a point there.

For example, if a reviewer says that your critique of the literature, policy of some other dimension of context is 'well worn', you do not necessarily have to dig up the original and intervening critiques and reference them, nor do you have to invent a new type of critique, since that might not work well with the rest of your paper, nor do you have to delete it, if you think it is an important foundation for your argument. Perhaps all that you need to do is to follow the reviewer's lead by acknowledging that it is a well-worn critique, but an important one that is still current and, therefore, all the more serious for not being new and, worse, for not being 'fixed'. Your revised text might therefore read, 'Although it is now well established that there are weaknesses in the current method of XXX, it seems that, as yet, no action had been taken to address these weaknesses', or 'The argument that XXX is a weak method of YYY has been much rehearsed/discussed in the literature; however . . .' or 'It has been argued convincingly elsewhere (references) that . . .'.

If you are accused by a reviewer of being over-critical or even 'vituperative', you could, again, acknowledge that your criticism is harsh, but well founded or strongly stated for a purpose, such as to draw attention to the seriousness of the issue or the severity of a problem that has been allowed to persist. Of course, if you are going to say that, you will have to be sure that it is both true and accurate. You can always take the moral high ground and say that you have to do this difficult harsh critique because there are those who are suffering in some way, or that research itself is weakened in some way. You can modulate such assertions, so as to avoid drawing a new form of critique from the editor when you resubmit, by adding the odd 'perhaps' and 'potentially'.

Check with someone who has been published in your target journal recently, but start thinking about changes you can make and, as you go through the reviewers' comments note the types of changes they are suggesting:

- One section seems to have drawn a lot of fire – consider cutting it.
- You do not agree with a reviewer's comment – take it up with the editor.
- A couple of comments are 'beyond the scope of this paper' – say so.
- Offer to discuss your revisions further, if you think/know this particular editor usually/ever takes time to do this.

Once you have had six or seven papers published, you will have your own list of the types of changes you have to make.

Responding to feedback from editors and reviewers

Reply immediately:

1 Be positive; thank the editor for the 'useful feedback'.
2 Say that you will revise your paper.
3 Ask for a deadline.
(4 Follow the editor's interpretation of the reviewers' comments.)
5 'Translate' each comment into a revision action.

    For example: Page 2   Cut . . .
               Page 6   Explain . . .
               Page 11   Add . . .
6 Discuss them with someone.
7 Do revisions immediately; return the revised paper as soon as you can.

When you send in the revisions:

1 Attach a letter/attach it to an email.
2 Give a point-by-point account of how you have acted on the editor's/ reviewers' suggestions, using your revision action list. Keep these brief, easy to scan.
  For example: Page 2   Cut . . .
              Page 6   Explained . . .
              Page 11   Added . . .
3 Do this in bullet points or a numbered list, or two lists, if there were two reviewers.

What now?

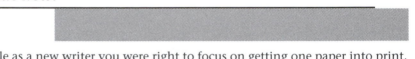

While as a new writer you were right to focus on getting one paper into print, in reality, and perhaps from now on, you have to have more than one piece of writing on the go at any one time. If you feel up to it, you can put in place a more complex programme of writing, particularly if your institution has set a target of two publications per year.

> Nobody hates writers more than writers do. . . . Nobody loves them more, either.
>
> (Atwood 2002: 97)

Are other people happy with your success? Does it matter? Margaret Atwood's description of the love-hate relationship between writers may apply less to you in the context of your writers' group, if you have one, but it rings true for some of the more competitive and even actively undermining reactions of some colleagues.

Do not be shocked if some colleagues ignore your success while others belittle it by, for example, remarking that the journal in which you have just been published does not have much standing. Even when you write a best-selling book, you can find some senior colleague who is keen to tell you that he or she had a book published that did not sell well because it was 'not that kind of book'. In other words, the put-downs may come thick and fast and you may find this heartily disappointing, if you were expecting collegial mutual respect, but it is not just you – it's them. Some people cannot stand others' success. They are not going to change, and they need not change your attitude to your own work. You did what you set out to do. Time to set a new writing goal and get on with that.

Focus on your writing: once you have had a paper accepted, take time to take stock. What, if anything, did you learn in the course of becoming a published writer? Did you find that there were things you still had to learn? As you look to your next paper, can you gather some informal 'intelligence' about other journals from other writers? Other newly published writers may be willing to trade information with you.

Changing your first name to 'Professor' might open some doors, but not for long. Another option is to make some effort to join another élite conversation, perhaps by working with a Professor. The top journals represent perhaps an even more select group. There may be even more nepotism at that level, a highly contentious statement, but people do tell me that there is evidence of this. Since much of it is anecdotal, you will have to make up your own mind, perhaps not being swayed by any one person's anecdotes. Yet it has been said to me on numerous occasions, in many institutions and in several countries, that there is discrimination on the basis of gender, race and class in all aspects of academic life, and we only have to do a quick scan of posts, publications and senior appointments to see that they are not representative of the general academic population. Nevertheless, if you are to be a publishing academic writer, you have to find a way to join the debate that they are effectively running. This is a discussion that was covered in an earlier chapter, but these issues may raise their ugly heads again as you set off on your next paper(s), particularly if you are thinking of targeting one of the 'élite' journals.

Acceptance

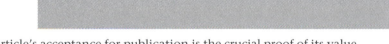

The article's acceptance for publication is the crucial proof of its value.
(Rossen 1993: 161)

What does acceptance of your article signify to you? That you have finally reached the high standard required? That you have packaged your work in such a way that it can be easily assimilated into the academic community? Or that you have, with the help of the reviewers, learned how to make your writing persuasive to that community?

What will it signify to others? It may indeed signal to others that your work should be taken more seriously, since someone with power – the editor – has accepted it. It may be time, therefore, for you to acknowledge, if you have not already done so, that your work is important and that your writing can persuade others that it is important. This may be all the more important if, as you go on to write more and more, colleagues challenge not only your publications but also, oddly, the processes by which you produced them, as if you were practising some dark art of writing, when all you were doing was putting into practice the tried and tested methods for productive academic writing:

> As long as I had only written and published one or two books no one ever inquired or commented on my writing process, on how long it took me to

complete the writing of a book. Once I began to write books regularly, sometimes publishing two at the same time, more and more comments were made to me about how much I was writing. Many of these comments conveyed the sense that I was either doing something wrong by writing so much, or at least engaged in writing acts that needed to be viewed with suspicion.

(hooks 1999: 14)

Let's assume that there will always be people who excel at 'damning with faint praise' and that publication will not give you immunity from that type of assault; in fact, it may increase it.

Do not expect that the new status accorded to your work will be 'accepted' within your department. Colleagues or heads of department may actively undermine your work, perhaps questioning the status of the journal in which you have just been published. You already know who is and is not likely to behave in this way. Welcome, therefore, those who 'damn with faint praise', since that is a relatively mild attack. Above all, do not expect them to change simply because you have. Your goal was to get published; it was not to convert your peers to congenial collegiality.

To complicate matters – and motivations – further, you may have a sense of anti-climax: it is so long since you started your paper, and you are so aware of the modesty of its contribution and are now certain that it will make no more than a gentle ripple in the sea of published work. You may find yourself agreeing with your colleagues' critiques. Remember that their criticisms are probably not based on a reading of your paper; they will criticize freely whether or not they have even read the sentence or two on your web site about this paper.

If their criticisms seem to be marginalizing you – and not just your work – remind them of the relevance and value of your work for the university and the department at opportune moments, such as appraisals, reviews and even staff meetings. Don't wait to be asked; just tell them. If this does not work, persist. Do not expect to see or hear any marked change in their attitudes. They are not going to say 'Oh, yes, I see it now – your work is indeed very important. I'm sorry I missed that before.'

If you feel you are genuinely being marginalized or even bullied, it may be time to take a different course of action, rather than trying to sort it all out yourself. You could start with an informal discussion, seeking advice from your head of department, or manager, or personnel or human resources. If need be, you have a right to take some formal action. Some people will tirelessly undermine their colleagues; be ready to look for ways to make sure that does not happen to you or to stop it if or when it does.

Once your paper has been accepted, you may feel a bit cynical – now you *know* it's all just a game, and it has to be played by their rules. You knew this would happen. You have had to compromise your work and hedge your state-ments so much that you feel your voice will not be heard and the value of your work is diminished. You still feel that you should be allowed to write what you think; even if people do not want to know, they should be made to hear it.

In some ways, you may still feel exactly as you did when you started. Although you are about to be published, you may be even more convinced that academic power is wielded by a very select group, that they are not out to share their power and that you will never be able to develop the kind of authority they enjoy when they write. Your writing will always be coming from a more contested place.

In some disciplines, of course, these issues have no relevance; it is the quality of the work that matters. If your work is good enough, the argument goes, you will be published in chemistry, for example. No question. Perhaps this is truer for other disciplines than new writers realize or are prepared to admit.

Proofs

The proofs show you exactly what your paper will look like when it is printed in the journal. This is editors' and authors' last chance to make final corrections to errors. This is not the time to make final revisions. Make essential corrections only, since any changes could be costly. Editors will tell you what they want you to do and, more importantly, what they do not want you to do, so check their instructions carefully and follow them to the letter. Check every word against your original file. Check all your references. There is usually a very quick turn around at the proof stage, often as little as three days.

If you have to make a change that adds even as little as one line, try to 'catch up' by cutting a line elsewhere on the same page. There is no point in saving a line on another page, as that would require them to reset two whole pages. You should have a really good reason for doing this, probably drawn to your atten- tion by the proof reader, such as including a reference in your list at the end of the paper that you have not actually referred to in the paper. This means that you either have to add the reference to your text, if you can find somewhere that it will fit on an existing line, or you may have to simply cut the reference. It may be a reference left over from an earlier draft that can be cut. The key motivation here is not to use this as an opportunity to 'polish' or 'perfect' your paper, but to make no changes at all, if at all possible.

Once you are at this stage, when you know that the next stage is the arrival of proofs, check with the editor about roughly when that will be. This is a courtesy that may save you all some grief later. If you are going to be off campus or out of the office for even a day or two, this will cause problems for a journal that has a three-day turn around time. Some journals allow longer for authors to check the proofs. You need to know exactly what you are dealing with. The editor may be able to tell you exactly when the proofs will be sent out and expected back. You can then arrange for them to be sent to you – if you are away – or emailed to another address.

Offprints

Offprints are quality prints of your paper, sometimes with a paper cover, sometimes just stapled together like a high-quality photocopy on good paper. They look a lot better than photocopies. Whether or not that means that it is worth paying for extra copies is up to you. Some journals no longer provide them.

If you have some money in a special fund, or if your department has, then this might be a good use of what is bound to be a small proportion of the total fund. It is good for the department and the university, not just for you, to publicize your work by distributing offprints. If even part of the fund is designated for support of research, then you can make the case that this is one way of doing that.

Some journals offer you a set of offprints – perhaps 20 or 50 – at no charge. Others will send you a note of their rate for additional copies, sometimes charging for orders of 50 or 100. Some will give you a complete copy of the issue of the journal in which your paper appears.

The key use of offprints is to send them to people whom you know have an interest in your work, either because they have supported you or because they are working in the area themselves. Send them offprints as soon as they come in. Send them to people you want to know about your publication, even if they are not interested in your area and are unlikely to even read it. Give one to your boss. If your department has one of those glass cases for publications, get one in there now. If it does not, suggest it. At the very least, you can make your publication more visible in your department by sticking an offprint on your wall, leaving your door open, so that everyone sees it. Or you could stick it on the outside of your door, though it may 'walk'.

Take your offprints to conferences and distribute them to those interested people who come up to talk to you after your session. It may seem a bit arrogant to buy copies of your paper with the express purpose of sending them out to people whom you think will want to read them, but this is just another means of continuing the dialogue with your peers. They will probably read your abstract and then flick to your references to see if there is anything new there, anything they have missed in the literature or any new connections you make.

If you were worried about sending your paper to your peers, you may be even more reticent about sending offprints to people you do not know, but, as with any other aspect of research, you can find out who is likely to be receptive and who is likely to be insulted, if that is what you are worried about. If you have not done so already, research the peers – those writing in your area – whom you do not know and ask around: who knows who? Finally, if there is someone with whom you would like to collaborate or write, this is a good way to introduce yourself to them.

Whatever you do with offprints, make sure that you file them in a sensible place so that you can find them if someone does ask for a copy. Start a new file, even if it only has one paper in it for the moment. Above all, do not just leave your offprints in a pile to gather dust. Put them to work.

Marketing your writing

Given that a small number of people may read your article once it is published in the journal, there is a case for marketing published articles. No one will do this for you; it's up to you. Since getting people to read, or at least know about, your writing is crucial for getting further responses and feedback, and possibly invitations to write, this is a much more important topic than new writers generally realize. Yet, with a few exceptions (Thyer 1994), this step is given surprisingly little consideration in descriptions of the process of writing for academic journals.

Some, of course, will tell you that if your work is good enough it does not need to be 'marketed'. Even when you successfully market your writing, some will come out with veiled or quite openly snide remarks such as, 'I'll say this for you, you certainly know how to *promote* your work'. Some people will make that a compliment; others will always make it sound like an insult.

You can even try to get your work featured in the newspapers or educational press. Most newspapers have an education day, often with a higher education section. If you can interest the relevant editor, providing him or her with an 'angle' on your work – make it topical, find something in your work that will be of interest to people outside your field – then you will reach a much larger audience than you did with your journal publications. Can you relate your work to recent events, trends or crises? Is there anything interestingly contentious about your work? This may be your chance to have a say about some of the issues you had to leave out of your paper.

There are also professional journals and magazines, for which you might be able to write a short piece yourself. This will not, of course, 'count' in the great scheme of things, but it will let many more people know about your publication. It may also develop your profile and network. Again, this may be your chance to bring in some of the issues, perhaps concerning practice or implementation – real-world issues – that you had to leave out of your more academic paper.

Finally, remember that you can and should still be talking about your subject at conferences and other meetings. Just because you have published a paper does not mean that you have to move on to a completely new area; your published paper, itself possibly the development of a conference paper, can be the subject of your next presentation. If this seems like just so much recycling, think again: writing about the same subject more than once, in more than one way and for more than one outlet is the way to develop your expertise and understanding. It is not just a matter of getting the maximum number of 'hits' from your material; it is about getting the maximum amount of learning out of your publishing.

Publishers, and perhaps others, have certain likes and dislikes (Baverstock 2001: 47–8), which may be instructive to writers for academic journals:

Publishers' likes and dislikes

Dislikes   Rudeness . . . . Not thanking them
Failure to give information on request or help with promotion
Unrealistic expectations of advertising

Likes   Focus: think about what you want to discuss before you call/email
Efficiency: ask for things in plenty of time
Contact: Send your contacts the occasional note of forthcoming key events and what might happen (for example, meetings at which you are speaking and at which information on your book [or paper] could be handed out) and a note of thanks if things have gone well! This is not just good nature – you will be remembered, and if any additional opportunities come up (for example, 'filler' advertisements available at last-minute prices), maybe it will be your book that gets included (p. 48).

While this may not all seem relevant to your paper, remember that some journals do feature papers in their leaflets and web sites. One paper I had featured in this way has been the one that most people have requested copies of, leading to new contacts and, more importantly, contact with people who are interested in my work.

What next?

One of the aims of this final chapter is to prompt you to think strategically, tactically and creatively about the potential subjects and stories of your papers:

- Which journals should you be writing for now or soon?
- Which ones do you think you have little or no chance of getting into?
- Why exactly is that?
- Can you convert that into a plus?
- How could your topic complement their papers?
- What would it take to make them consider your topics/ideas/work?
- Can you make explicit connections with their publication?

If you are doubtful about these suggestions, remember how doubtful you felt about your first paper – possibly at every single stage of writing – and recognize that having it accepted means that your work is worth something. Talk yourself into thinking this way – or get someone to help you to do so – about some other aspect of your work. Be creative. What would it take for one of the top journals in your field to give serious consideration to a paper from you, particularly if you have limited research data, profile or experience?

Just because you have been through the process once does not mean that you can dodge the systematic process of targeting a journal. In fact, if you are planning to target a different journal for your next publication, you should perhaps go through the same process of analysing it in some detail. This may take you less time, but it should, I would argue, be no less thorough. As before, you can learn a lot about writing from working out how published articles are put together.

Consider collaborating with colleagues or students. There may be others, in your writers' group, for example, who are keen to publish in different areas. You can also write about your teaching and supervision roles. Other aspects of academic practice are open to debate. You may want to join current debates on such matters as research training. In some systems these types of publication will not count in the scoring system, but they can demonstrate your willing-ness to develop in these roles and you might also learn something about academic writing.

In some disciplines this will seem nonsensical: surely you can only learn about writing for your journals by writing for your journals? Surely those who have research to write about do so, and those who do not, write about their teaching and supervision instead? Again, as teacher accreditation becomes more established in higher education, it is a mistake to discount altogether the practice of learning and writing about your teaching, at the very least. That is one way of demonstrating your knowledge in this area, as in any other.

If you are thinking of writing in another area, you might want to co-author with a colleague who is already established in that area, or whose home discip-line it is. They will have more background than you; you will have a new perspective to offer them. It can be an interesting combination.

Many outputs that do not 'count' can be useful stepping stones to publica-tion and regular academic writing. They also get your name noticed in the journals: book reviews, letters about published papers or current debates.

There is no need to wait until you are asked to review a book; write to the reviews editor and offer to do so.

As before, you should start looking for your next paper in all the obvious places: your conference presentations, workshops, consultancies and briefing papers can all work as starters for further papers, for disseminating your work and 'marketing your writing' (Thyer 1994; Baverstock 2001). While in some fields, none of these would be considered as 'research', they can be the starting point for a piece of academic writing that might at some stage become a paper. As always, you have to find the right journal to publish it in.

The key step at this stage is therefore balancing three factors in your writing decision:

* Which journal do you want to target now?
* Which topic do you want to write about now?
* What work have you done that is potentially publishable?

In some fields academics know exactly where their next paper is coming from, since it follows on immediately from the one before. But in others the process is a matter of juggling answers to these three questions; it is unlikely that you will be able to answer all three questions right away and come up with an instant topic. Your answer to one question may not match the others. For example, your preferred topic may be the least likely one for your preferred journal, and you will have to decide whether or not to persevere with it.

Whatever field you are in, there are almost always things you left out of the paper you have just completed. There are things that occurred to you as you wrote. There are questions you did not answer and possibly new questions generated by your work. There were matters – worth discussing in another forum – that were beyond the scope of that paper. In your conclusion you referred to other questions that merit further study or simply consideration. These can, in some disciplines, be starting points for your next few papers, your future research or for future collaborations.

Recycling and 'salami-slicing'

A variant on duplicate publication is 'salami publishing', in which each bit of research is divided into the thinnest possible slices (sometimes referred to as 'LPUs', for 'least publishable units'), with each slice submitted as a separate article. This is marginally more ethical than duplicate submission, but it is equally wasteful.

(Luey 2002: 16)

Yet, if you are to develop a profile in a certain area, you will have to write about it several times. It is a mistake, in any case, to look around for a new topic, once your paper has been published. Therefore the term 'salami-slicing' – often taken to be a cynical strategy – can be recovered to define the strategy of planning a series of papers from any piece of work or project. It is also a useful reminder to new writers not to put the whole salami into any one paper.

Similarly, 'recycling' can be a useful term for describing the process of covering the same ground in a series of papers, not in the sense that you are repeating yourself, but in the sense that you are taking up in a new paper where your previous paper left off. This is a prompt to go back to all that material that you cut from your first paper and kept in a separate file. Can that now be the subject of your next paper?

Writing a book

> ... the so-called research assessment exercise, a crazy Soviet-style set of production targets for goods that nobody wants. It coerces even those who have the decency not to want to publish much into fulfilling their production norms.
>
> (Allison 2004: 14)

Thinking of writing a book because you want to? Or because you think it is expected of you? Or because a publisher has asked you to? Or some combination of the three? Writing a book can be one way of bringing all your papers together – in a new form – to establish a synthesis and a coherent body of work. The book form can allow you more freedom of expression than is possible in academic journals. In terms of time, it can take just as long to get a paper from inception to publication, sometimes as much as two years, as it does to write a book.

See publishers' web sites for guidance on how to put together a proposal, but, as for academic journals, contact the appropriate editor first with an initial enquiry to see if they are interested in your topic.

Developing a programme for writing

There are several ways in which you could draw up a programme of writing for yourself for the next five years or so.

Year 1   First paper submitted/published (plus ideas for others)
Year 2   Draw up list of other possible papers, convert conference papers into publications, writing several papers at the same time, target new journal

Year 3   Targeting higher level of journal
Year 4   Writing for journals and other outlets for dissemination
Year 5   Pulling papers together for a book (depending on academic discipline),
          major research proposals and collaborations

Use the 'Page 98 paper' (Murray 2002a) to develop your ideas, beyond simply being 'ideas', and to contextualize them in the literature. This is an activity that postgraduates have found useful – to the extent of referring to it as a type of paper – in helping them to map out the context and focus for their work. It might also work for sketching a paper.

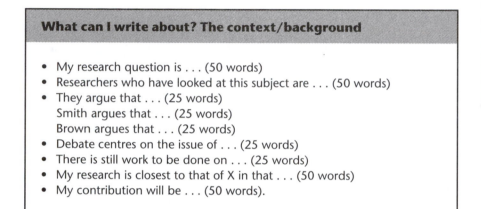

What can I write about? The context/background

- My research question is . . . (50 words)
- Researchers who have looked at this subject are . . . (50 words)
- They argue that . . . (25 words)
  Smith argues that . . . (25 words)
  Brown argues that . . . (25 words)
- Debate centres on the issue of . . . (25 words)
- There is still work to be done on . . . (25 words)
- My research is closest to that of X in that . . . (50 words)
- My contribution will be . . . (50 words).

Once your paper has been accepted, you may find that you have a slightly different view of the publishing game. You may have learned a lot from the reviewers' feedback, and you may have picked up a few dos and don'ts from how they have played their role. Whatever you have got out of the experience, it is time to move on.

If you do not yet feel that you have a set of productive academic writing practices, that will not necessarily be because you are slow on the uptake; these skills take time to learn. In time, you will also develop your own strategies. In the meantime, writing to prompts, freewriting, generative writing and the outlining strategies in this book will serve as a reminder of the range of writing activities that lie behind many published papers, even if their authors would not all use these terms.

Writing for academic journals is always instructive. It makes us test our ideas and forces us to submit to others' testing. Publication can give you a qualified confidence in your writing, qualified by the knowledge that your future work and writing will have to be tested in these ways if they are genuinely to amount to anything. Ultimately, this is where the genuine rewards of academic writing lie.

Checklist

- Translate reviewers' comments into revision actions.
- Learn from their feedback.
- Once you are published, promote your papers.

Bibliography

Albert, T. (2000) *Winning the Publications Game: How To Write a Scientific Paper without Neglecting Your Patients*, 2nd edn. Abingdon: Radcliffe.

Allison, L. (2004) Why I . . . think we have too many books, *The Times Higher*, 9 April, p. 14.

Anglin, J. (1999) The uniqueness of child and youth care: A personal perspective, *Child and Youth Care Forum*, 28(2): 143–50.

Appelbaum, J. (1998) *How to Get Happily Published: A Complete and Candid Guide*, 5th edn. New York: HarperCollins.

Atwood, M. (2002) *Negotiating with the Dead*. Cambridge: Cambridge University Press.

Ballenger, B. (2004) *The Curious Researcher: A Guide to Writing Research Papers*, 4th edn. New York: Pearson Longman.

Barrass, R. (2002) *Scientists Must Write: A Guide To Better Writing for Scientists, Engineers and Students*, 2nd edn. London: Routledge.

Baverstock, A. (2001) *Marketing Your Book: An Author's Guide*. London: A. and C. Black.

Belton, V. (1985) The use of a simple multiple-criteria model to assist in selection from a shortlist, *Journal of the Occupational Research Society*, 36(4): 265–74.

Bennett, J.B. (2003) *Academic Life: Hospitality, Ethics and Spirituality*. Bolton, MA: Anker.

Bensimon, E.M. (1995) Total quality management in the academy: A rebellious reading, *Harvard Educational Review*, 65(4): 593–611.

Bereiter, C. and Scardamalia, M. (1987) *The Psychology of Written Composition*. London: Lawrence Erlbaum.

Black, D., Brown, S., Day, A. and Race, P. (1998) *500 Tips for Getting Published: A Guide for Educators, Researchers and Professionals*. London: Kogan Page.

Blaxter, L., Hughes, C. and Tight, M. (1998a) *The Academic Career Handbook*. Buckingham: Open University Press.

Blaxter, L., Hughes, C. and Tight, M. (1998b) Writing on academic careers, *Studies in Higher Education*, 23(3): 281–95.

Boice, R. (1987) Is released time an effective component of faculty development programs?, *Research in Higher Education*, 26(3): 311–26.

Boice, R. (1990) *Professors as Writers: A Self-Help Guide to Productive Writing*. Stillwater, OK: New Forums.

Boice, R. (1990) Faculty resistance to writing-intensive courses, *Teaching of Psychology*, 17(1): 13–17.

Boud, D. (1999) Situating development in professional work: Using peer learning, *International Journal for Academic Development*, 4(1): 3–10.

Boud, D. and Walker, D. (1998) Promoting reflection in professional courses: The challenge of context, *Studies in Higher Education*, 23(2): 191–206.

Bradbury, R. (1994) *Zen in the Art of Writing*. Santa Barbara, CA: Joshua Bell.

Brew, A. (2001) *The Nature of Research: Inquiry in Academic Contexts*. London: Routledge.

Brew, A. (2004) Conceptions of research: A phenomenographic study, in M. Tight (ed.) *The RoutledgeFalmer Reader in Higher Education*. London: RoutledgeFalmer.

Brown, R. (1994/95) Write right first time, *Literati Newsline*, Special Issue, 1–8 (http://www.literaticlub.co.uk/writing/articles/write.html).

Burton, S. and Steane, P. (eds) (2004) *Surviving Your Thesis*. London: Routledge.

Bykofsky, S. and Sander, J.B. (2000) *The Complete Idiot's Guide to Getting Published*, 2nd edn. Indianapolis, IN: Alpha Books.

Caffarella, R.S. and Barnett, B.G. (2000) Teaching doctoral students to become scholarly writers: the importance of giving and receiving critiques, *Studies in Higher Education*, 25(1): 39–51.

Caldwell, J.J., Colman, R., Kerr, W.J. and Magennis, E.J. (2001) Novel use of a selenoalkyne within untraditionally mild Dötz benzannulation processes; total synthesis of a *Calceolaria andica L.* natural hydroxylated naphthoquinone, *Synlett*, 9: 1428–30.

Cameron, J. (1998) *The Right to Write: An Invitation and Initiation into the Writing Life*. London: Macmillan.

Carra, J., Candau, R., Keslacy, S. et al. (2003) Addition of inspiratory resistance increases the amplitude of the slow component of O_2 uptake kinetics, *Journal of Applied Physiology*, 94: 2448–55.

Cummings, L.L. and Frost, P.J. (1995) *Publishing in the Organizational Sciences*, 2nd edn. London: Sage.

Damarell, B. (1999) Just forging, or seeking love and approval: An investigation into the phenomenon of the forged art object and the copied picture in art therapy involving people with learning disabilities, *Inscape*, 4(2): 44–50.

Davis, M.S. (1971) That's interesting!: Towards a phenomenology of sociology and a sociology of phenomenology, *Philosophy of Social Science*, 1: 309–44.

Davis, R. and Shadle, M. (2000) 'Building a mystery': Alternative research writing and the academic act of seeking, *College Composition and Communication*, 51(3): 417–46.

Day, A. (1996) *How to Get Research Published in Journals*. Aldershot: Gower.

Drake, S. and Jones, G.A. (1997) *Finding Your Own Voice in Academic Publishing: Writing Your Way to Success*. Stillwater, OK: New Forums.

Elbow, P. (1973) *Writing Without Teachers*. Oxford: Oxford University Press.

Ely, M., Vinz, R., Downing, M. and Anzul, M. (1997) *On Writing Qualitative Research: Living by Words*. London: Falmer.

Emerson, C. (1996) *The 30-Minute Writer*. Cincinnati, OH: Writers' Digest.

Estrin, S. and Wright, M. (1999) Corporate governance in the former Soviet Union: An overview, *Journal of Comparative Economics*, 27: 398–421.

Fahnestock, J. and Secor, M. (1990) *A Rhetoric of Argument*, 2nd edn. New York: McGraw-Hill.

Fiala, Z., Hinz, M., Meissner, K. and Wehner, F. (2003) A component-based approach for adaptive dynamic web documents, *Journal of Web Engineering*, 2(1 & 2): 58–73.

Fiske, D.W. and Fogg, L. (1990) But the reviewers are making different criticisms of my paper!: Diversity and uniqueness in reviewer comments, *American Psychologist*, 45(5): 591–8.

Flower, L. and Hayes, J.R. (1981) A cognitive process theory of writing, *College Composition and Communication*, 32: 365–87.

Frost, P.J. and Taylor, M.S. (1996) *Rhythms of Academic Life: Personal Accounts of Careers in Academia*. London: Sage.

Gavin, J. and Lister, S. (2001) The strategic use of sports and fitness activities for promoting psycho-social skill development in childhood and adolescence, *Journal of Child and Youth Care Work*, 16: 325–39.

Gere, A.R. (1987) *Writing Groups: History, Theory, and Implications*. Carbondale, IL: Southern Illinois University.

Germano, W. (2001) *Getting it Published: A Guide for Scholars and Anyone Else Serious about Serious Books*. London: University of Chicago Press.

Grant, B. and Knowles, S. (2000) Flights of imagination: Academic writers be(com)ing writers, *International Journal for Academic Development*, 5(1): 6–19.

Greenhalgh, T. (2001) *How to Read a Paper: The Basics of Evidence-based Medicine*, 2nd edn. London: British Medical Journal Books.

Greer, G. (1991) *The Change: Women, Ageing and the Menopause*. London: Penguin.

Griffiths, M. (1993) Productive writing, *The New Academic*, Autumn: 29–30.

Haines, D.D., Newcomer, S. and Raphael, J. (1997) *Writing Together: How to Transform Your Writing in a Writing Group*, New York: Perigree.

Hall, G.M. (ed.) (1998) *How to Write a Paper*, 2nd edn. London: British Medical Journal Books.

Halliday, M.A.K. and Martin, J.R. (1993) *Writing Science: Literacy and Discursive Power*. London: Falmer.

Hanks, R. (2003) Let them eat cake, *The Independent Magazine*, 25 January, p. 20.

Hartley, J. and Branthwaite, A. (1989) The psychologist as wordsmith: a questionnaire study of the writing strategies of productive British psychologists, *Higher Education*, 18: 423–52.

Hartley, J., Sotto, E. and Pennebaker, J. (2002) Style and substance in psychology: Are influential articles more readable than less influential ones?, *Social Studies of Science*, 32(2): 321–34.

Hayes, R.L. (1996) Writing for publication: Solutions to common problems, *Australian Occupational Therapy Journal*, 43: 24–9.

Henderson, K.W., Kerr, W.J. and Moir, J.H. (2000) Enantioselective depronotation reactions using a novel homochiral magnesium amide base, *Chemical Communications*, 6: 479–80.

Hicks, W. (1999) *Writing for Journalists*, London: Routledge.

Ho, S.P., Riester, L., Drews, M., Boland, T. and LaBerge, M. (2003) Nanoindentation properties of compression-moulded ultra-high molecular weight polyethylene, *Proceedings of the Institution of Mechanical Engineers, H, Journal of Engineering in Medicine*, 217: 357–66.

hooks, b (1999) *remembered rapture: the writer at work*. New York: Henry Holt.

Hough, J. (2000) Commentary on Belton (1985): The use of a simple multi-criteria model to assist in selection from a shortlist, *Journal of the Occupational Research Society*, 51: 895–6.

Huff, A.S. (1999) *Writing for Scholarly Publication*. London: Sage.

Kaye, S. (1989) *Writing Under Pressure: The Quick Writing Process*, Oxford: Oxford University Press.

Kitson, A.L. (2001) Does nursing education have a future?, *Nurse Education Today*, 21: 86–96.

Lea, M.R. and Street, B.V. (1998) Student writing in higher education: An academic literacies approach, *Studies in Higher Education*, 23(2): 157–72.

Lee, A. and Boud, D. (2003) Writing groups, change and academic identity: research development as local practice, *Studies in Higher Education*, 28(2): 187–200.

Lodge, D. (1996) *The Practice of Writing: Essays, Lectures, Reviews and a Diary*. London: Penguin.

Luey, B. (2002) *Handbook for Academic Authors*, 4th edn. Cambridge: Cambridge University Press.

MacDonald, S.P. (1994) *Professional Academic Writing in the Humanities and Social Sciences*. Carbondale, IL: Southern Illinois University.

Mailer, N. (2003) *The Spooky Art: Some Thoughts on Writing*. London: Little, Brown.

Matejka, K. (1990) Unpublished? Perish the thought, *Management Decision*, 28(6): 9–11.

McCall Smith, A. (2003) *Portuguese Irregular Verbs*. Edinburgh: Polygon.

Montgomery, S.L. (2003) *The Chicago Guide to Communicating Science*. Chicago, IL: University of Chicago Press.

Moore, S. (2003) Writers' retreats for academics: exploring and increasing the motivation to write, *Journal of Further and Higher Education*, 27(3): 333–42.

Morss, K. and Murray, R. (2001) Researching academic writing within a structured programme: insights and outcomes, *Studies in Higher Education*, 26(1): 35–51.

Moxley, J.M. and Taylor, T. (1997) *Writing and Publishing for Academic Authors*, 2nd edn. London: Rowman and Littlefield.

Mullen, C.A. (2001) The need for a curricular writing model for graduate students, *Journal of Further and Higher Education*, 25(1): 117–26.

Murray, R. (2000) *Writing for Publication* (video and notes). Glasgow: University of Strathclyde.

Murray, R. (2001) Integrating teaching and research through writing development for students and staff, *Active Learning in Higher Education*, 2(1): 31–45.

Murray, R. (2002a) *How to Write a Thesis*. Buckingham: Open University Press.

Murray, R. (2002b) Writing development for lecturers moving from further to higher education, *Journal of Further and Higher Education*, 26(3): 229–39.

Murray, R. and MacKay, G. (1998a) Supporting academic development in public output: Reflections and propositions, *International Journal for Academic Development*, 3(1): 54–63.

Murray, R. and MacKay, G. (1998b) Writers' groups for researchers and how to run them, Universities' and Colleges' Staff Development Agency, Sheffield.

Navarra, T. (1998) *Toward Painless Writing: A Guide for Health Professionals*. Thorofare, NJ: SLACK.

Palumbo, D. (2000) *Writing from the Inside Out: Transforming Your Psychological Blocks to Release the Writer Within*. New York: John Wiley.

Pasco, A.H. (2002) Basic advice for novice authors, *Journal of Scholarly Publishing*, January: 75–89.

Pazaratz, D. (2001) Defining and describing the child and youth care worker's role in residential treatment, *Journal of Child and Youth Care*, 14(3): 76–7.

Peat, J., Elliott, E., Baur, L. and Keena, V. (2002) *Scientific Writing: Easy When You Know How*. London: British Medical Journal Books.

Peter, D.P. and Ceci, S.J. (1982) Peer-review practices of psychological journals: The fate of published articles, submitted again, *The Behavioural and Brain Sciences*, 5: 187–255.

Powell, W.W. (1985) *Getting into Print: The Decision Making Process in Scholarly Publishing*. London: University of Chicago.

Rachlin, H. (2000) *The Science of Self-Control*. Cambridge, MA: Harvard University Press.

Reif-Lehrer, L. (2000) The Beauty of Outlines (http://nextwave-uk.sciencemag.org/cgi/content/full/2000/06/07/2).

Rich, A. (1986) *Blood, Bread and Poetry, Selected Prose 1979–1985*. London: Virago.

Rich, A. (2001) *Arts of the Possible*. New York: Norton.

Roberts, J., Mitchell, B. and Zubrinich, R. (eds) (2002) *Writers on Writing*. London: Penguin.

Rodrigues, D. (1997) *The Research Paper and the World Wide Web*. Upper Saddle River, NJ: Prentice Hall.

Rossen, J. (1993) *The University in Modern Fiction: When Power is Academic*. New York: St Martin's Press.

Rozakis, L. (1999) *Writing Great Research Papers*. London: McGraw-Hill.

Rymer, J. (1988) Scientific composing processes: How eminent scientists write journal articles, in D.A. Jolliffe (ed.) *Advances in Writing Research: Volume 2 – Writing in Academic Disciplines*. Norwood, NJ: Ablex.

Sadler, D.R. (1990) *Up the Publication Road: A Guide To Publishing in Scholarly Journals for Academics, Researchers and Graduate Students*, 2nd edn, Green Guide No. 2. Campbelltown, New South Wales: Higher Education Research and Development Society of Australasia.

Sanders, S.R. (1995) *Writing from the Centre*. Bloomington, IN: Indiana University Press.

Selzer, J.L. (1981) Merit and degree in Webster's *The Duchess of Malfi, English Literary Renaissance*, 11(1): 70–80.

Smith, A. and Eysenck, M. (2002) Letter, *Times Higher Education Supplement*, 1 March, p. 15.

Steinbeck, J. (1962) *Travels with Charley: In Search of America*. London: Pan.

Steinbeck, J. (1970) *Journal of a Novel: The East of Eden Letters*. London: Pan.

Sternberg, R.J. (ed.) (2000) *Guide to Publishing in Psychology Journals*. Cambridge: Cambridge University Press.

Swales, J.M. and Feak, C.B. (2000) *English in Today's Research World: A Writing Guide*. Ann Arbor: University of Michigan Press.

Thow, M., Rafferty, D. and Armstrong, G. (2004) A United Kingdom survey of physiotherapists' involvement in cardiac rehabilitation and their perceived skills and attributes, *Physiotherapy*, 90(2): 97–102.

Thyer, B.A. (1994) *Successful Publishing in Scholarly Journals*. London: Sage.

Torrance, M., Thomas, G. and Robinson, E.J. (1991) Strategies for answering examination essay questions: Is it helpful to write a plan?, *British Journal of Educational Psychology*, 61: 46–54.

Torrance, M., Thomas, M. and Robinson, E.J. (1993) Training in thesis writing: An evaluation of three conceptual orientations, *British Journal of Educational Psychology*, 63: 170–84.

Truss, L. (2003) *Eats, Shoots and Leaves*. London: Profile Books.

Van der Geest, T. (1996) Professional writing studied: Authors' accounts of planning in document production processes, in M. Sharples and T. Van der Geest (eds) *The New Writing Environment: Writers at Work in a World of Technology*. Berlin: Springer, pp. 7–24.

Wager, E., Godlee, F. and Jefferson, T. (2002) *How to Survive Peer Review*. London: British Medical Journal Books.

Wellington, J. (2003) *Getting Published: A Guide for Lecturers and Researchers*. London: Routledge Falmer.

Wheatley, M.J. (2002) *Turning to One Another: Simple Conversations to Restore Hope to the Future*. San Francisco, CA: Berrett-Koehler.

Wilk, K.E., Voight, M.L., Keirns, M.A. et al. (1993) Stretch-shortening drills for the upper extremities: Theory and clinical application, *Journal of Sports Physical Therapy*, 17(5): 225–39.

Williams, J. (1996) Writing in concert, in H.A. Veeser (ed.) *Confessions of the Critics*. London: Routledge, pp. 156–76.

Williams, J. and Coldron, J. (eds) (1996) *Writing for Publication: An Introductory Guide for People Working in Education*. Sheffield: PAVIC.

Ziegler, D. (2001) To hold, or not to hold . . . Is that the right question?, *Residential Treatment for Children and Youth*, 18(4): 33–45.

Index

HOW TO WRITE A THESIS

Rowena Murray

This is the book that all PhD supervisors and their students have been waiting for: the first comprehensive overview of the many different writing practices, and processes, involved in the production of a doctoral thesis. Crammed full of explanations, shortcuts and tips, this book demystifies academic writing in one fell swoop. Everyone who reads it will be massively enabled as a writer.

> Professor Lynne Pearce, Associate Dean for
> Postgraduate Teaching, University of Lancaster

Rowena Murray's down-to-earth approach both recognises and relieves some of the agony of writing a PhD. The advice in this book is both practical and motivational; sometimes it's 'PhD-saving' too. By using Rowena Murray's techniques of regular snacking, instead of occasional bingeing, I managed to rescue my PhD from near-death at a time of work overload.

> Christine Sinclair, part-time PhD student and Lecturer in
> Educational Development, University of Paisley

This book evolved from 15 years' experience of teaching thesis writing. The contents have been tried and tested with postgraduates and academics. Early chapters explore the ambiguities and subtleties of thesis writing in detail. Later chapters are more compact, listing steps in the writing process. All chapters provide examples to illustrate techniques and activities to progress writing.

When you write a thesis be ready to develop new modes of writing. The harsh reality is that:

> If you like to work to goals, you are likely to have to submit to floundering around, reconstructing your well laid plans;

While if you are the kind of person who hates to be driven by goals, or does not see the point of them, you will have to submit to deadlines and milestones that may seem like millstones. This book will help you cope with the challenges inherent in writing your thesis.

Contents

Introduction – How to write 1000 words an hour – Thinking about writing a doctorate – Starting to write – Seeking structure – The first milestone – Becoming a serial writer – Creating closure – Fear and loathing: revising – It is never too late to start – The last 385 yards – After the viva: more writing? – References – Index.

304pp   0 335 20718 9 (Paperback)   0 335 20719 7 (Hardback)

HOW TO SURVIVE YOUR VIVA

Rowena Murray

The oral examination is a new type of communication event. It requires the highest standard of communication skills. Writing a thesis or dissertation requires students to pull their ideas together into a unified whole; oral examinations take it all apart again.

Typical questions, and strategies for answering them, are provided in order to help participants prepare and practise.

The book features:

- Real examples of questions and answers
- Narratives of experiences
- Planning tools
- Preparation framework
- Specific verbal strategies to use in the viva to do justice to the thesis
- User-friendly writing style
- Reading list

This is the first book to provide comprehensive coverage of the viva. It is an essential handbook for all involved in oral examinations: students, supervisors, tutors and examiners, including undergraduate, Masters and doctoral examinations.

Contents
Introduction – What is a viva? – Roles and responsibilities – Countdown to the viva – Questions – Answers – Interactions – Practice – Outcomes – A new type of communication event – Bibliography – Index.

176pp   0 335 21284 0 (Paperback)   0 335 21285 9 (Hardback)